D1524630

# Philosophy and AI

# Philosophy and AI
Essays at the Interface

edited by Robert Cummins and John Pollock

A Bradford Book
The MIT Press
Cambridge, Massachusetts
London, England

This book was set in Times Roman by Asco Trade Typesetting Ltd., Hong Kong and printed and bound in the United States of America.

Library of Congress Cataloging-in-Publication Data

Philosophy and AI : essays at the interface / edited by Robert Cummins
and John Pollock.
   p.   cm.
Includes bibliographical references and index.
ISBN 0-262-03180-9
  1. Reasoning. 2. Artificial intelligence. 3. Computers. I. Cummins, Robert.
II. Pollock, John L.
BC177.P48   1991
128′.3—dc20
91-16817
CIP

# Contents

# List of Contributors

**Michael Bratman** is professor of philosophy at Stanford University, and a researcher at the Center for the Study of Language and Information. He received a Ph.D. in philosophy from Rockefeller University in 1974. He is the author of *Intention, Plans, and Practical Reason* (Harvard University Press, 1987). His main research interests are in the philosophy of action and related areas in the philosophy of mind, moral philosophy, and foundational issues in artificial intelligence and the social sciences.

**Robert Cummins** is professor of philosophy and research scientist in cognitive science at the University of Arizona. His Ph.D. is from the University of Michigan in philosophy (1970). He is author of *Meaning and Mental Representation* and *The Nature of Psychological Explanation*, both from MIT Press/Bradford Books. His current research interests include mental representation, cross-domain inference, and the automatic acquisition and use of conventions governing the communicative use of symbols and syntactic constructions.

**Jon Doyle** took his B.A. in mathematics at the University of Houston before beginning work on artificial intelligence at the Massachusetts Institute of Technology. He received his master's degree in 1977 for his work on truth maintenance systems (which he now prefers to call reason maintenance systems), and invented nonmonotonic logic the next summer with Drew McDermott. He received the doctorate in 1980 for a dissertation about controlling reasoning and action through dialectical deliberation and introspection. He has held research positions at Stanford University and Carnegie-Mellon University, and is currently a principal research scientist in the Laboratory for Computer Science at MIT. His recent work concerns economic theories of default reasoning and belief revision, new approaches to reason maintenance, knowledge representation languages, qualitative physics, rational self-government, and the mathematical foundations of artificial intelligence.

**Jennifer J. Elgot-Drapkin** received her B.A. in mathematics from the University of Virginia in 1980, and her M.S. and Ph.D. in computer science from the University of Maryland in 1985 and 1988, respectively. She is currently an assistant professor in the Department of Computer Science and Engineering at Arizona State University. Her research interests are in the logical foundations of artificial intelligence, real-time commonsense reasoning, nonmonotonic reasoning, and knowledge representation.

**Clark Glymour** is Alumni Professor of Philosophy at Carnegie Mellon University and adjunct professor of history and philosophy of science at the University of Pittsburgh. His recent work has focused on computational learning theory, automated causal inference, and the foundations of psychology.

**David Israel** received his B.A. in philosophy from Harvard College in 1965. He entered graduate school at the University of California,

Berkeley in 1965, again in philosophy. He was awarded his Ph.D. in philosophy from Berkeley in 1974. Israel's thesis was in the areas of philosophy of logic and philosophy of science. From 1970 to 1979, Israel taught philosophy, principally at Tufts University. During the academic year 1978–79, he was a consultant in formal semantics to a knowledge representation and natural language understanding project at the Artificial Intelligence Department of Bolt Beranek and Newman in Cambridge and joined the AI Department as a computer scientist in September 1979. In September 1984 Israel moved to the Artificial Intelligence Center at SRI International as a senior computer scientist. Since 1986, he has been one of the four principal investigators of the Situated Language Research Project at the Center for the Study of Language and Information. Israel's main research interests are in formal semantics, knowledge representation and reasoning, and theories of rational action.

**Kevin Kelly** is assistant professor of philosophy at Carnegie Mellon University. He works on a variety of topics in computational learning theory and philosophy of science.

**Henry E. Kyburg, Jr.**, received a B.E. from Yale University in Chemical engineering in 1948, and a Ph. D. in philosophy from Columbia University in 1955. He is currently professor of philosophy at the University of Rochester. He is author of fourteen books in both philosophy and mathematics; a hundred and fifty articles and reviews in books and journals in philosophy, mathematics, computer science, and even agriculture. He is especially well known for his work in probability and induction.

**Ronald P. Loui** has principal interests in artificial intelligence and philosophy of science, especially in reasoning and decision. He holds his degrees from Harvard (B.A., m.c.l., 1982, applied mathematics: Decision and Control) and the University of Rochester (M.S., 1985, computer science, and Ph.D., 1987, computer science and philosophy). At Stanford, he was a postdoctoral research affiliate, and at Washington University he is assistant professor of computer science and adjunct assistant professor of philosophy. He organized a workshop on defeasible reasoning (1989), was on the program committee of AAAI 1988, was on a reviewer for IJCAI 1989, and was an NSF RIA funding review panelist (1989). He has been an invited presenter at ORSA/TIMS (1984), at TARK II (1988), at SEP 17 (1988), at the Workshop on Human and Machine Cognition (1989), and at Uncertainty Workshop V (1989). His undergraduate thesis won the ACM George S. Forsythe Student Paper Competition first prize (1983). His doctoral dissertation was runner-up for the Journal of Philosophy Johnsonian Prize (1989). He is co-editor of *Knowledge Representation and Defeasible Reasoning* with H. Kyburg, and G. Carlson (Kluwer. 1989).

**Michael Miller's** undergraduate degree is a B.A. from Temple University. He holds an M.A. in communication arts from the University of Wisconsin, Madison and an M.S. in computer science from the University of Maryland. Currently he is working on a Ph.D. at Maryland, also in computer science. His research interests are primarily centered around commonsense reasoning.

**Don Perlis** received a Ph.D. in math (New York University) and another in computer science (University of Rochester) before taking up his current position as associate professor of computer science at the University of Maryland. His interests center on computational approaches to understanding mind and cognitive behavior.

**Martha E. Pollack** received her B.A. in linguistics in 1979 from Dartmouth College, and her M.S.E.E. (1984) and Ph.D. (1986) in computer and information science from the University of Pennsylvania. Her doctoral thesis, on plan recognition in discourse, was awarded the University of Pennsylvania's Rubinoff Dissertation Prize. Since 1985, Pollack has been a computer scientist at the Artificial Intelligence Center at SRI International, as well as a senior researcher at the Center for the Study of Language and Information. She is also consulting assistant professor of computer science at Stanford University. Her research interests are in plan generation and plan recognition, theories of rational action, experimental evaluation of AI systems, and natural-language semantics and pragmatics. She is co-editor of the recently published *Intentions in Communication* (MIT Press, 1990), an interdisciplinary volume bringing together related work by researchers in philosophy, computer science, linguistics, and psychology.

**John L. Pollock** is professor of philosophy and research scientist in cognitive science at the University of Arizona. His Ph.D. is from the University of California at Berkeley in philosophy (1965). His books include *Knowledge and Justification* (Princeton, 1974), *The Language of Thought* (Princeton, 1981), *The Foundations of Philosophical Semantics* (Princeton, 1983), *Contemporary Theories of Knowledge* (Rowman and Littlefield, 1986), *Nomic Probability and the Foundations of Induction* (Oxford, 1989), and *How to Build a Person* (MIT Press, 1990). His current research interests include automated deduction, defeasible reasoning, and general questions about rationality.

**William J. Rapaport** is associate professor of computer science, associate director of the SNePS Research Group, and was interim director of the Center for Cognitive Science, all at SUNY Buffalo. He received his Ph.D. in philosophy from Indiana University in 1976 and his M.S. in computer science from SUNY Buffalo in 1984. Previously, he was associate professor of philosophy at SUNY Fredonia. He received the SUNY Chancellor's Award for Excellence in Teaching (1981) and the Northeastern Association of Graduate Schools Master's Scholar Award

(1987). His research interests are in cognitive science, knowledge representation, and computational linguistics. He has published articles in artificial intelligence, cognitive science, computational linguistics, philosophy of mind, and philosophy of language; received the American Philosophical Quarterly Essay Prize (1982); and is co-author of a text, *Logic: A Computer Approach* (McGraw-Hill, 1985). He is (or has been) on the editorial boards of the journals *Computational Linguistics, Machine Translation*, and *Nous*, and of the Kluwer book series Studies in Cognitive Systems. He is the book review editor of the journal *Minds and Machines*. He has supervised or is currently supervising three Ph.D. dissertations and six master's degrees, and has served on ten Ph.D. committees in computer science, psychology, and linguistics. He has received grants and fellowships from NSF, NEH, and Research Foundation of SUNY, for work on cognitive and computer systems for understanding narrative text, the logical foundations of belief representation, and natural-language semantics. He has served on the American Philosophical Association Committee on Pre-College Instruction in Philosophy, and is currently on the APA Committee on Computers and Philosophy.

**Stuart C. Shapiro** received the S.B. degree in mathematics from the Massachusetts Institute of Technology in 1966, and the M.S. and Ph.D. degrees in computer sciences from the University of Wisconsin, Madison, in 1968 and 1971, respectively. He is currently professor of computer science at SUNY Buffalo, where he was department chairman from 1984 to 1990. In 1971, he was a lecturer in computer sciences at the University of Wisconsin, Madison. Between then and going to Buffalo in 1977, he was at the Computer Science Department of Indiana University, where he held positions of assistant and associate professor. In summer 1974 he was a visiting research assistant professor at the Computer Science Department of the University of Illinois at Urbana-Champaign. He spent the 1987–88 academic year on sabbatical at the University of Southern California/Information Sciences Institute. Shapiro's research interests are in artificial intelligence, specifically knowledge representation, reasoning, and natural language processing. His Ph.D. dissertation is considered to be one of the seminal works in the development of semantic networks as a representation of knowledge. He is editor-in-chief of *The Encyclopedia of Artificial Intelligence* (John Wiley & Sons, 1987), which was named Best New Book in Technology and Engineering for 1987 by the Association of American Publishers Professional and Scholarly Publishing Division. He is also the author of *Techniques of Artificial Intelligence* (D. Van Nostrand, 1979), *LISP: An Interactive Approach* (Computer Science Press, 1986), and over one hundred technical articles and reports. He has served on several National Research Council review panels, as a consultant on artificial intelligence for several companies, as department editor of the journal *Cognition and Brain Theory for artificial intelligence*, and has served on the editorial board of the *American Journal of Computational Linguistics*. Prof. Shapiro is a member of the ACM, the IEEE, the Association for Computational Linguistics, the Cognitive Science Society, the American Association for Artificial Intelligence, and Sigma Xi. He is listed in *Who's Who in America, American Men and Women of Science, Contemporary Authors, Who's Who in Technology*, and *Who's Who in Artificial Intelligence*.

**Yoav Shoham** received a B.A. in computer science from the Technion in Israel in 1981, and a Ph.D. in computer science from Yale University in 1987. He is currently an assistant professor of computer science at Stanford University, and holds a university chair endowed by Finmeccanica. Shoham's research has concentrated on several areas of knowledge representation, including temporal, nonmonotonic, and epistemic reasoning. His current research concerns the ascription of mental qualities to machines and the relationship between logical statements and sensory-motor activity.

**Peter Spirtes** is assistant professor of philosophy at Carnegie Mellon University. His recent work has been devoted to computerized causal inference; he has also worked on the development of a number of expert systems.

**Paul Thagard** is Senior Research Cognitive Scientist at the Princeton University Cognitive Science Laboratory. His degrees include a Ph.D. in philosophy and an M.S. in computer science. He is co-author of *Induction: Processes of Inference, Learning, and Discovery* (MIT Press, 1986) and author of *Computational Philosophy of Science* (MIT Press, 1988) and *Conceptual Revolutions* (Princeton University Press, forthcoming).

# Introduction

## Some Recent History

A number of philosophers have recently been led into artificial intelligence by their interests in the mind, especially in knowledge and reason. Similarly, a number of researchers in artificial intelligence have recently found themselves writing, without any conscious intent, what philosophers recognize as philosophy. In many cases, the latter has occurred without any conscious realization that they were writing philosophy and without any intent to do so. Instead, computationally driven interests have motivated research that is only indirectly concerned with computation, and the result is that the field of artificial intelligence has expanded in such a way that its borders have come to overlap those of philosophy. In some cases, the overlap is so substantial that it is no longer possible to distinguish the two fields or to say that a particular problem belongs most properly to one rather than the other.

## How Philosophers Drift into Artificial Intelligence

Some just like the toys, of course. But there are good intellectual reasons as well, many already recognized but worth rehearsing.

Twentieth-century English-speaking philosophy has, like the positivists who influenced it, been profoundly conditioned by its demand for rigor. The origin of this demand is the positivist's requirement that theories be testable. At the very least, a respectable philosophical theory should be stated with sufficient precision that one can tell what it says about *something* and whether its predictions about that subject matter are borne out. We should be able to tell, at least in some cases, whether we are faced with a counterexample or a confirming instance. For many years, this minimal requirement of rigor meant, in practice, that respectable philosophy had to be capable of being articulated in the formalism of logic. As time passed, however, the awareness grew that formal rigor was not sufficient to guarantee unambiguous content or to ensure sufficient philosophical clarity to meet even this minimal criterion of testability. For instance, a model-theoretic investigation of a concept accomplishes little without some explanation of how the model-theoretic semantics is supposed to represent the world, and the latter is a topic that cannot be addressed in the same formal manner as the construction of the semantics itself. There must be more to philosophical analysis than logical formalism.

In some cases, this realization has led contemporary philosophers to eschew rigor altogether. Even in investigations shrouded in a façade of formalism, there is often a lamentable tendency toward handwaving when the going gets difficult. The trend is toward painting pictures rather than constructing detailed theories. Perhaps *most* contemporary philosophy is too vague and unfinished to satisfy even a minimal requirement of testability. The solution is not to symbolize it all in the predicate calculus. Perhaps the solution is just to strive for clarity, and not get lazy when the going gets tough. Instead of waving his or her hands, a philosopher needs to work out the details. If that cannot be done, it is an indication that the theory is wrong.

To some of us, the concepts and technology of artificial intelligence provide at least a partial resolution of the problem of ensuring some degree of testability. As Paul Thagard (1988) has pointed out, artificial intelligence liberates us from the narrow constraints of standard logic by enforcing rigor in a different way, namely via the constraint of computational realizability. You cannot make a computer do anything by waving your hands at it. If a theory is to be implementable on a computer, the details have to be there. You cannot get away with concealing intellectual sloppiness behind a mask of vague profundities.

Computational realizability is no guarantee of truth or of explanatory interest, of course, but it does guarantee a certain kind of rigor. Those philosophers who have begun to test their theories by trying actually to implement them in computer programs have found that the discipline required almost invariably reveals ambiguity, vagueness, incompleteness and downright error in places where traditional philosophical reflection was blind. Implementing a theory requires that the theory has really been completed, in the sense that the details have been worked out and that it has been formulated precisely and unambiguously. Furthermore, a running implementation of a theory makes it possible to apply the theory to more complicated test cases than would be possible by armchair reflection, and experience indicates that this usually reveals counterexamples that would not otherwise have been apparent.

A (partial) guarantee of philosophical rigor and clarity is not the only attraction artificial intelligence holds for philosophers. The discipline of programming also leads to a shift in perspective on the traditional issues. It invites—or rather requires—one to adopt what Dennett (1968) calls the design stance toward the mind. Rather than ask what rationality is, or what "our concept" of rationality is, for example, we must ask how a rational agent might be designed. Rather than ask under what conditions someone can be said to know something, we are led to ask how an agent might be designed that acquires information and applies it in the service of some goal, and what such an agent's environment must be like for the design to work. We are led, as Kyburg points out in his chapter, to blur the received distinction between the normative and the descriptive. Rather than ask how things (practical reason, belief fixation, justification, etc.) ought to work, we are led to ask how things could work. An example of this is the growing suspicion (conviction?) that it is not possible to understand reason as a competence that idealizes away from resource constraints. It is a commonplace in cognitive psychology that a potential prey must tolerate a lot of false positives from its predator recognition system if it is to get answers fast enough to be of any use in directing evasive action. What is not so obvious, but may nevertheless be true, is that you cannot build a satisfactory predator recognition system by building a system that is as infallible as possible and then adding a time constraint. The principles that underlie the design of a real time system may be entirely distinct from those that underlie a system that is optimal with respect to error avoidance. Similarly, bounds on memory size require a computational system to be selective about what information it retains. This is probably the explanation for the fact that human beings tend to remember the reasons for their beliefs only briefly. This brute psychological fact makes it impossible for humans, in many cases, to correct their beliefs in the face of new discoveries that refute the reasons they originally had for those beliefs. These kinds of considerations indicate that a good deal of traditional epistemology radically oversimplifies the computational problems involved in rationality. An adequate epistemology must be sensitive to the kinds of resource constraints that are tediously familiar to the computer scientist.

A corollary to the proposition that design matters essentially is the proposition that architecture and hardware matter, for these have consequences for computational space and time as well as for the range of operations available to the system. It is likely, for example, that some parallel processing is essential to rationality in the biological world because serial processing is just too slow. Thus the distinction between how it ought to be done "ideally" and how it is actually done begins to break down. Moreover, none of this is the sort of thing that is likely to leap to the eye of the philosopher employing traditional methods.

The forgoing is meant only as a crude—though dramatic—illustration of how the conceptions and technology of artificial intelligence can alter one's perspective, and consequently one's ideas, on a traditional philosophical problem. The chapters in this volume are, of course, the real illustrations.

## How Artificial Intelligence Researchers Drift into Philosophy

In the early days of artificial intelligence, the attitude seems to have been that the problems were just programming problems and could be solved by the same kind of engineering approach that computer scientists had successfully applied to other problems. In some sense, that is no doubt true. But the problems of artificial intelligence have proved unexpectedly resistant to this approach. The problems have proved to be too difficult to be solved by brute force.

Artificial intelligence embraces a variety of problems, only some of which are recognizably "philosophical." But an important subclass of problems concerns the construction of information processing systems that digest information and produce conclusions or perform actions that are "reasonable". Ultimately, the criterion of reasonableness is what human beings regard as rationally acceptable. It has become increasingly apparent that the production of such information processing systems requires a prior theory of rationality. Successful implementation must be driven by theory. The recognition of this fact has led researchers in AI to address fundamental questions in the theory of rationality. In some cases, AI researchers have addressed topics largely ignored by philosophers (for example, temporal reasoning), but in other cases they have addressed questions that are quite literally the same as those that have occupied philosophers. The articulation of a theory of rationality is a complicated matter and has been the topic of philosophical investigations in epistemology, decision theory, and practical reasoning literally for centuries. Philosophical theories of rationality have often been naïve in ignoring resource constraints, but despite this, philosophers have over the years learned a lot about rationality and reasoning, and AI researchers cannot afford to ignore this body of information. As Shoham points out in his contribution to this book, philosophy has a big head start when it comes to thinking about the mind.

Philosophy and artificial intelligence bring different perspectives and techniques to the theory of rationality, and each can profitably learn from the other. For example, one of the most significant advances in epistemology in the second half of the twentieth century has been the recognition that most reasoning is defeasible. That observation is now firmly entrenched in epistemology and has been used extensively as a tool in epistemological investigation. Researchers in artificial intelligence made the same discovery independently, without realizing that there was a pre-existing parallel literature in philosophy. This had the salutory effect that research on defeasible reasoning proceeded differently in the two fields, producing more original ideas than would likely have been the case if they had been more strongly influenced by each other. But it also had the unfortunate effect that the two fields did not profit from each other's discoveries. Somewhat perversely, the AI work on defeasible reasoning (nonmonotonic logic) has been more abstract and formal, the philosophical work more concerned with how defeasible reasoning works in relatively concrete epistemological contexts. The philosophical work has often ignored the need to get the general logic of defeasible reasoning right. Interaction with AI work on defeasible reasoning is now forcing philosophers to address that problem. On the other hand, the AI work has tended to be epistemologically simplistic. It has tended to proceed in an epistemological vaccuum, and has often been driven more by considerations of formal elegance than by an understanding of how defeasible reasoning must work in order to accommodate actual human standards of rationality. Interaction with philosophers should go a long way towards rectifying this shortcoming.

## Philosophy and Artificial Intelligence

The upshot of this is that philosophical theories of rationality need to be more strongly influenced by considerations of "computational engineering." The theories must be formulated with an eye to implementability. Conversely, AI theories of rationality need to be better informed by what philosophers have painstakingly learned about what is required of rationality to solve concrete epistemological and decision-theoretic problems. The result will be (and to some extent already is) theories that are equally at home in philosophy and artificial intelligence. We get a spectrum of theories, ranging from the very abstract to the highly concrete. Very abstract speculation about how the mind might work is obviously philosophy, whether it is done by Immanuel Kant or by Jon Doyle. Highly concrete theories about database management or search algorithms may be of philosophical interest, but they belong most properly to computer science. In between, we find theories that are less abstract and more constrained by computational and psychological reality. These theories belong equally to both disciplines. It is just when you can't tell what it is any more—philosophy or science? normative or descriptive?—that things get really interesting to those of us who have contributed to this volume.

## References

Dennett, Daniel (1968) *Brainstorms*. Cambridge, MA: MIT Press. A Bradford book.

Thagard, Paul (1988) *Computational Philosophy of Science*. Cambridge, MA: MIT Press. A Bradford book.

# 1 Plans and Resource-Bounded Practical Reasoning

**Michael E. Bratman, David J. Israel, and Martha E. Pollack**

## 1.1 Two Problems

Rational behavior—the production of actions that further the goals of an agent, based upon her conception of the world—has long interested researchers in artificial intelligence, who are attempting to build machines that behave rationally, as well as philosophers of mind and action, decision theorists, and others who are attempting to provide an account of human rationality. Each of these research traditions has tended to concern itself with a different facet of the problem.

Within AI much attention has been given to the "planning problem," namely, the problem of automating means–end reasoning. AI solutions to the planning problem generally consist of methods for searching the space of possible actions to compute some sequence of actions that will achieve a particular goal or conjunction of goals. Work in this area has resulted in a number of extremely useful techniques for representing and reasoning about actions and their effects (Fikes and Nilsson 1971, Sacerdoti 1977, Georgeff and Lansky 1987, Georgeff 1987b).

Within decision theory (DiFinetti 1975, Jeffrey 1983, Savage 1972), the primary concern has been somewhat different: competing alternatives are taken as given, and the problem is to weigh these alternatives and decide on one of them. A completed means–end analysis is implicit in the specification of the competing alternatives.

It is clear that rational agents must both perform means–end reasoning and weigh alternative courses of action; so an adequate architecture of intelligent artificial agents must therefore include capabilities for both. The design of such an architecture must also specify how these capacities interact. But there is yet another problem. All this must be done in a way that recognizes the fact that agents, whether humans or robots, are *resource bounded*: they are unable to perform arbitrarily large computations in constant time.[1] To what extent have the AI and decision-theoretic traditions faced up to questions raised by the phenomenon of resource boundedness?

In decision-theoretic accounts, an agent is seen as selecting a course of action on the basis of her subjective expected utility, which is a function

---

[1] Problems of resource boundedness have been forcefully pointed out by Herbert Simon; see, for example, Simon 1957.

of the agent's beliefs and desires. For an idealized, resource-*un*bounded agent, this may be a plausible model: perhaps such an agent could, at each instant of time, compute which course of action currently available would maximize its expected utility. But, of course, for real agents it takes time to do such computations—and the more complicated they are, the more time it takes. This is a problem because the more time spent on deliberation, the more chance there is that the world will change in important ways— ways that will undermine the very assumptions on which the deliberation is proceeding.

What about AI planning systems? Until recently, these have typically been designed to construct plans prior to, and distinct from, their execution.[2] It is recognized that the construction of plans takes time. However, these plans have been constructed for a set of future conditions that are known in advance and are frozen. The implicit assumption is that the conditions for which a plan is being formed, the so-called start state, will not change prior to execution. And when it is assumed that the plans will be executed in single-agent environments, in which the only state changes are a result of the single agent's actions, there is no concern that the world will change in unexpected ways during execution. But of course, the world does not actually stay fixed during an indefinitely long planning period. Nor do true single-agent environments exist: even if the environment contains no other human or robot agents, nature often intrudes.[3]

---

[2] In the past few years, there has been a burgeoning interest in the AI community in the problem of "real time" behavior, which has, in turn, led to a concern with the challenge of resource boundedness. One strategy has involved the use of knowledge compilation techniques to do away with explicit symbol manipulation at execution time (Brooks 1986; Rosenschein and Kaelbling 1986). A second line of research has studied the application of decision-analytic techniques to meta-level reasoning (Horvitz et al. 1988; Russell and Wefeld 1989). Finally, there have been a number of complete systems actually implemented, systems that are capable of performing real-time behavior in certain restricted dynamic domains (Georgeff and Ingrand 1989; Fehling and Wilber 1989; Dodhiawala et al. 1989). See also Boddy and Dean 1989 for the theory of algorithms appropriate for real-time behavior under resource bounds.

[3] Even when it is assumed that the world changes only as a result of the agent's actions, it is still infeasible for that agent to consider all possibilities ahead of time. In consequence, the primary capabilities of many practical planning systems were augmented to allow for the monitoring of plan execution and for replanning (Fikes and Nilsson 1971; Sridharan and Bresina 1982; Wilkins 1984). However, the replanning modules that were built had much the same character as the planning modules themselves: they operated under the assumption that the world around them was frozen during replanning. Recently there has been a growing concern with developing representations for multi-agent domains (Georgeff 1987a; Lansky 1987; McDermott 1985).

During the time it takes to engage in practical reasoning, the world can change in important ways. This fact poses the problem of resource boundedness that concerns us here.

So we have two problems. First, an architecture for a rational agent must allow for means-end analysis, for the weighing of competing alternatives, and for interactions between these two forms of reasoning. Second, this architecture must address the problem of resource boundedness. We sketch a solution of the first problem that points the way to a solution of the second. In particular, we present a high-level specification of the practical-reasoning component of an architecture for a resource-bounded rational agent. In this architecture, a major role of the agent's plans is to constrain the amount of further practical reasoning she must do.

## 1.2    The Functional Roles of Plans

Figure 1.1 is a block diagram of an architecture for practical reasoning in resource-bounded agents. It can be classified as a belief/desire/intention (BDI)-architecture: it includes fairly direct representations of the agent's beliefs, desires, and intentions. We view the agent's intentions as structured into larger plans. We distinguish between the plans that the agent has actually adopted, which are represented in figure 1.1 in the oval labeled "Intentions Structured into Plans," and the plans-as-recipes, or operators, that the agent knows about, which are represented in the oval labeled "Plan Library." The plan library might be seen as a subset of the agent's beliefs: specifically, her beliefs about what actions would be useful for achieving which effects under specified conditions. We shall reserve the term "plan" to refer to those plans an agent has actually adopted.

In addition to the information stores, which are denoted by ovals in the figure, there are a number of processes, denoted by rectangles. Our concern will be with four of these: the "Means–End Reasoner," the "Opportunity Analyzer," the "Filtering Process," and the "Deliberation Process." To-gether these constitute a practical-reasoning system, that is, a system by which an agent forms, fills in, revises, and excecutes plans.

Underlying the architecture depicted in figure 1.1 is an account of the functional roles of an agent's plans not just in producing action, but also in constraining further, practical reasoning—an account so far developed largely by Bratman (1987). In this account, an agent's existing plans make

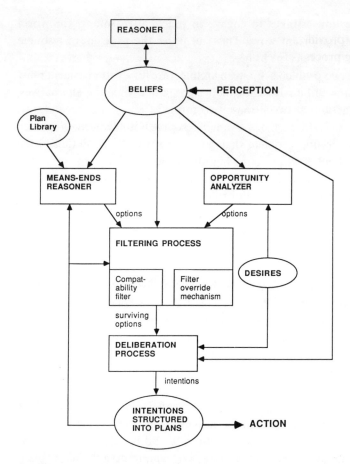

**Figure 1.1**
An architecture for resource-bounded agents

practical reasoning more tractable in two ways: as input to the means–end reasoner, they provide a clear, concrete purpose for reasoning, and as input to the filtering process, they narrow the scope of deliberation to a limited set of options. We shall briefly describe this conception and then explain how it is realized in the architecture depicted in figure 1.1.

The fundamental observation of our approach is that a rational agent is committed to doing what she plans.[4] The nature of this commitment is quite complex (Bratman 1987), but involves at least certain characteristic roles in further practical reasoning.[5] For example, once an agent has formed a plan to attend a particular meeting at 1:00, she need not continually weigh the situation at hand in a wholly unfocused manner. Instead, she should reason about how to get there by 1:00; she need not consider options incompatible with her getting there by 1:00; and she can typically ground her further reasoning on the assumption that she will indeed attend the meeting at 1:00. This example illustrates three roles that an agent's plans will play in her further reasoning: they will drive means–end reasoning, they will provide constraints on what options need be seriously considered, and they will influence the beliefs on which further practical reasoning will be based. In this paper, we focus primarily on the first two roles.

Consider the constraining role of plans. Other things being equal, an agent's plans should be consistent, both internally and with her beliefs. Roughly speaking, it should be possible for her plans, taken together, to be executed successfully in a world in which her beliefs are true. As a result of this demand for consistency, options that are inconsistent with her existing plans and beliefs will be filtered out.

Of course, prior plans may be subject to reconsideration or abandonment in light of changes in belief. But if an agent constantly reconsiders her plans, they will not limit her deliberation in the way they need to for a resource-bounded agent. This means that an agent's plans should be reasonably stable, that is, they should be relatively resistant to reconsideration and abandonment.[6]

Given the requirement of stability, plans should also be partial. In addition to bounded computational resources, agents have bounded know-

---

[4] The reader should recall our distinction between intended plans and plans-as-recipes.
[5] An attempt at constructing a formal model of commitment is made by Cohen and Levesque (1990).
[6] We discuss these matters further in section 1.5.

ledge. They are neither prescient nor omniscient: the world may change around them in ways they are not in a position to anticipate. Hence highly detailed plans about the far future will often be of little use, the details not worth bothering about.

Plans can be partial in at least two different ways. They may be *temporally partial*, accounting for some periods of time and not for others. An agent may plan to give a lecture from 10:00 until noon, to pick up a book at the bookstore on the way back from the lecture, to attend a meeting from 1:00 to 2:30, and to pick up her child at school at 4:00; she may not yet have decided what to do between 2:30 and the time she leaves for her child's school.

More important for our purposes is the potential for *structural partiality* in plans. Agents frequently decide upon ends, leaving open for later deliberation questions about means to those ends.[7] An agent may, for example, first decide to pick up a book at the bookstore, postponing decisions about what route to take to get there and whether to use Visa or MasterCard to pay. The structural partiality of plans is the reason we speak of their decomposition into intentions: for example, we shall speak, of an agent's "filling in" her plan to buy a book with an intention to pay for it with her MasterCard. We shall also be concerned with the interaction between a plan's decomposition and the requirement of consistency. A plan to spend all of one's cash at lunch is inconsistent with a plan to buy a book that includes an intention to pay for it with cash, but is not necessarily inconsistent with a partial plan merely to purchase a book, since the book may be paid for with a credit card.

The characteristic process of means–end reasoning suggests the second way in which plans focus the practical-reasoning process. Plans, while potentially partial, must be *means-end coherent*: as time goes by, they must be filled in with subplans that are at least as extensive as the agent believes necessary to execute the plan successfully.[8] As a result of the demand for means–end coherence, prior, partial plans can be seen to pose problems for

[7] Hence, structural partiality is related to the partiality of plans produced by traditional, hierarchial planners, such as NOAH (Sacerdoti 1977). However, whereas these planners used partial plans only as intermediate representations in the plan formation process, we are suggesting the usefulness of acting on the basis of partial plans. PRS (Georgeff and Ingrand 1989) is an example of a system that makes use of structurally partial plans during execution.
[8] Further development of this architecture requires the construction of techniques for detecting threats to means–ends coherence, techniques that are compatible with the demands of relative computational efficiency.

further practical reasoning. Once the agent has decided to read a certain book today, a means–end problem is posed: how will she get the book? Will she go to the library to borrow a copy of it, or will she stop by the bookstore and purchase one? Once she has formed an intention to read the book, her reasoning can focus on deciding how to do so, rather than on assessing all the options that are currently available.

## 1.3   The Larger Architecture

We can now return to the architecture illustrated in figure 1.1. Let us assume, for expository purposes, an agent who embodies this architecture and who has already adopted some structurally partial plans, and let us consider the practical reasoning she will perform. Her means–end reasoner will be invoked for each of her existing partial plans, to propose subplans that complete it. Means–end reasoning may occur at any time up to the point at which a plan is in danger of becoming means–end incoherent; at that point it must occur, proposing options that may serve as subplans for the plan in question. The means–end reasoner may propose a number of options, all of which are means to a particular end: for example, it may propose going to the bookstore and going to the library as alternative means to getting a desired book.

Not all options are proposed as a result of means–end reasoning. Changes in the agent's environment may lead to changes in her beliefs, which in turn may result in her considering new options that are not means to any already intended end. The opportunity analyzer in figure 1.1 is the component that proposes options in response to perceived changes in the environment. Such opportunities may be welcome or unwelcome. Some changes may lead to previously unexpected opportunities for satisfying desires; others to opportunities for avoiding unexpected threats.

Once options have been proposed, either by the means–end reasoner or by the opportunity analyzer, they are subject to filtering. So far, we have suggested how one of the components of the filtering process, the compatibility filter, operates. (In section 1.4, we explain how the behavior of the overall filtering process is affected by the other component, the filter override mechanism.) The compatibility filter checks options to determine compatibility with the agent's existing plans. Options deemed compatible are *surviving options*. Surviving options are passed along to the deliberation process and, when there are competing surviving options. they are weighed against one another. The deliberation process produces intentions, which are incorporated into the agent's plans.

It is essential that the filtering process be computationally efficient relative to deliberation itself. After all, the motivation for introducing this process into the architecture was to reduce the amount of computation in practical reasoning. Here a variety of ideas can be explored. One is to delimit types of incompatibility that can be checked in a computationally tractable manner. Thus, for example, one might define a measure of spatio-temporal separation between options and design the compatibility filter so that it rules out all and only those options that overlap inappropriately with already intended actions. For an important class of cases, such a scheme can be implemented as a polynomial-time constraint-propagation algorithm over intervals (Kautz and Vilain 1986). Another idea would be to employ a tractable system of defeasible reasoning involving imperfect, albeit still useful, filters. Such filters may be "leaky," in that they sometimes let through options that are in fact incompatible, or they may be "clogged," in that they sometimes block options that are in fact compatible.

What happens when the agent comes to believe that a prior plan of hers is no longer achievable? A full development of this architecture would have to give an account of the ways in which a resource-bounded agent would monitor her prior plans in the light of changes in belief. However this is developed, there will of course be times when an agent will have to give up a prior plan in light of a new belief that this plan is no longer executable. When this happens, a new process of deliberation may be triggered indirectly in one of two ways. First, the abandoned plan may be the specification of the agent's means to some intended end. In this case, the agent's larger plan will be threatened with means–end incoherence, which would normally trigger reasoning of the sort we have already described. But sometimes the abandoned plan may not be the specification of a means to a presently intended end. Still, we can suppose that this plan was initially adopted as a way of satisfying some desire. If the agent still has this desire, it may lead to further deliberation should an appropriate opportunity arise.

## 1.4   Filtering and Overriding

The account of practical reasoning given so far is incomplete in an important way. Recall that agents are not only resource-bounded, but also knowledge-bounded. So a rational agent's current plans must not have irrevocable control over her future deliberation and behavior. Rather, a rational agent should sometimes be willing to reconsider her plans in light of unanticipated events. There thus exists a tension between the stability that plans must exhibit to play their role in focusing practical reasoning and the revocability that must also be inherent in them, given that they are formed on the basis of incomplete information about the future.

In the architecture of figure 1.1, this tension is mediated by the second component of the filtering process: the "filter override mechanism." The filter override mechanism encodes the agent's sensitivities to problems and opportunities in her environment—that is, the conditions under which some portion of her existing plans is to be suspended and weighed against some other option. The filter override mechanism operates in parallel with the compatibility filter. As we noted above, an option that survives the compatibility filter is subject to consideration by the deliberation process: deliberation is not affected by the filter override mechanism. However, an option that does not survive the compatibility filter may still be subject to consideration if it triggers a filter override, that is, if it satisfies one of the conditions encoded by the override mechanism. If an option fails to survive the compatibility filter but does trigger a filter override, the intended act that is incompatible with the new option is up for reconsideration.

An agent's filter override mechanism must be carefully designed to embody the right degree of sensitivity to the problems and opportunities that arise in her environment. If the agent is overly sensitive, willing to reconsider her plans in response to every unanticipated event, then her plans will not serve sufficiently to limit the number of options about which she must deliberate. On the other hand, if the agent is not sensitive enough, she will fail to react to significant deviations from her expectations.

Consider what can happen to a proposed option. It may not survive the compatibility filter. Such an incompatible option may or may not trigger a filter override. If it does, the deliberation process will be invoked to decide between the incompatible option and the previously intended act that is now up for reconsideration. There is no guarantee that the agent will decide in favor of the new incompatible option; the result of deliberation may be a decision to maintain the previous intention.

If an incompatible option does not trigger a filter override, the agent does not deliberate about it. However, the designer (or other observer) of the agent may be able to determine what the result of properly functioning

**Table 1.1**
A taxonomy of practical-reasoning situations

|   | Survives compatibility filter | Triggers filter override | Deliberation leads to change of plan | Deliberation *would have* led to change of plan |
|---|---|---|---|---|
| 1 | N | Y | Y | |
| 2 | N | Y | N | |
| 3 | N | N | | N |
| 4 | N | N | | Y |
| 5 | Y | | | |

**Table 1.2**
Further complications

|   | Survives compatibility filter | Triggers filter override | Deliberation leads to change of plan | Deliberation *would have* led to change of plan | Deliberation worthwhile |
|---|---|---|---|---|---|
| 1a | N | Y | Y | | Y |
| 1b | N | Y | Y | | N |
| 4a | N | N | | Y | Y |
| 4b | N | N | | Y | N |

deliberation would have been, that is, whether or not the agent's current beliefs and desires are such that deliberation would reasonably have led to her changing her plans to incorporate the new option.

Finally, it is of course possible that a proposed option will be compatible with the agent's existing plans, in which case it will be considered in deliberation. So we now have five possible situations, which are summarized in table 1.1.

The next step is to note certain complications in situations 1 and 4. In both cases, these stem from the same fact: even deliberation that reasonably results in a change of intention takes time and so precludes other useful activities. This means that, in some instances of situation 1, the benefits achieved by the change in intention may be outweighed by the cost of deliberation. Similarly, in some instances of situation 4, the benefits that would have been obtained by the change in intention would have been outweighed by the deliberation required for this change. So there are two subcases of each of these situations, summarized in table 1.2. In situation

1a, the change in intention has benefits which outweigh the cost of the extra deliberation, whereas in situation 1b, the cost of the deliberation outweighs the benefits of the change in intention. In situation 4a, the change that would have occurred would have had benefits outweighing the cost of the deliberation that would have been required, while in situation 4b, the opposite is the case.

## 1.5  Caution and Boldness

Situations 1b and 2 have an important property in common: the agent engages in deliberation that is not on balance worth its cost. In constrast, in situation 4a; the agent fails to engage in deliberation that would have been worth its cost. Thus, an architecture that guaranteed that any agent embodying it would never be in these situations would be, at least in that respect, ideal.

Unfortunately, such an architecture is an impossibility.[9] Using the architecture we describe, one of the jobs of the robot designer is to construct the filter override mechanism so that, other things equal, it minimizes the frequency with which the agent will be in these situations.[10]

We can develop this last point and set the stage for some examples by introducing some terminology. When a proposed but incompatible option triggers a filter override, thereby leading to reconsideration of an existing intention, the agent is being *cautious*. When a proposed but incompatible option fails to trigger a filter override, the agent is being, *bold*. What we have seen in our previous discussion is that sometimes caution pays and sometimes it doesn't; by the same token, sometimes boldness pays and sometimes it doesn't. In situation 1a, caution pays, whereas in situations 1b and 2, it doesn't. In situations 3 and 4b, boldness pays, whereas in situation 4a, it doesn't.

A filter override mechanism that results too often in cautious behavior that doesn't pay is *overly cautious*; one that results too often in bold

[9] Indeed, if such an architecture were possible, it would seem to have an odd consequence. Consider an agent who is disposed to deliberate about an incompatible option when and only when that deliberation would lead to a worthwhile change. Such an agent might as well be designed to decide in favor of the new option whenever she is disposed to deliberate about it.

[10] In fact, one might ultimately want the filter override mechanism to be capable of being altered by the agent herself: if she realizes that she is spending too much time in fruitless deliberation, she should raise the sensitivity thresholds in the override mechanism; and if she notices too many missed opportunities, she should lower the thresholds.

behavior that doesn't pay is *overly bold*. In a well-designed agent, the filter override mechanism will be neither overly cautious nor overly bold.

Consider a robot Rosie, whose task it is to repair computer equipment. We present six different scenarios involving Rosie, scenarios that illustrate the situations described above in which an option fails to survive the compatibility filter. In each of the scenarios, we imagine that Rosie has been assigned several tasks, the first of which is to fix a malfunctioning video display on some terminal. We assume that Rosie does some means–end reasoning before setting off to do the repair: she determines that the best way to fix the problem is to replace the CRT, basing this decision upon a belief that CRTs burn out regularly as well as on an assumption that this is the cause of the malfunction. She thus brings a replacement tube along with her.

In the first scenario, Rosie arrives and discovers that the problem with the video display is caused by the contrast on the terminal being turned off. The opportunity analyzer proposes a new option: to fix the malfunction by simply turning up the contrast. This option is incompatible with Rosie's intention to fix the problem by replacing the CRT, yet she reconsiders her plan because her filter override mechanism has been triggered. Rosie's deliberation leads her to change her plan: she drops her intention to replace the CRT, and instead forms an intention to fix the malfunction by adjusting the contrast. Not only is this new option superior to the CRT replacement, but it is sufficiently superior to outweigh the costs of reconsideration. After all, turning up the contrast is known by Rosie to be a significantly cheaper solution than replacing the CRT. So Rosie is being cautious and her caution pays (situation 1a).

In the second scenario, Rosie discovers that the existing CRT is repairable. As in the last example, Rosie is cautious and, in light of this new information, reconsiders her prior intention to replace the CRT. This involves weighing the pros and cons of replacement versus repair, a complicated exercise. Her deliberation results in a decision to repair rather than replace. And, indeed, repairing is a slightly better option. However, instead of deliberating, Rosie could have simply gone ahead with her intention to replace the CRT, and proceeded more quickly to her next task. Given this cost of her deliberation, her caution doesn't pay in this case (situation 1b).

Now suppose instead that replacing the CRT is the superior option, say, because the existing one is quite old and hence likely to break down again soon. Hence, when Rosie reconsiders, she decides not to change her prior intention, but instead to go ahead and replace the CRT. Here again Rosie is cautious, and her caution doesn't pay (situation 2).

In the remaining three scenarios, which illustrate Rosie's being bold, we suppose that, upon arrival, she discovers the presence of a spare CRT of a slightly different kind, one that she could use for the replacement, instead of the one she brought.

In the first case, despite this new information, Rosie does not reconsider her prior plan to replace the CRT. And, in fact, even had she reconsidered, she would have stuck with her prior plan, since the type of CRT she brought with her is superior. Rosie has been bold, and her boldness has paid off (situation 3).

Next, suppose that the opposite is true: had Rosie reconsidered, she would have found the new CRT to be slightly superior. Still, we can ask whether or not the deliberation that would have been required would have been worth it. In one case, the deliberation is relatively easy and does not interfere in any serious way with Rosie's other activities. In this case, then, Rosie's boldness doesn't pay (situation 4a). Alternatively, the deliberation would have precluded important activities of Rosie's, in which case, despite the slight superiority of the new CRT, Rosie's boldness pays (situation 4b).

This last pair of examples highlights an interesting fact about the difference between situations 4a and 4b. In both cases, the agent performs an action that is inferior to a known alternative: in both cases she would have favored the alternative, had she deliberated. So in both cases there is a kind of suboptimality. However, situation 4b differs from situation 4a in the following respect: in 4b, the combination of deliberation and the change of intention, taken together, is inferior to simply going ahead with the original intention. So it is no criticism of a well-designed agent that she ends up in situation 4b.

An agent instantiating a well-designed architecture, then, will tend to be in situations 1a, 3, and 4b, and to avoid situations 1b, 2, and 4a. So other things being equal, we want to design a filter override mechanism that has this effect. But, of course, there are limits to fine-tuning. We cannot expect even a well-designed architecture always to avoid situations 1b, 2, and 4a.

Consider Rosie. Suppose that CRTs are very expensive, and Rosie knows this. It might be a good strategy for her to reconsider an intention to replace a CRT when an alternative means is proposed. After all, such reconsideration will, on many occasions, save the cost of a new CRT. Of course, there may also be times when this strategy lands Rosie in situations of type 1b or 2, in which her caution doesn't pay: recall the case of the very old CRT. Nonetheless, this strategy might, on balance, be a good one. A more finely tuned filter, one that would be more successful in avoiding these undesirable situations, would run increased risks of ending up in situation 4a. As we try to avoid caution that doesn't pay, we run an increased risk of boldness that doesn't pay.

And, of course, the opposite is true as well: as we try to avoid boldness that doesn't pay, we run an increased risk of undesirable cautiousness. Suppose that the difference between one CRT and another is minimal. Then it might be a good strategy for Rosie not to reconsider her original intention to use a specific CRT replacement when an alternative replacement becomes available. This might be so even though such a strategy might sometimes land Rosie in situations of type 4a. If we try to fine-tune Rosie's strategy so as to avoid this risk, we shall simultaneously increase the risk of having her end up in situations 1b or 2.

## 1.6   Conclusion

We have presented the outlines of an architecture that can be used in the design of artifical agents who are, after all, resource-bounded. A key feature of this architecture is a filtering process that constrains the overall amount of practical reasoning necessary. The operation of this filtering process is based upon a theory of the functional roles of plans in practical reasoning. While this is a fairly abstract architecture, it does pose several specific design problems. In particular, procedures are needed for:

- Detecting threats to means–end coherence
- Proposing new options in light of perceived changes in the environment
- Monitoring prior plans in light of changes in belief
- Checking compatibility with prior plans
- Overriding the compatibility filter

Of course, there are other design problems, such as means–end analysis and the weighing of conflicting options, that are common to a wide range of architectures for rational agency. Here we have highlighted problems specific to the architecture we are proposing.

## Acknowledgments

This is a slightly revised version of a paper that originally appeared in *Computational Intelligence* (1988). Reprinted with permission.

This work has been partially supported by a gift from the Systems Development Foundation. For their discussion of this work, the authors are grateful to other members of the Rational Agency Project at CSLI: Phil Cohen, Michael Georgeff, Kurt Konolige, Amy Lansky, and Ron Nash. The authors would also like to thank an anonymous reviewer.

## References

M. Boddy and T. Dean. 1989. Solving time-dependent planning problems. In *Proceedings of the International Joint Conference on Artificial Intelligence*. Morgan Kaufmann, San Mateo, California, pp. 979–984.

M. E. Bratman. 1987. *Intention, Plans, and Practical Reason*. Harvard University Press, Cambridge, Massachusetts.

R. A. Brooks. 1986. A robust layered control system for a mobile robot. In *IEEE Journal of Robotics and Automation*, 14–23.

P. R. Cohen and H. Levesque. 1990. Persistence, Intention, and Commitment. In *Intentions in Communication*. Edited by P. R Cohen, J. Morgan, and M. E. Pollack. MIT Press, Cambridge, Massachusetts.

B. DiFinetti. 1975. *Theory of Probability*. John Wiley and Sons, Inc., New York.

R. Dodhiawala, N. S. Sridharan, P. Raulefs, and C. Pickering. 1989. Real-time AI systems: A definition and an architecture. In *Proceedings of the International Joint Conference on Artificial Intelligence*. Morgan Kaufmann, San Mateo, California, pp. 256–261.

M. R Fehling and B. M. Wilber. 1989. *Schemer-II: An architecture for reflective, resource-bounded problem solving*. Technical Report 837–89–30, Rockwell International Science Center, Palo Alto Laboratory, Palo Alto, California.

R. E. Fikes and N. J. Nilsson. 1971. Strips: A New Approach to the Application of Theorem Proving to Problem Solving. *Artificial Intelligence* 2:189–208.

M. P. Georgeff. 1987a. Actions, Processes, and Causality. In *Reasoning about Actions and Plans: Proceedings of the 1986 Workshop*. Morgan Kaufmann, Los Altos, California, pp. 99–122.

M. P. Georgeff. 1987b. Planning. In *Annual Review of Computer Science, Vol. 2*. Edited by J. Traub. Annual Reviews, Inc., Palo Alto, California, pp. 359–400.

M. P. Georgeff and F. F. Ingrand. 1989. Decision-making in an embedded reasoning system. In *Proceedings of the International Joint Conference on Artficial Intelligence*. Morgan Kaufmann, San Mateo, California, pp. 972–978.

M. P. Georgeff and A. L. Lansky, editors. 1987. *Reasoning about Actions and Plans: Proceedings of the 1986 Workshop*. Morgan Kaufmann, Los Altos, California.

E. J. Horvitz, J. S. Breese, and M. Henrion. 1988. Decision theory in expert systems and artificial intelligence. *Journal of Approximate Reasoning* 2: 247–302.

R. Jeffrey. 1983. *The Logic of Decision*. Second edition. University of Chicago Press, Chicago, Illinois.

H. A. Kautz and M. Vilain. 1986. Constraint Propogation Algorithms for Temporal Reasoning. In *AAAI-86, Proceedings of the Fifth National Conference of the American Association for Artificial Intelligence*. Morgan Kaufmann, Los Altos, California, pp. 377–382.

A. L. Lansky. 1987. A Representation of Parallel Activity Based on Events, Structure, and Causality. In *Reasoning about Actions and Plans: Proceedings of the 1986 Workshop*. Morgan Kaufmann, Los Altos, California, pp. 123–159.

D. McDermott. 1985. Reasoning about Plans. In *Formal Theories of the Commonsense World*. Edited by J. R. Hobbs and R. C. Moore. Ablex Publishing Company, Norwood, New Jersey, pp. 269–317.

S. J. Rosenschein and L. P. Kaelbling. 1986. The synthesis of digital machines with provable epistemic properties. In *Proceedings of the Conference on Theoretical Aspects of Reasoning about Knowledge*. Morgan Kaufmann, Los Altos, California, pp. 83–98.

S. Russell and E. Wefald. 1989. Principles of metareasoning. In *Proceedings of the First International Conference on Principles of Knowledge Representation and Reasoning*. Morgan Kaufmann, San Mateo, California, pp. 400–411.

E. D. Sacerdoti. 1977. *A Structure for Plans and Behavior*. American Elsevier, New York.

L. J. Savage. 1972. *The Foundations of Statistics*. Second edition. Dover Press, New York.

H. Simon. 1957. *Models of Man*. Macmillan Press, New York.

N. S. Sridharan and J. Bresina. 1982. Plan Formation in Large, Realistic Domains. In *Proceedings of the Fourth National Conference of the Canadian Society for Computational Studies of Intelligence*. Canadian Society for Computational Studies of Intelligence, Saskatoon, Saskatchewan. pp. 12–18.

D. E. Wilkins. 1984. Domain-Independent Planning: Representation and Plan Generation. *Artificial Intelligence* 22:269–301.

# 2 Cross-Domain Inference and Problem Embedding

Robert Cummins

## 2.1 Introduction

### 2.1.1 Two Reasons for Studying Inference

Inference is studied for two distinct reasons: for its bearing on *justification* and for its bearing on *learning*. By and large, philosophy has focused on the role of inference in justification, leaving its role in learning to psychology and artificial intelligence. This difference of role leads to a difference of conception. An inference-based theory of learning does not require a conception of inference according to which a good inference is one that justifies its conclusion, whereas, obviously, an inference-based theory of justification does require such a conception.[1] Because of its focus on normative issues of justification, philosophy has taken a retrospective approach to inference, whereas a focus on learning naturally leads to a prospective approach. A focus on learning leads us to ask, Given what is known, what should be inferred? How can what is known lead, via inference, to new knowledge? A focus on justification has led philosophers to concentrate instead on a retrospective question: Given a belief, can it be validly inferred from what is known? How can what is known justify, via inference, a new belief? Thus, for philosophy, inference can be regarded as permissive: one needn't worry about what to infer, only about whether what has been arrived at somehow or other is or can be inferentially justified. A theory of learning, on the other hand, requires a conception of inference that is directive, for the problem of inference based learning is precisely the problem of what to infer.

### 2.1.2 Inference and Learning

Inference is relevant to learning because it is a method of expanding or revising existing knowledge. There are two main limitations of inference based accounts of learning.

---

[1] Acquiring a concept or a motor or intellectual skill is a standard case of learning, yet neither concepts nor skills need be justified to count as learned. Indeed, it isn't even obvious what it would mean to say that a concept or skill is justified. Even knowledge acquisition, as this is conceived in psychology and AI need not, and typically does not, involve justification: Knowledge, as this concept is used in the theory of learning, need not be true, let alone justified.

(1) Inference has to be inference *from* something; it requires premises. Inference based learners must be "seeded". Thus, inference based theories of learning must either be nativist, or they must acknowledge some non-inferential learning. This consequence is well known, and I will say no more about it.

(2) Less often noticed is a difficulty that arises in connection with the acquisition of knowledge expressed in novel concepts or terms. Inference, on the face of it, cannot lead from existing knowledge K to new knowledge K' in cases in which K and K' are representationally disjoint. Premises expressed on one vocabulary do not relate inferentially to conclusions expressed in another. Thus "cross-domain" learning, as I shall call it, poses a problem for inference based accounts of learning. The problem has a Kantian ring: How is cross-domain inference possible?

We deny the possibility of cross-domain inference at some cost. If there is no cross-domain inference then each domain must be seeded by its own proprietary innate knowledge, or by some kind of non-inferential learning. Pan-nativism is preposterous, however, and non-inferential learning mechanisms are thin on the ground, and not plausible for the introduction of "higher knowledge" in any case. We do well, therefore, to inquire what resources there are for cross-domain inference.

### 2.1.3   Cross-Domain Inference

Only two kinds of cross-domain inference have received any extended attention: explanation by and confirmation of theory, and analogy.

**Theoretical explanation and confirmation.**   Many scientific theories are expressed in a vocabulary that is disjoint from the vocabulary appropriate to the expression of the theory's intended explananda and confirming data. Given that explanation and confirmation are typically explicated in terms of (or as forms of) inference, the problems of theoretical explanation and confirmation have long been recognized as instances of cross-domain inference in the philosophy of science. But although there is a large literature on these issues, there is nothing in it to help us with the problem of learning by cross-domain inference. There are two reasons for this. First, as has been typical in philosophy, a normative, retrospective approach to the problem has dominated (but see Hanson 1958). The distinction between the context of discovery and the context of justification, made popular by positivist philosophy of science, was designed to canonize such an approach by relegating problems of discovery—that is of learning—to psychology on the grounds that they were not amenable to rational assessment. Thus, the problem of how knowledge in one domain might lead to knowledge in another was ruled out of bounds in this context in favor of the standard normative and retrospective problem: Given a theory and a body of data, or an alleged explanandum, what inferential relations must hold if the one is to be confirmed by or explain the other? (The classic text is Hempel 1965.)

In spite of this neglect of the problem of learning, one might hope that the literature on theoretical explanation and theory confirmation might provide some ideas about how distinct domains can be linked inferentially. Unfortunately, the only idea one finds is that there must be "bridge principles," laws linking the two domains explicitly. Little is said about where bridge principles come from. Again, the worry is only about what, if anything, might justify them once they have been formulated. Form the point of view of the learning theorist, nothing could be more disappointing: one is presented with the most obvious brute-force patch— to link $\Sigma$'s to S's, introduce a conditional "If $\Sigma$ then S'"—and no hint as to how the patches might be generated.[2]

**Analogy.**   Surprisingly, analogy is the only recognized *form* of inference that explicitly addresses the cross-domain problem. For this reason, I am not here to bury analogy, but to praise it. Perhaps the discussion so far will stimulate more research on analogy by indicating its unique importance. Still, it would be nice if there were another tool in the box to help cope with cross-domain inference.

## 2.2   Task Embedding

There is another way that cross-domain inference can be facilitated. The basic idea is to embed a task requiring knowledge of domain $D'$ in a task requiring knowledge of D in such a way that success in the D task is contingent on success in the $D'$ task. Reasoning about D thus constrains reasoning about $D'$. I propose to illustrate this approach in some detail by

---

[2] In the context of justification, this isn't a problem: theorists typically supply the intended connections between theory and observation or explanandum. It is not my intent to criticize the literature on theory justification; my point is only that we cannot hope that that literature has already invented the wheel learning theory is looking for.

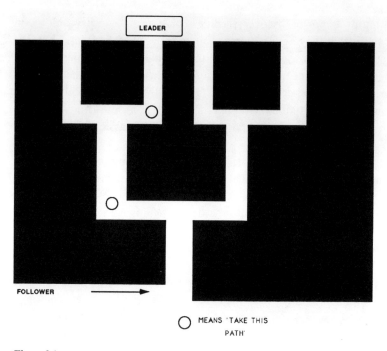

Figure 2.1

describing a technique for learning the meanings of arbitrary symbols or icons and simple syntactic constructions for combining them.

### 2.2.1    Illustration: Learning to Understand Simple Symbols and Syntax

**The embedding task.**    Someone, call her Leader, blazes a trail through a simple branching maze like that shown in figure 2.1. The blazes consist of arbitrary icons having no meaning for the task at hand, for example, a circle, a square, a wavy line. Follower then attempts to find Leader and, in the process, to discover the meaning of the "blazes." It is understood that Leader is trying to be helpful, to make things easy for Follower. Either part—Follower or Leader—can be played by the computer, with a human subject playing the other part. At any given time, the human subject sees only one intersection, as in figure 2.2. One can move left or right, or retrace one's steps to a previous intersection.

**Learning.**    A typical trial, described from the point of view of Follower, will give the flavor of the task. Consider the maze in figure one. You come

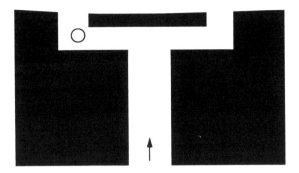

**Figure 2.2**

to the first intersection and observe the circle to the left, nothing to the right. You recall no meaning for a circle in this context. Reasoning that Leader probably marked the route taken rather than the one avoided, since the mark is well down the path, not in the intersection itself, you take the route marked. At the next intersection, you find a circle to the right. Evidently, Leader did come this way, or there would be no blaze at this point in the maze. You continue to follow the circles until you come to Leader. You now have a (perhaps tentative) convention with Leader governing the use of the circle.[3] Presented next with a maze like figure 2.3, you go directly to Leader with no false steps. The convention is no longer tentative.

Now consider figure 2.4. At the first intersection, you encounter a square. Most subjects take the path with the square for the same reason they take the path with the circle. This time, however, you encounter no marks whatever at the second intersection, and, in particular, no squares. Had Leader come this way, there would be some mark, so Leader must have gone the other way at the last intersection. New hypothesis: the square marks the route to avoid. You retrace your steps to the previous intersection and take the unmarked path. At the next intersection, you discover a square to your left. You go right, in accordance with your current hypothesis, and find Leader. Your hypothesis is confirmed. Presented with other mazes blazed (correctly) with squares, you go directly to Leader without

---

[3] A *convention* in the sense of Lewis 1969, that is, a shared plan for achieving a shared goal. When agents act in a certain way A to coordinate on the basis of mutual knowledge that A is how they have achieved coordination in the past, they have a convention for achieving coordination in that situation.

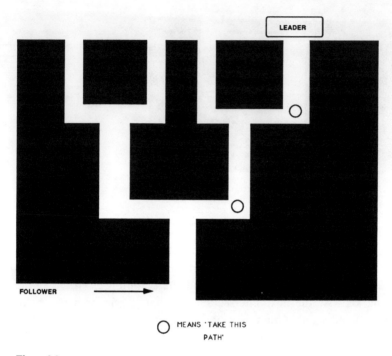

○  MEANS 'TAKE THIS
     PATH'

**Figure 2.3**

any false steps. You now have a convention with Leader governing the use of the square.

Next, consider figure 2.5. You know what the circle means, but not the bar. If you are like most subjects, you stick with what you know, taking the path with the circle. The next intersection prompts you to retrace your steps, and subsequently to avoid paths with the circle–bar blaze, a policy that takes you to Leader with no further problems. You now know what the circle–bar combination means, and what the circle means by itself. If you are like most subjects, asked what the bar means, you will say something like this: It means: do the opposite of what the other symbol means. That is, you will do a kind of subtraction problem:

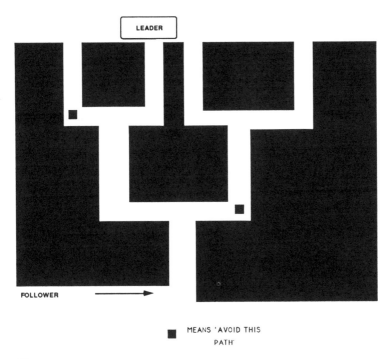

Figure 2.4

Moreover, presented with the maze of figure 2.6, you will find Leader with no false steps.

Comparable experience with figures 2.7 and 2.8 will provide conventions for symbols for "go left" and "go right," both of which combine un-problematically with the bar to form "don't go left" and "don't go right," as in figures 2.9 and 2.10.

Figure 2.11 introduces a new twist: symbols that refer to particular objects in the maze. Having no experience with the "squiggle," subjects typically ignore it and proceed on the basis of the vertical bar which they know to mean "go right." Eventually, they discover that going right meets with success when it is done at the church. After a few mazes blazed in this way, subjects will say the squiggle means "church." Analogous experience with ⊟, combined with previous experience, allows for rather complex situations such as those in figures 2.12 and 2.13.

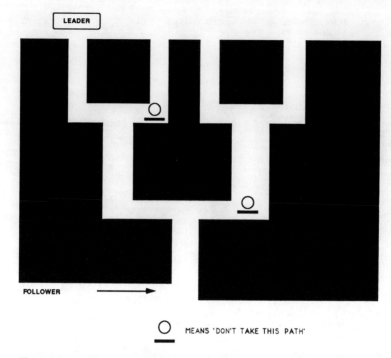

MEANS 'DON'T TAKE THIS PATH'

**Figure 2.5**

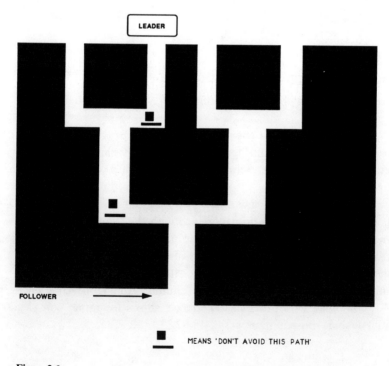

MEANS 'DON'T AVOID THIS PATH'

**Figure 2.6**

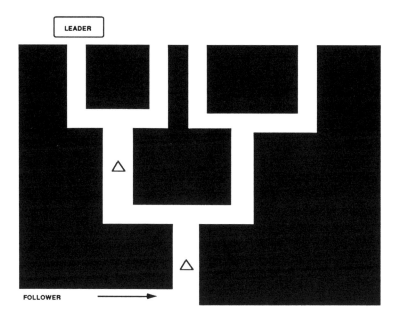

Figure 2.7

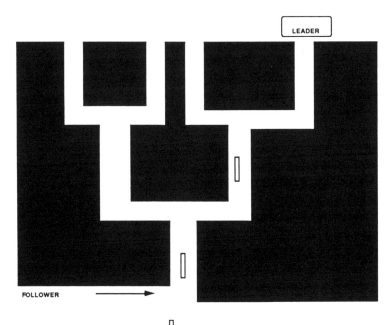

Figure 2.8

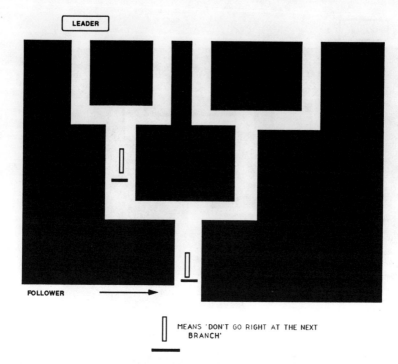

Figure 2.9

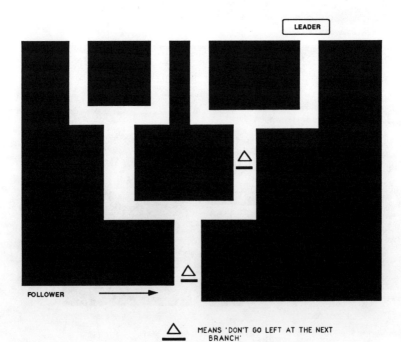

Figure 2.10

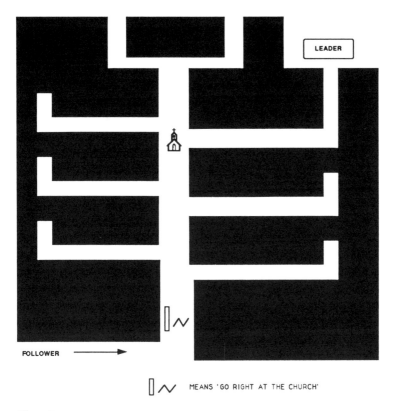

MEANS 'GO RIGHT AT THE CHURCH'

**Figure 2.11**

### 2.2.2   Remarks about the Illustration

In the illustration just rehearsed, both the embedded task and the embedding task are coordination problems (Lewis 1969), that is, problems in which two or more agents share a goal and must coordinate their actions in order to achieve it. While it is obvious that the embedding task is a coordination problem, it isn't so obvious that the embedded task is a coordination problem. To see that it is, notice that it is a communication problem: the shared goal is successful communication between Leader and Follower. What successful communication requires, roughly, is that Understander adopt correct beliefs about Meaner's intentions in producing the

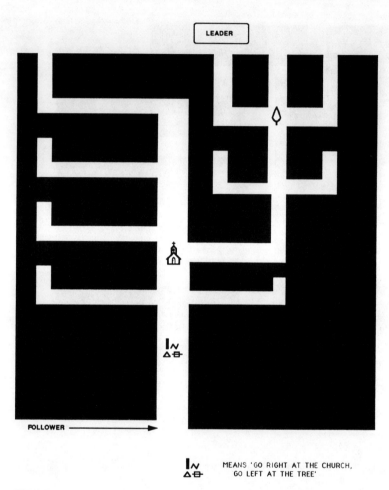

MEANS 'GO RIGHT AT THE CHURCH,
GO LEFT AT THE TREE'

**Figure 2.12**

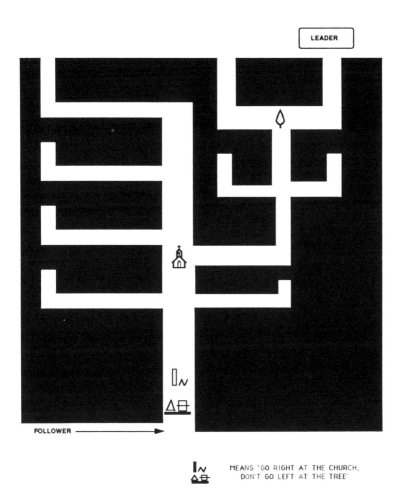

MEANS 'GO RIGHT AT THE CHURCH,
DON'T GO LEFT AT THE TREE'

Figure 2.13

communicative signals—blazes, in this case; Understander's beliefs must coordinate with Meaner's intentions.[4]

Communication is an especially difficult coordination problem for two reasons: (i) Intentions and beliefs are hidden, hence it is difficult to determine whether coordination has been achieved. (ii) Because any symbol or construction could mean anything, the range of hypotheses Understander might have to canvass is essentially unbounded. Embedding the communication task in the maze task allows a solution to both of these problems by allowing knowledge of the embedding task to constrain inferences required to perform the embedded task. Feedback about success or failure properly to recognize Leader's communicative intentions is provided in a readily accessible and easily appreciated manner by the fact that success in the maze task is contingent in an obvious way on success in guessing Leader's communicative intentions. Embedding the communication task in the maze task has the effect of turning the communication task into a case of supervised learning, even though there is no teacher. The environment, together with knowledge about the embedding task, play the role of a teacher in an entirely natural way, allowing Follower easy access to information about Leader's communicative intentions.

Working together with the feedback provided by the embedding task is the equally important fact that the embedding task severely limits the range of hypotheses that Follower needs to consider. Early in the learning task, Follower's hypotheses about Leader's communicative intentions (i.e., about the meanings of the blazes encountered) are effectively limited to direct correlates of Follower's possible actions. Subjects faced with the figure 2.1 maze always regard themselves as faced initially with two possibilities: The square means that Leader went down the path with the square, or the square means that Leader went down the path without the square. Given knowledge of the embedding task, there is simply nothing else relevant that the square could mean.

An important feature of the learning achieved via task embedding is that the acquired knowledge can be applied successfully in the absence of the embedding task that enabled learning in the first place. Subjects who learn the meaning of symbols for *left, right, take, avoid, tree, church*, and the like in the maze context have no trouble applying this knowledge when the symbols are encountered in different contexts.

---

[4] See Grice 1959, Bennett 1973, Lewis 1969, and Cummins 1979 for more on the analysis of communication in terms of intentions and beliefs.

**Canoe paddling.** The subject is in the rear paddling position and can paddle either forward or backward on the left or right. Instructions are issued from the forward position in the form of arbitrary icons for which conventions have been established in the maze context. Although both paddlers can see the destination, the person in the forward position is the only one who can see obstacles (e.g., submerged rocks). Conventions for "left," "right," "forward," and "back," acquired in the maze context, generalize to this context without difficulty.

**Giving/following directions.** This is very similar to the maze task. Director gives directions to a specified location in a city, and Traveler attempts to follow them. "Left," "right," "tree," and so on transfer unproblematically.

## 2.3 Caveats and Conclusions

This project demonstrates that task embedding can effect cross-domain inference in the broad sense in which this means that knowledge of one domain constrains inferences in another. It is important, however, to be clear about what the illustration does not show.

First, the illustration involves embedding coordination problems, and the learning involved is a species of convention acquisition. While it seems clear that the technique will work for other kinds of tasks and learning, I haven't actually tried it.

Second, you can't learn—at least not inferentially—what a symbol means if you don't already have the capacity to represent the meaning in question (Fodor 1975). This point *does* generalize: task embedding constrains hypothesis formation and confirmation, but it does not provide new representational resources.

Third, task embedding, like analogy, presupposes appropriately structured knowledge of the source (embedding) domain. Just as knowing that A is analogous to B doesn't help you infer things about A if you don't know anything, or the wrong things, about B, so embedding A in B doesn't help you infer things about A unless you know the right things about B.

Taken together, the second and third points must temper optimism about inference-based learning. Cross-domain inference (analogy, task embedding) allow the inference-based learning theorist to avoid one kind of pan-nativism, namely, seed-knowledge in every domain, but leaves nativism of two other kinds intact: You have to know about the source domain, and you have to have the representational power already in place. We still have to explain the origin of the knowledge of the source domain, and we still have to explain the origin of the concepts used to formulate hypotheses in the new domain. These are the central challenges to inference-based learning. Compared to these problems, the problem of cross-domain inference, while interesting and important, is just detail.

## References

Bennett, J. 1973. The Meaning-Nominalist Strategy. *Foundations of Language* 10, 141–168.

Cummins, R. 1979. Intention, Meaning and Truth-Conditions. *Philosophical Studies* 35, 345–360.

Fodor, J. 1975. *The Language of Thought*. New York: Crowell.

Grice, H. 1957. Meaning. *Philosophical Review* 78, 147–177.

Hanson, N. 1958. *Patterns of Discovery*. Cambridge: Cambridge University Press.

Hempel, C. 1965. *Aspects of Scientific Explanation*. New York: The Free Press. See chapter 4, "Empiricist Criteria of Cognitive Significance," and chapter 8, "The Theoretician's Dilemma."

Lewis, D. 1969. *Convention*. Cambridge: Cambridge University Press.

# 3 The Foundations of Psychology: A Logico-Computational Inquiry into the Concept of Mind

Jon Doyle

If today one asks, What is the brain?, one receives volumes of material from the neuroscientists. This material may not be very complete, nor terribly revealing about the operation of the brain, but it is a beginning one can hope to continue. On the other hand, if one asks, What is the mind?, or What is thinking?, one receives today little information more certain than that supplied by the quaint theories of antiquity. On these latter questions one finds not just volumes of material, but volumes of material for each of many diverse theories of mind. Philosophers alone supply dozens, but they are not exceptional, for so do the psychologists, linguists, decision-theorists, artificial intelligence researchers, and novelists. These and other answers are in turn assumed by the social sciences, each of which depends on a conception of man for its formulation, and by moral thinkers in philosophy, theology, and politics for similar reasons. What's a body to think?

Is it not a scandal that such common notions as mind and thought enter so prominently in our understanding of the world, yet find so little definiteness in the sciences they underlie? How are the sciences to look for facts, to measure, analyze, or construct minds without a clear notion of the object of their study? Without a clear conception of mind, how can the sciences tell if they are studying minds or if they have accidentally drifted to studying something else instead? How, indeed!

In spite of the great wealth of theories extant, my purpose here is to present yet another, one which underlies many of my recent studies.[1] The concept of mind is ultimately a philosophical or metaphysical subject, and as a consequence my inquiry begins in largely philosophical terms. I approach the subject from backgrounds in mathematics and artificial intelligence, and use of mathematical, logical, and computational methods soon join philosophical methods in my investigations. I believe the use of both philosophical and mathematical tools necessary to this project. If successful, these results will inform researchers in artificial intelligence of the logical foundations and implications of their techniques, and will inform philosophical and mathematical logicians of both psychological applications of their theories and possible areas for new mathematical developments. I permit myself the hope that even the philosophers, if they

---

[1] Doyle 1983a, 1983b, 1983c, 1983d, 1988.

examine what I have written without prejudice, will find in it something of use to them.

The best of tools is powerless, however, if the nature of the investigation is not clear. Sadly, there is some confusion about the aims of artificial intelligence and the other cognitive sciences. One finds views of artificial intelligence ranging from "frontier applications of computers," to "knowledge engineering," to "making machines act more intelligently," to "making machines simulate human thought," to "making intelligent machines." A glance at introductions to cognitive science reveals scant definition beyond a melding of artificial intelligence and psychology, together with hopes that maybe bits of philosophy, linguistics, education, neurosciences, and so forth will make their way into the field. This is a recipe for a stew, not a statement of the scientific aims of a field. Artificial intelligence and cognitive science may in fact be or turn out to be all these things, but these must be consequences of the pursuit of yet unarticulated scientific aims rather than the aims themselves.

Clarity about scientific aims is especially important for the present work, for our investigations will not make much sense or will be misconstrued without a proper understanding of their intended contribution. The title of this paper is "The Foundation of Psychology," yet one will find virtually nothing from modern psychological theories here. This paper is not so much about the modern discipline of psychology as it is about all possible organizations for minds, that is, psychologies. These are the objects of study of what I call *rational psychology*, which, in analogy with rational mechanics, is the conceptual investigation of psychology by means of the most fit mathematical concepts.[2] The disciplines of psychology and artificial intelligence are simply particular subdisciplines of cognitive science with special interests to pursue. I share this last conclusion with the views mentioned above, but the former conclusion, upon which to me the latter is based, seems much less widely held, if others hold it at all. To avoid misconstrual of these investigations, the remainder of this introduction sets out the assumed scientific aims of rational psychology, psychology, and artificial intelligence.

Rational psychology is the study of all possible minds. It may not be possible to set out in advance a definite class containing all possible minds, just as biologists have had to abandon all definitions of "living things"

[2] See Truesdell 1966 and Doyle 1983a, 1983b.

and adopt an accommodating approach to newly discovered life forms. Nevertheless, this paper formulates a definition of what minds are as an initial foundation for their study. To jump ahead of ourselves, we view minds as narrowly realized theories, so that minds are not natural objects but theory-relative instead. The theories realized as minds are psychologies (not to be confused with the discipline psychology), ways of viewing the organizations of minds. This definition can hardly mean much now, but we do assume some definite range of objects as minds. The task of rational psychology is to discover classifications of minds so that each mind can be uniquely characterized in terms of the system of classifications, and so that identically characterized minds are isomorphic in some natural sense. In other words, the aim of rational psychology is to characterize the equivalence classes of possible minds. Some classifications of minds will involve the sorts of constituents (e.g., beliefs, pains, etc.) from which mental states are constructed. In addition to internal structural classifications, other classifications involve relations between psychologies and other things. In the case of relating one psychology to another, one has classifications involving homomorphism, embeddability, or compatibility, of one psychology being a form of another. For example, if humans typically realize a general psychology $\psi$, then a psychology $\psi'$ realized by a particular normal human, will be a more detailed version of the general psychology, and so will admit a homomorphism onto $\psi$. In the case of relating psychologies to non-psychological entities, the principal question is whether a particular psychology $\psi$ is realizable in entities of class E. For example, the task of the familiar discipline of psychology is to find psychologies that can be and typically are realized in human beings. One view of the task of artificial intelligence can be phrased as discovering "interesting" (e.g., human-like) psychologies which can be realized in Turing-equivalent machines.

Human beings and Turing-equivalent machines need not exhaust the range of entities in which to realize psychologies. Many interesting psychologies may lie beyond the realm of what is realizable given the physics of our universe. Consideration of this possibility may seem strange to those steeped in traditions involving empirical psychology and Church's thesis (see Minsky 1967), but limiting the scope of rational psychology by the laws of physics is mistaken. The questions of rational psychology have content independent of the particular characteristics of our universe. This can be understood in several steps as follows.

Individual psychologies are particular theories of mind, precise specifications of mental organizations. If a psychology is a formal theory of a mental organization, realizations of this psychology are models of the theory. There is no normative or descriptive content in the notion of psychology itself, just the notion of a theory and its possible models. However, we may view psychologies from both normative and descriptive perspectives. We can ask for the psychologies describing some individual human, for example, and we can say some psychology specifies normal human mental organization. When viewed normatively, psychologies are competence theories in Chomsky's sense, where realizations of the normative psychology are mentally "competent" agents, and realizations of differing psychologies are mentally "incompetent" agents (although their incompetence may involve being stronger as well as weaker in their faculties, unavoidable supercompetence considered a form of incompetence at meeting normative limitations).

Chomsky's idea of competence theories has influenced much work in the cognitive sciences, but the applications of this idea may have been unnecessarily limited in comparison with the more basic notion of normative theory due to the context in which the idea was introduced. In the beginning of *Aspects of the Theory of Syntax*,[3] Chomsky develops his competence/performance distinction as a tool in explaining how a finite mind can use an apparently infinite language, to say how a grammar makes possible the "infinite use of finite means." Chomsky motivates the notion of competence with a picture of an idealized speaker as one free of all memory limitations and free of certain computational limitations such as distractions, shifts of attention and interest, and random or characteristic errors. Since Chomsky speaks from a linguistic tradition which gathers yes-or-no judgments of grammaticality from subject speakers, it is easy to assume he assumes recursiveness of spoken languages. But to extend the requirement of recursiveness to the idea of competence seems unwarranted.[4] "Finite means" might be finitely axiomatized second-order theories like arithmetic, beyond the pale of recursive enumerability. Once one widens one's interest from human languages to rational psychology, limitations of recursiveness can be viewed as merely a characteristic error for the

[3] Chomsky 1965.
[4] Thomason (1979) discusses some problems with the notion of competence theories for cognitive scientists wedded to the assumption of recursiveness.

speakers of a nonrecursive language. The aim of a normative or competence theory is to give an ideal against which to measure the performance of supposed practitioners. There is nothing in the notion of ideal *simpliciter* which entails recursiveness or even recursive enumerability. We should be able to consider an ideal consisting of just the true sentences of arithmetic. Of course, we can prove that no Turing-equivalent speaker can achieve this ideal of competence, but that is nothing new in the world. Suppose, for example, we try to formulate weightlifting competence and performance. It seems plausible to take the notion of weightlifting competence to be that one can lift barbells of any weight. Of course, there are many "processing" limitations idiosyncratic to all humans. Moreover, one can prove from physical laws that there are weights humans can never lift. Is this provable physical incompetence somehow specially different from provable mental incompetence? It seems unlikely that Church's thesis is anything but an empirical fact, just like the ordinary laws of physics. Gandy, for instance, has outlined a proof of Church's thesis from physical laws.[5] The apparent equivalence of effective computability and recursive enumerability may be nothing more than an amazing coincidence of our universe. But if the limitations of Church's thesis are empirical rather than logically necessary, there might exist universes in which machines have super-Turing powers of computation, and excluding these universes and their inhabitants from the domain of normative theories is nothing but chauvinism.

By virtue of their use as normative theories, we must conclude that psychologies need not be actually realizable to be of interest to rational psychology. This range of concern frees rational psychology to calmly study controversial assumptions. Rational psychology studies in part the range of psychologies realizable by machines limited to the effectively computable, where what may be computable effectively by machines may vary with the laws of physics. Artificial intelligence will be the main research vehicle for studying mechanical intelligence in our universe. Rational psychology also studies the full range of psychologies realizable by arbitrary physical systems. In some universes, these may include nonmechanical psychologies, and in others, these may be the same as the mechanical psychologies. For example, human psychologies may or may not be mechanically realizable in our universe, but this is no cause for heated debates to impede the progress of rational psychology. Mechanists will relate their

[5] Gandy 1980.

studies to the comparable but independent questions of artificial intelligence, and non-mechanists will not be so bothered unless it is to demon-
strate the non-effectiveness of some aspects of human psychologies.

In addition to this argument from antichauvinism, one might arrive at
the proposed scope of rational psychology as one more fruitful scientifically
than one limited to our universe. Arbitrarily limiting the range of acceptable psychologies may unnecessarily prevent discovery of important facts
about uncontroversial psychologies. The more generally posed problem
may admit an easy solution even when the special case presents intractable
difficulties. For example, real and complex numbers may be "unreal" in
some sense in which integers are not, but some facts about integers and
integer functions (e.g., the prime number theorem) are obtained most easily
as facts about real and complex numbers and functions, and can be obtained only with extreme difficulty as facts about integers alone. In the same
way we may most easily see things about the minds of men by looking, so
to speak, to the mind of God. Limiting the domain of rational psychology
to the boundaries of our own universe and excluding the trans-computable
is analogous to limiting mathematics to the integers and excluding the
transfinite. This analogy has a moral. Cantor led mathematicians into a
paradise many will not abandon due to the rich harvest they find there.
Other mathematicians stay outside to see what fruits hang on branches
reaching over the walls. In comparison, rational psychologists have hardly
begun to taste the fruit of their field. Perhaps our paradise grows only sour
grapes, but we must taste them to see.

## 3.1   Rigor in Psychological Theories

After proceeding for centuries without exceptional standards of rigor,
philosophy of mind within this century has been the beneficiary of three
great boons. The first of these was the development, beginning primarily
with Frege, Russell, and Hilbert, of modern mathematical logic and metamathematics.[6] The second boon was the development, beginning with
Wundt, Freud, and Watson, of modern scientific psychology.[7] The third
boon was the development, with the advice of Turing and Von Neumann,
of the general-purpose electronic computer.[8] Mathematical logic has pro-

[6] See, for example, Frege 1884, Whitehead and Russell 1910, and Hilbert 1900.
[7] See, for example, Wundt 1874, Freud 1895, and Watson 1914.
[8] See Goldstein 1972 and Randell 1975 for histories.

vided the language for precise formulations of problems of mind and their solutions. Scientific psychology has provided many careful observations of human behavior and performance to account for in theories. And the high-speed electronic computer has provided the means for experimentally investigating the consequences of partial and comprehensive theories of mind in ways that were previously infeasible. Together these three developments have stimulated the new field of artificial intelligence. With the intellectual and practical tools at hand, artificial intelligence promises the most precisely formulated and visibly detailed theories of mind yet developed. Where previous centuries served as grounds for battles between imprecise, ill-understood proposals, battles allowing little hope for eventual comprehension of or agreement on the nature of the issues at stake, the new tools permit far greater clarity in formulating the concepts and structures of theories, so that parties to debates at least can agree on the issues, if not on the answers. Properly applied, the new tools ruthlessly expose inadequacies of theories previously hidden behind the general vagueness of formulations of the theories, and this shows up in the aphorism of artificial intelligence which states that about the nature of mind, the first twenty obvious ideas are wrong. More clearly than ever before, the new tools prove that in psychology simple moral conviction, even supported by a mass of successful applications, is not enough. Rigor in formulation must accompany conviction if the field is to visibly progress.

Precision in formulating psychological theories leads quickly to a need for clear conceptions of the nature of mind and the nature of thinking. In the past, psychological theories have all too often lacked clarity through vagueness about the object of the theory. Routinely, investigators would propose hypotheses in great detail about some particular component of mind or thought, while merely alluding to an overall structure never made precise. This course holds two dangers: first, that not being closely tied to a definite conception of mind, the component theory will wander off to become an abstract plaything of its creator; and second, that the component theory will become vacuous by pushing all important theoretical burdens onto the vaguely defined theory of the whole. To avoid these dangers, we must strive for as much precision in setting out concepts of mind as in proposing theories of particular mental components.

If the first aim of psychology must be to set out at least skeletal theories of mind, lest any empirical or detailed studies of supposed mental components risk triviality or irrelevance, then the first step toward this aim must be to understand the possible forms of psychological theories, to understand the range of possible conceptions of mind. Care is required in this enterprise, for historically there has been frequent temptation to confuse the theoretical tools used to formulate theories with the theories themselves, and this confuses the aims of psychology with the aims of mathematics, logic, computer science, and other fields. For example, logic is not part of psychology, and neither is psychology a part of logic. Nevertheless, the temptation is frequently great to transfer the methods of logic to the methods of thinking and *vice versa*. Just as Modus Ponens is well established in logic, many nondeductive inferential processes are well established in psychology, and confusing the logical notions of entailment and proof with the psychological notions of argument and thinking is just wrong. Yet numerous students of mind make this confusion, and in consequence many works in artificial intelligence place psychological burdens on logic, faulting it for remaining silent on properly psychological problems, and mistakenly turning away from the clarity of formulation logical tools provide. Complementing this, other works view the purpose of thinking as the production of new knowledge from old, to which logical deduction is well suited if anything is. This transference of purpose oversteps the proper role of logical rigor in psychology. The purpose of thinking is insight, not knowledge. The aim of reasoning is not merely to ensure the truth or drawing of a conclusion, but more fundamentally, to afford insight into the dependence of conclusions upon one another. From certain interdependencies of conclusions, we can tell that one conclusion will be true if others are; and from other interdependencies, that one conclusion will be held by the agent if others are. On the face of it, these are different relations between conclusions. It is not difficult to think of further interesting relations between conclusions, such as confirmation or falsification in inductive reasoning. In fact, each of the disciplines brought to bear in formulating a conception of mind may have its own special interdependencies, but these must not be confused with each other. The separate disciplines must enhance each other, not replace each other.

Although I am led to ask these questions in the course of formulating psychological theories, philosophical motives too have prompted me to enquiries of this kind. Our understanding of the questions traditionally raised about the relation of mind and matter, of free will and determinism, and of the limitations of effective computability all must increase from consideration of the nature of psychological theories. We may, if lucky, arrive at answers to these questions, or at formulations of possible positions if not answers. Even if no conclusions result, at least the outlines of the mysteries will be clarified.

Surprisingly, starting from these theoretical and philosophical questions about the nature of mind, we are led to formulate the same demand as that which had arisen independently in the practice of artificial intelligence, namely that psychological theories be cast as sets of narrowly interpreted self-specifications; for only if a theory is suitably narrow in the range of its references can it be realized in humans or machines; and only if a theory can be used in isolation to reconstruct states of mind after changes does it facilitate the design of artificial agents. Our story is largely a tale of the two theories leading to this remarkable convergence.

## 3.2 Views of Certain Writers on the Nature of Mind

### 3.2.1 Are There Thoughts?

During most of the history of philosophy, men have been assumed to have thoughts. More often than not, thoughts and their vehicle, the mind, were taken to be different somehow than the ordinary stuff from which our bodies are composed. A high point in this train of thought was the skeptical argument of Descartes.[9] By elementary considerations, Descartes managed to convince himself that his mind existed. He required substantial additional hypotheses and arguments to convince himself that his body and other ordinary things existed as well. Based on these considerations, Descartes divided the world into two parts: the realm of matter, from which our bodies are composed, and the realm of an immaterial sort of substance, from which our minds are composed. For a long time after Descartes, the principal themes in discussions of mind consisted of speculative theories about the relation and possible interaction of immaterial mind and material body. These theories were hampered by the growth of the physical sciences, for as more and more of the universe came under the domain claimed by physics, it became increasingly difficult to supply a plausible account of how an immaterial object, not subject to physical law, could influence or be influenced by a material object subject to those laws.

Fortunately for the growth of a somewhat less speculative psychology, another train of thought was developing in the wings. Long ago, the

---

[9] Descartes 1637.

Epicurians, taken with Democritus's ideas about atoms, proclaimed that all the world was composed of atoms.[10] Men's minds, no less than their bodies, were made up of atoms, and the behavior of minds could be explained like the behavior of bodies, in terms of the mechanical laws governing the motions of atoms. However, the Epicurians proposed no details of these explanations and laws. Instead, they simply claimed the soul was composed of atoms lighter and more mobile than ordinary atoms, so presumably accounting for the rapidity with which thoughts can progress while leaving no outward sign of change visible to observers.

After some delay, the Epicurean program was taken up by Hobbes, who tried to give some explanation of the workings of the material mind. Hobbes took his models of mechanics from the new physics, which clarified the notions of forces and inertia. With these, he explained thought and imagination as the decaying motion of the atoms of the sense organs as they stimulate other atoms and are stimulated by new impressions. In spite of the possibilities of this program, Hobbes was limited by contemporary ignorance about neurophysiology and non-naïve psychological phenomena, so his theory remained largely speculative and general about mental mechanics.

After yet another delay, these ideas received their first detailed treatment. An experimental, scientific psychology developed under the impetus of Wundt and others, and much information became available about psychological phenomena.[11] However, much of this information still depended on uncritical speculation in the form of introspective evidence. Watson urged that psychology secure its foundations and either shore up introspection or avoid it altogether in favor of theories of overt and neurophysical behavior.[12] He took the latter course, and his program, psychological behaviorism, became widely influential, and led to much progress in matters such as neurophysiology, neurochemistry, and neuropsychology.

Given this development of ideas, it seems like a small step from psychological behaviorism to philosophical behaviorism. Where psychological behaviorism, in modest formulations at least, seeks simply to determine the laws of mind and thought and their realization in the body, philosophical behaviorism, as championed by Ryle and Skinner, claims reducibility to

[10] Much of my knowledge of these fragments of history comes from Boring 1950 and Peters and Mace 1967.
[11] Wundt 1874.
[12] Watson 1914.

overt behavior as well.[13] For the philosophical behaviorist, mental phenomena can not only be realized in terms of neurological hardware, but can also be reduced to those functionings of that hardware, in the sense that all theories about belief, desire, inference, and action can be formulated purely in terms of the overt behavior of the body. In this view, mental entities and processes are simply unreal, and their use is as unscientific as phlogiston descriptions of combustion. Ryle, for example, sought descriptions of human behavior strictly in terms of overt acts, dispositions to behave, and changes in dispositions to behave, where dispositions to behave were formulated purely as physical states and physical laws.

Philosophical behaviorism eschewed the mind. Indeed, some of its adherents went so far as to deny any introspective self-awareness in their own cases: not a tactic unknown to philosophy, but one never before practiced on such a grand scale. Cartesian skepticism seems meager compared to that of the philosophical behaviorists.

Philosophical behaviorism is implausible, and for very simple reasons. Suppose one attempts to analyze an ascription of belief, for example, "Fred believes his computer program has a bug" in terms of behavior and dispositions to behave. We can of course guess at predictive generalizations about Fred's behavior given this belief, such as "Fred is disposed to log in and debug his program," but for any of these predictions to have any plausibility, they cannot be formulated simply in terms of behavior and states of the world; they must refer to other of Fred's beliefs and desires that might influence his dispositions, for example, "Fred believes the computer is down" or "Fred wants to take his time so as to increase his wages." Because predictions of Fred's behavior must refer to his thoughts about things as well as to the actual state of things, philosophical behaviorism is untenable.

With Cartesian dualism indefensible, but with its prime alternative inadequate, philosophers developed several replacement theories which identified mental states and processes with the physical states and processes of the brain and connecting parts of the body.[14] These identity theories, as they are known, hoped to analyze beliefs and desires, for example, as physical predicates of brains, thus allowing the objections to philosophical behaviorism to be overcome by phrasing references to beliefs and desires as references to certain sorts of brain states. The identity theorists returned

---

[13] Ryle 1949, Skinner 1957.
[14] See, for instance, Place 1956, Feigl 1958, and Smart 1959.

to a position much like that of Hobbes, although unlike Hobbes, they had a stronger physics and neurophysiology to draw upon for formulation and examples.

Although the identity theories avoid the obvious problems with philosophical behaviorism, they suffer from inadequacies of their own. Curiously, these inadequacies are made all the sharper by the development of somewhat intelligent machines in artificial intelligence, although the inadequacies can be brought out without using those machines as examples.

Identity theories claim that all statements about mental phenomena are reducible to statements purely about physical brain states, with the implication that perhaps we are better off studying the brain states in psychology and leaving the mind alone. The first objection to this idea, at least to its implication, is that even if such a reduction is possible, it is useless in practice and so even theoretically uninteresting (at least to those who include practical power as a measure of a good theory). Putnam gives as example the analogous case of a description of a hole in a board in terms of the location and momentum of elementary particles.[15] If the hole is round, we cannot insert a square peg of equal cross-section area, and presumably this fact can be explained in terms of the locations of and forces between the particles comprising the board and peg. But such an explanation must be astronomically long, and must involve many details that are in some sense irrelevant to the important facts, namely, the roundness of the hole and squareness of the peg. Dennett gives as another example chess-playing computers.[16] Unless one is a chess master, one's best tactic in playing such a machine is to treat it as a rational agent with beliefs, desires, and knowledge of the game, for the actual sequence of computational steps the machine employs to develop its moves is incomprehensible (at least in any reasonable amount of time for individual humans). Dennett describes this observation as the notion of "intentional stance": that no matter what other theories are possible concerning the realization of mental phenomena, we still must use a psychology formulated in mental terms, because mentalist ascriptions are the ones of practical predictive power (for humans, at any rate).

The identity theories also fall prey to a stronger criticism: that their supposed reduction of psychological physical laws cannot be done, even in

[15] Putnam 1975c.
[16] Dennett 1978.

principle, without severely gutting the notion of law. Suppose one has a psychological theory formalized in mental terms, a physical theory formalized in terms of particles and fields, and, as the identity theorists suggest, a set of "bridging laws" or "bridging definitions" connecting the two theories. Fodor points out that because there are presumably many, many ways of realizing minds in matter (just as many physical objects can be used as money), the bridging statements cannot be laws unless they are so wildly disjunctive as to ridicule our ordinary conception of what it means to be a law.[17] Fodor continues by pointing out that if the bridging statements are reasonably informative or concise definitions, then the psychological theory that results cannot aspire to the title of law either—its applicability need not be wide, nor need its conditionals have counterfactual force.

These criticisms of identity theories contain the seeds of a theory to replace the identity theories, functionalism. Functionalists contend that mental states are functional states; that is, what makes something a belief or a desire of the agent is the fact that that something plays a certain role in the processes of the agent, independent of any other properties possessed by its particular realizations in brains, computers, or ghosts.[18] Expressions of functionalist psychological theories take the form of physical theory plus a collection of Ramsey sentences: existentially quantified statements asserting the existence of something that bears certain relations to other things which, in light of the criticism of psychological behaviorism, will include some of the other entities asserted to exist by the Ramsey sentences. For example, a ten-cent soda machine accepting either nickels or dimes might be described by the two sentences "There exists a state $S_0$ such that receiving a nickel in $S_0$ results in a change to state $S_5$, and receiving a dime in $S_0$ results in dispensing a soda and remaining in $S_0$" and "There exists a state $S_5$ such that receiving a nickel in $S_5$ results in dispensing a soda and a change to state $S_0$, and receiving a dime in $S_5$ results in dispensing a soda, dispensing a nickel, and a change to state $S_0$." Functionalism thus permits some separation between the development of a psychological theory and the delineation of the ways in which the theory may be realized in humans or machines. However, functionalism is not without problems of its own, and some of these concerning surprises about what things can and cannot be functional states will arise in the following.

[17] Fodor 1975.
[18] See, for instance, Putnam 1975b and Fodor 1968.

### 3.2.2 Have Thoughts Content?

Even if one accepts functionalism as a hopeful theory of the mental, there are many serious difficulties that must be overcome. The first of these is the nature of thoughts as conceived in functionalist terms. To understand this problem, we must examine the functions thoughts play in mental activity.

To begin a functional characterization of the role of particular thoughts in thinking, we can take as a crude approximation all the truisms about rational thought and action. For example, a functionalist psychology might have specifications like the following: (1) "If agent $A$ desires $p$ and believes $M$ a method for achieving $p$, then $A$ desires to do $M$, other things being equal," and (2) "If $A$ desires to do $M$, and believes doing $M$ is better than doing any other action $A$ desires, then $A$ does $M$." Our lazy programmer Fred might desire to earn a living without the necessity of toil, might believe that being slow to debug his programs a way of doing this, and might in fact be slow in his chores thinking this the easiest way of life. Of course, specifications (1) and (2) are woefully simplistic, and any careful treatment would have to be based on a better theory of rationality and practical reasoning, but the example serves to illustrate the basic idea.

In addition to basing functional specifications for the mind on sound theories of thinking and doing, we must take care to ensure that the specifications are suitably narrow in scope. For example, we might consider a specification like (1') "If $A$ desires $p$, and $M$ is a method for achieving $p$, then $A$ desires to do $M$, other things being equal." The problem with (1') is that it puts a measure of omniscience into the specifications, omniscience that offends our notion of what a psychology should involve. While one might give such specifications in ecological theories of how well agents fit into their environments, for psychology proper we eschew any specifications which do not express what Putnam terms "psychology in the narrow sense."[19] Psychology in the narrow sense is concerned only with narrowly realized psychological theories, where narrowly realized psychological theories refer only to the agent's personal mental structures, and do not refer to any correspondence or lack of correspondence between the agent's thoughts and its environment, such as the truth of its beliefs or the physical possibility of its desires. Narrowness is a property of realizations or interpretations of psychological theories, rather than a property of the theories

---

[19] Putnam 1975a.

themselves, since a particular theory might admit interpretations stepping outside the agent as well as strictly internal interpretations. For example, to return to the ten-cent soda machine introduced above, the functional specifications given there were not narrowly realized. Those specifications referred to dispensing of sodas, objects presumably beyond the machine's ken. Ordinary soda machines (at least the ones I have lost money to) only send signals to the dispenser for its jaws to open, thus allowing a soda to fall if one is there, but failing to dispense a soda (unbeknownst to the machine) if the soda rack is empty or jammed. To describe the machine's structure narrowly, we must replace references to sodas by references to signals sent from the cashier to the dispenser. Fodor terms such restrictions of narrowness on acceptable interpretations of psychological specifications "methodological solipsism."[20]

Adherence to the methodology of psychological solipsism requires that we re-examine our naïve psychological theories to excise all externalities. The example specifications (1) and (2) given above seem to refer to the content or meaning of the agents beliefs, desires, and so on, but notions of meaning or interpretation are usually external relations of the agent to the world, hence the use of such notions in our psychological theory is suspect. We could immediately excise these notions from our psychology, but this would be hasty since there are many reasons why we would like to have some notion of content available for thoughts. The agent must be able to compare or distinguish its thoughts, one from another, lest its psychology be completely trivial and implausible. Some notion of content is also required for comparing thoughts of the agent at different times, and with the thoughts of other agents. We clearly can make some powers of discrimination between thoughts available to the agent simply by relying on a formal syntax of thoughts, but it is less clear whether these discriminations will match or can match the discriminations needed in diachronic and interagent comparisons. These latter comparisons are more clearly dependent on interpretations external to the agent, but all of these cases call for careful examination.

Before considering the answers that have been proposed for these questions, we introduce a new bit of terminology. Functional specifications of psychologies have thoughts playing certain roles in the agent. We can turn this relation around and for convenience say that the agent bears a certain

---

[20] Fodor 1981.

relation to its thoughts. Indeed, this latter phrasing suggests some of the motivation for Russell's "propositional attitude" terminology, since the agent-thought relation can be viewed as a certain stance or attitude taken by the agent toward a possible thought. In this phraseology, the requirement of methodological solipsism becomes the requirement that thoughts are graspable, that is, some how manipulable and determinable by the agent itself. The agent presumably bears some relation to the real world, but if the agent is only a small part of the world and the weakest forms of skepticism are justified, the agent cannot fully grasp its relation to the external world.

The first suggestion we consider about the nature of thoughts holds that the content of thoughts are abstract entities called *propositions*. The term "propositional attitude" stems from this orientation. Propositions as the content of thoughts comes as a suggestion from two quarters: Brentano's theory of intentionality and Frege's theory of language.

Brentano distinguished mental states from physical states of an agent with the idea of intentionality.[21] He claimed that all acts of consciousness, such as beliefs and desires, are *directed towards* or *about* some object or objects. For example, a hatred of paperclips is an act of consciousness whose intentional objects are all paperclips. In the case of the belief or desire that some condition obtains, Brentano maintained that the object of the belief or desire is a proposition.

From another orientation, Frege distinguished the sense of names or terms from their reference.[22] To use the celebrated example, the terms "author of *Waverley*" and "Scott" have different senses, but refer to the same person. Frege claimed that thoughts express propositions as their sense, and may be either true or false as their reference. (Actually, this takes liberties with Frege's conception, but the details are not crucial here. Moreover, he used a term translated as both "thought" and "proposition", calling what we call thoughts "ideas" or "concepts".)

These suggestions have attracted many critics and defenders, but the main point we note about these suggestions is that such propositions cannot be part of a suitably narrow psychological specification for agent's structure, that is to say, propositions are not graspable. Putnam observed that one can distinguish between real and apparent propositional content

[21] Brentano 1874.
[22] Frege 1892.

in beliefs, just as earlier skeptical arguments distinguish between the real and apparent truth of beliefs.[23] Putnam's examples are rather involved, but Kaplan gives the simpler examples of thoughts involving indexicals, that is, implicit self or temporal reference.[24] For example, on Monday I think the thought "Today is beautiful." In the propositional theory, I can think exactly the same thought on Tuesday by thinking "Yesterday was beautiful." But this identity of actual content between these thoughts is indiscernible to me, since I might lose track of the days and think "Yesterday was beautiful" on Wednesday, thus actually expressing a proposition about Tuesday while thinking I am merely reminiscing on Monday's glories. Thus what proposition I actually express with my thought is not determined by my narrow psychological state.

One can back off from propositions with the suggestion that thoughts are the relation of the agent to sentences. This suggestion has been motivated both in terms of an aversion for introducing abstract objects like propositions, and in terms of seeking graspable thoughts. Rather than introduce propositions as the meaning of sentences, and having propositions be true or false depending on circumstances, Quine recommends simply having the sentences themselves be true or false in circumstances directly, rather than indirectly through the medium of propositions.[25] And rather than have an agent's thoughts involve grasping ungraspable abstractions, Fodor recommends having thoughts involve realizable representations, such as electrical patterns in the brain, markings on paper, or data structures in computer storage.[26] While this suggestion avoids the pitfall of a non-narrow psychological specification for the structure of mind, it raises other serious questions.

The first problem for the sentential view is that of the language of thought (sometimes called "brain-writing" or "Mentalese"). Since the sentences involved in thoughts are not just abstract entities but members of some language or representational system, they have a concrete syntax, and this places the sentential theory on the horns of a dilemma. Either the language of thought is common to all agents at all times, in which case diachronic and interagent comparisons of thoughts can be made within the confines of solipsistic psychology, or else the language of thought can depend on

---

[23] Putnam 1975a.
[24] Kaplan 1977.
[25] Quine 1970.
[26] Fodor 1975.

the temporal development of individual agents, in which case functionalism's claims to general applicability are sabotaged.

The hypothesis of a universal language of thought is difficult to accept
for many reasons. The first objection is that if there are several (actual or
possible) species of agents, the hypotheses claims a universality that can
only be defended on grounds of cognitive necessity, on grounds that the
very nature of successful or rational thought and action entails, by means
of physical or computational necessity, the features of Universal Mentalese.
While it seems plausible (perhaps weakly so) that some general features of
language must be forced by the necessities of the task, it requires considerable demonstration that all features of the languages must be the same.
One might claim that all agents of a certain species begin with the same
innate language, or grow to accept the same language through learning of
cultural conventions, but these suggestions are suspect on the grounds of
simple genetic and educational variability.

But if the hypothesis of a universal language of thought is implausible,
the acceptance of individual evolving languages is not without theoretical
difficulties or unpleasant consequences. Theoretically, one may have to
retreat from the view that a language has a definite set of sentences as
members, for actual questions of membership may be infeasible or may
change the language, so challenging the sensibility of determining the
language by combining hypothetical judgments. Practically, acceptance of
this hypothesis means that the accuracy of memory becomes much more
problematic, since sentences brain-written in the past may play a different
role in the agent's language in the future, if they still are in the language
at all. This entails either continuous rephrasing of memories when the
language changes, or loss of the power to interpret memories. This last
possibility is not without attraction, since it fits well with Piagetian-style
theories of psychological development, in which the conceptualization of
the world changes radically as a child grows. I can hardly recall a thing
of my childhood: perhaps I still have all my brain-records, yet cannot recall
or make sense of them any more in terms of my present mental language.

Psychological solipsism seems to force us to accept individual, evolving
languages of thought with their attendant temporal and contentual ambiguities for the agent. This conclusion seems in some ways to defeat the
motivation for functional specifications of psychologies. For example, recall specification (1): "If agent $A$ desires $p$, and believes $M$ a method for
achieving $p$, then $A$ desires to do $M$." Since narrowly interpreted psychol-

ogy cannot refer to actual content, we cannot include specifications like "$A$ desires $p$", since that refers to our interpretation of $A$'s attitude. We cannot even say instead "$A$ thinks that $A$ desires $p$", since that merely shifts the problem to the accuracy of $A$'s introspective beliefs. Instead, we are driven to write instead things like (1″): "If agent $A$ incorporates $A$-now-Mentalese sentence $S_1$ and $A$-now-Mentalese sentence $S_2$, then $A$ incorporates (or adopts) $A$-now-Mentalese sentence $S_3$," where we must write the concrete $A$-now-Mentalese sentences $S_1$, $S_2$, and $S_3$ in our theory, since we cannot refer to their external interpretation. But does such a theory fit our intentions for a psychological theory? We started by thinking we could sharpen up our naive beliefs about psychology by expressing them as a functional theory, but we find that if we want a narrowly interpreted theory, we get a purely formal set of specifications like (1″) for each individual agent at each atomic interval of time. Such a theory may leave open some questions about the details by which the agent actually realizes all these sentences and computes with them: but it certainly seems to have abandoned the generality of realization motivating functionalism in the first place. It may be possible to salvage these ideas by formulating general psychological theories which describe both universals of a species's psychology and which postulate the existence, for each agent at each time, a personal language instantiating or approximating the general one, but we have none to propose at this point.

Another suggestion about the nature of thoughts is less easy to place within a nonbehavioristic theory of mind, and that is the idea of possible-world interpretations of propositional attitude ascriptions.[27] In this approach one says $A$ believes $p$ if $p$ is true in every possible world compatible with what $A$ believes. This may seem circular, but one can take as primitive $A$'s acceptance or grasping of a set of possible worlds, among which $A$'s actual world is supposed to lie. With such a primitive conception, talk about beliefs is reduced to talk that does not involve beliefs in an attractive way.

However, this approach suffers from several difficulties. First, it entails that an agent's beliefs are closed with respect to logical consequence. It is certainly not obvious that (or if) the functional specifications for beliefs of any sufficiently rigorous intuitive psychology entail deductive closure, yet such closure seems to be an inescapable consequence of the possible-world

---

[27] See, for instance, Hintikka 1971.

approach. A second difficulty is that the earlier arguments about the ungraspability of meaning would seem to have similar force for the graspability of a set of possible worlds. If these problems are not enough, the third difficulty with the possible world approach arises when we try to extend the idea to other attitudes. If we take exact analogies for interpreting ascriptions of desires, hopes, fears, angers, and the like, we get the same closure problem. But it is a strange psychology which does not allow for conflicting yet limited set of desires (or beliefs, for that matter). I can desire to have my cake and eat it too and still not desire nuclear war. In addition, a psychology should be sensitive not just to logical incompatibility between desires but also to compatibility with respect to the agent's beliefs, yet the straightforward possible-world approach cannot incorporate such a notion. Instead, the only way open for making sense of possible-world compatibility seems to be by using the psychological theories to determine possible worlds as compatible sets of mental attitudes. And this is simply an acknowledgement of the antireductionist arguments mentioned earlier in support of functionalism.

## 3.3  Views on the Nature of Machines

### 3.3.1  Models of Computation

For most of history, mankind has had only simple machines. Machines had at most a few parts, often fixed rather than moving, and the invention of a new useful machine was a significant event for civilization. Part of the reason for this contrast with current times, in which vast numbers of new machines are constructed each day, must be that machines were less reliable in the past, and so if a complex machine was constructed from simpler ones, its chance of working was small. The big advances were not simply the construction of new machines, but of ones simple enough to be reliable, rather than Rube Goldberg contraptions. Would any king today pine for a mechanical nightingale?

The obstacle of unreliability is serious. One of our most powerful intellectual tools for understanding the world and for taking action is *problem decomposition*. Problem decomposition is the technique of breaking one problem up into several hopefully simpler subproblems together with a way of combining the subproblem solutions into a composite solution to the original problem. When I make a cake, I do not throw all the ingredients into the oven and expect a cake to appear. Instead, I break the task into first making the batter, then baking it, then making the frosting, and finally assembling the finished cake. Moreover, this trick works for more serious problems than cooking. But for problem decomposition to work, the composition methods must be effective. When most machines were not terribly reliable or precise, new machines could not be designed by straightforward problem decomposition because the composite machine would be hopelessly unreliable, if it worked at all. Until science and technology had progressed to the point where most machines could be built to be reliable, invention of useful new machines remained largely a matter of inspiration, luck, or natural analogy.

The modern theory of machines developed with the advent of reliable machines, and has focussed mostly on computational devices, since modern computers and the specialized machines realized in them via programs are the most complex machines ever known. Yet though modern machines are more reliable and can be combined in more complex constructions, theoretical models of machines do not always reflect this. Instead, the earliest developed models of machines offered little sense of machines decomposable into parts, and concentrated solely on a notion of the machine as a whole.[28]

Whatever their inadequacies regarding decomposability, machine models fulfill the subsequently formulated philosophical demands about narrowness. Normal uses of machine specifications involve narrow interpretations of the machine states. The idea of machine is closely connected with the idea of effective calculability, and non-narrow interpretations of machine specifications make the machine operations non-effective. In fact, effectiveness is a stronger requirement than simple narrowness, and later we see what things might fill this gap.

One of the first models of machines was that of the *finite state machine*, introduced at least as early as 1936 by Turing.[29] A finite state machine is simply a transducer of input strings into output strings, with a finite amount of memory. Each finite state machine M is completely described by two functions $F_M$ and $G_M$, such that if M is in state $S_i \in \{S_1, \ldots, S_k\}$ and receives input $I_j \in \{I_1, \ldots, I_l\}$, it emits the output $F_M(S_i, I_j) \in \{O_1, \ldots, O_m\}$ and moves to state $G_M(S_i, I_j) \in \{S_1, \ldots, S_k\}$. The finite set of states of the machine limits

---

[28] For presentation of many machine models, consult Minsky 1967 and Aho, Hopcroft, and Ullman 1974.
[29] Turing 1936.

its memory capacity, so that there are severe restrictions on what can be computed with a finite-state machine. Nevertheless, finite-state machines are theoretically interesting and frequently useful in practice. Unfortunately, this model of machines provides a relatively poor foundation for understanding machines by means of problem decomposition. Each of the states of a finite-state machine is atomic, so there is no overt sense of a finite state machine having parts or being constructed out of submachines. Indeed, one of the heights of the theory of finite-state machines is a characterization of when a finite-state machine is equivalent to the sum, product, or concatenation of smaller finite-state machines. We must look further to find models of machines congenial to problem decomposition.

Another early machine model is the *Turing machine*.[30] Turing machines are simply finite-state machines which can read and write symbols from a finite alphabet on an infinite tape. The tape symbols form the input alphabet of the finite-state controller, and combinations of symbols to write and tape motion signals form the output alphabet. Although Turing machines put some of their state onto the tape, where decompositions can be observed by using separate areas of the tape for separate subcomputations, Turing machines do not facilitate problem decomposition much more than do finite state machines, since the tape controllers are just finite state machines with the difficulties observed previously.

Machine models closer to the structure of modern computers were formalized in the *random access machine* (RAM) and *random access stored program machine* (RASP).[31] A RAM has a read-only input tape, a write-only output tape, an infinite array of memory cells, and a program. Each tape square or memory cell is either blank or may contain an integer. The machine's program is a finite list of numbered instructions from a certain fixed repertoire which can make arithmetic computations and comparisons on the memory cells as well as specifying the number of the next instruction to execute. RASPs are just like RAMs except that the program is stored in the memory cells, so that the machine can modify its own instructions by altering the contents of the memory cells storing the program.

RAMs and RASPs are much better than finite-state machines or Turing machines at facilitating problem decomposition. Because both the program and memory are broken into discrete components, RAMs and RASPs

[30] Turing 1936.
[31] See Shepherdson and Sturgis 1963 and Elgot and Robinson 1964.

computing a combination function can be built more or less by conca-tenating and renumbering the programs and by relocating the memory segments used by each submachine to disjoint (possibly interleaved) com-ponents of the combined memory. These are essentially the ideas of subroutines and linking loaders so important in modern programming systems. Such combination of machines is possible because each of the operations of the machine changes only a bounded component of the machine's state, i.e., a couple of cells and the program counter. This means that all operations ignore almost all of the machine state, so that separate submachines ignore each other when combined, except in their desired communication channels.

Models of computation moved most recently to a position of complete decomposability in the functional programming languages.[32] We must live with an unfortunate coincidence of terminology between "functional" spe-cifications of roles and "functional" programming languages. The notion of roles played by some object need not be the same as the mathematical notion of function. We try to minimize confusion by always referring to the latter notion as "functional programming." In the functional programming model, submachines realize self-contained, arbitrary type functions, and composite machines are constructed by functional composition and appli-cation from submachines. Since no machines share any structure, there can be no interference when they are combined. This greatly facilitates problem decomposition. In fact, the principal theoretical difficulties with functional programming languages involve how to reintroduce shared structures and side effects in a useful way. Shared structures are often important for economy of storage usage, and for economy of effort in updating a database common to a number of separate processes. Unfortunately, functional programming languages have gone too far in seeking decomposability, since structure sharing is outside the domain of a pure functional pro-gramming language, so that a less extreme position must be found.

### 3.3.2 Functional Specifications in Programming

Most actual computers in use today are organized something like RASPs in the so-called *von Neumann architecture*. Reflecting this common archi-tecture, most programming languages are based on the idea of combining procedures with local instruction and data sets communicating through

---

[32] See, for example, Backus 1978.

global or shared data sets, although there are a few languages like LISP and APL which come close to the functional language conception. One important consequence of the typical structure of computing machines and programming languages, if it is merely a consequence and not more deeply intertwined, is the phenomenon of procedural thinking among programmers. Most programmers find it easiest to compose programs by conceiving or imagining sequences of operations that wind up with the intended result. Only after they have composed the program in this way do they, if ever, reflect on what the program is computing to explain the functional relationships between the pieces of information it manipulates. This do-first, reflect-later, phenomenon may be simply a consequence of the intellectual culture in which the programmers were raised, or it might stem from the human mind being a decomposable system in which most of one's mental state is automatically conserved from one moment to the next, facilitating envisioning of individual actions. In any event, programming methodologists have had to develop ways by which conscious functional decomposition can be facilitated in programming. The popular methodologies ("structured programming," "stepwise refinement," and the like) are suggestions for how to break problems up into explicit subproblems, how to combine the separate subsolutions, and how to ensure or check the correctness of any non-interference assumptions made in the process of combination. Of course, these methodologies are still more hints about how to think than recipes for programming. The topic of how to decompose problems into subproblems is still more the domain of artists than of technicians, as only incomplete heuristics have been articulated, and the mechanization of these is still part of artificial intelligence. In contrast, much more is known about ways of checking the correctness of noninterference assumptions. There are two issues here: one of how to state what a machine is intended to compute, as opposed to how it is supposed to compute, and one of how to relate the intentions for submachines to intentions for the whole machine.

Although each computer program is a precise set of instructions written in an interpreted formal language, most programming languages provide no formal means for restating what the program's instructions are intended to accomplish. Most programming languages provide only a commenting facility, with which the programmer can attach to lines of program text comments in English (or some other natural language) to indicate what the individual program instructions mean in the larger scheme of the program. Unfortunately, these comments do not have equal force of specification as the program text, but instead are completely non-operative. In part this is due to the informal language of comments, to the lack of a formal language within the programming language for stating comments. The result is that the program forms a uniquely privileged specification of the machine realizing it, the only description that really matters to the operation of the machine. Some programming methodologists abhor the discretion this privileged status gives programmers in deciding whether or not to document their programs, but the number of machine descriptions does not seem to be the crucial issue. While undocumented programs are often odious, the underlying problem seems one of lack of force of specification (either to the computer or to programmers) rather than one of discretionary use.

To remedy these deficiencies of programming languages, computer scientists have developed numerous formal specification languages, logical metalanguages of programming languages with which one can state the intended effects of a program (its ecological specifications) and the intended roles of program components in program operation (its internal functional specifications). The ecological specifications for the program as a whole connect to the internal functional specifications by means of ecological descriptions of elementary program instructions. For example, one common type of instruction operates on certain data-structures so as to mimic arithmetic operations on numbers. Since almost everyone thinks of these instructions as arithmetic operations, or uses them for other purposes by means of arithmetic encodings, the axiomatizations of these instructions usually state the effects of the instructions' execution in terms of arithmetic operations on numerically interpreted data-structures. Similarly if computers had instructions mimicking the operations of sewing machines on cloths, one might axiomatize these instruction in terms of sewing operations on cloth-interpreted data-structures. Other instructions call for further fabrication of interpreting axioms.

Complementing the notion of formal specification of machines is the notion of verification of machine specifications, in which one checks that the specification of a composite machine follows from the specifications of the submachines and properties of the combination method. That is, one asks whether the ecological specifications of program operation follow from its functional specifications plus the ecological axiomatizations of instruction execution effects. Verifications can be approached syntactically or semantically, either by giving a logic of programs for formally deriving relations between specifications, or by giving a model which simultaneously satisfies all the specifications. While the syntactic approach is more immediately amenable to mechanization (and many attempts at mechanization populate the literature), the semantic approach is more fundamental, since a theory of models must underlie any logic of programs. Models of external domains like arithmetic, symbol strings, and cloths, present no difficulties peculiar to computer science, but many instructions operate on the internal components of machine states, affecting by their actions the meaning of the instructions themselves.[33] Models for these instructions are much more complex and much less familiar than everyday models involving ships and sealing wax. This unfamiliarity may be part of why programming seems so hard to teach; in any case, this complexity presented serious obstacles to development of satisfactory models for program specifications. However, much progress has been made, the most striking advance being the models for type-free functional programming languages developed by Scott, Plotkin, and others.[34] These developments make doubly appropriate the term "functional specification," since they allow functions to be elements of the domains of models as well as parts of the relational structures of the models.

### 3.3.3   Functional Specifications in Artificial Intelligence

While formal specifications fill the literature and textbooks of computer science, on first glance they seem almost totally absent from the artificial intelligence literature, their appearance there being restricted to attempts at mechanizing the problem decomposition and specification verification processes for "automatic" (i.e., machine-performed) programming. In actuality, however, formal specifications do play a significant role in artificial intelligence, but a very different role from that played in computer science. This difference in role stems partly from the nature of artificial intelligence research, where problems of formulation play so great a role. If the primary purpose of writing a program is to increase one's understanding of the psychology realized by the program, verifying the specifications of the program becomes a pointless activity compared to reformulating the psychology and the implementation to accord with the insights gained in the experiment. Most programs written in artificial intelligence are not meant to be solutions, but are meant to be rungs on the ladder of understanding,

---

[33] See Elgot and Robinson 1964 for instructive models of RASPs in these terms.
[34] See Scott 1973, Plotkin 1972, Barendregt 1981.

rungs which allow one to progress, but rungs to be discarded after use. This is quite a contrast with the usual situation in computer science, where the focus is on better algorithms for tasks with stable formulations. But however important this difference in the purposes of programming in the two fields, it is dwarfed by the difference between the audiences of specifications in the two fields.

In computer science, the study of machine specifications focuses on how a human programmer can think about programs and their use. This means that the principal contribution of formal specifications and semantics is a way of interpreting the structure of machines in terms of their real-world meaning. A hand calculator or slide rule is interesting only because we interpret the data-structures it manipulates as numbers, and because we interpret its operations on these data-structures as arithmetic operations. We do not care about changes in machine states, flip-flops, or bit patterns. We care about numbers and arithmetic. Similarly, we do not specify a bank's accounting machine in terms of patterns of bits and their manipulation, but in terms of customers, their deposits, their withdrawals, and their balances. The interpretations of interest are those relating the machine's state to the external world, and any discussion of the relations between machine states is merely part of a proof that the specifications of external interest are reflected in the structure and behavior of the machine. In our earlier language for describing psychological theories, the specifications of interest in most of computer programming are non-narrow, ecologically interpreted specifications which refer to circumstances external to the machine.

In artificial intelligence, however, the study of machine specifications focuses on how the machine can think about itself. One key component of intelligence seems to be adaptiveness, the ability of the agent to change itself or its surroundings when it so desires. Mundane adaptiveness involves, for example, the agent updating its beliefs to reflect the effects of its actions, to accommodate new information, or to adopt a stand on some question. Similarly, the agent might adapt by changing other mental structures, such as its desires and intentions (resolving inconsistencies, adopting stands, etc.) or its skills. In all these examples, the agent is acting as the designer of its new state, as its own programmer.

As its own programmer, the agent needs some way of guiding its adaptations, some way of stating its intentions about the relations of parts of its mental structure at single instants and over time so that it can modify itself to satisfy these intentions. But this is just the problem described above facing any programmer, one addressed by functional specifications relating parts of mental states to others at the same time, to others at other times, or to the mental state as a whole. The agent modifies itself so that its new state still satisfies (is a model of) the set of self-specifications. But since the machine is doing this revision itself with only its current state to work with, the machine's interpretation of these self-specifications cannot refer to external affairs, but must be narrowly interpreted specifications referring only to parts of the agent itself. In classical terminology, artificial-intelligence programs are not merely rule-obeying machines, but are rule-following machines, interpreters of the rules, and as such must be able to grasp the import of their rules.

Examples of such self-specifications are abundant in artificial-intelligence programs. Perhaps the clearest example is that of reason maintenance systems, also called truth maintenance, belief revision, or dependency network systems.[35] In a machine based on reason maintenance techniques, the fundamental sort of self-specification states that if the current state of mind contains certain components and lacks certain other components, then the current state of mind should also contain some further component. These specifications are termed *reasons* or *justifications*. The mental components related by reasons may be mental attitudes like beliefs and desire; descriptions and procedures; or whatever the psychology of the agent employs as building blocks for mental states. The agent follows these self-specifications by deriving its current mental state from the current set of reasons, using groundedness principles to construct a set of mental components satisfying all the reasons (i.e., by falsifying an antecedent or by including the conclusion). The agent's thinking and acting may change the state of mind by adding new reasons to or subtracting reasons from the current set, or by switching to another model of the current set. In each of these cases, the machine revises its current mental state by using the reasons as guides to what mental components should be adopted or abandoned.

Reasons are not the only sort of narrowly interpreted self-specification employed in artificial intelligence. The least complex self-specifications are those simply declaring the existence of some component of mental structure. Most of the declarations of the so-called "knowledge representation

---

[35] See Stallman and Sussman 1977, Doyle 1979, London 1978, McAllester 1980, Doyle 1983a, and de Kleer 1986. ·

languages" take this form, asserting the existence of a belief (a statement in a database), of a desire (a goal statement), or of an intention (an item on an agenda). More complex self-specifications relate two or more components of states of mind, including reference or coreference relationships (procedural attachments and equalities).[36] The structure sharing, inheritance, or "virtual copy" relationships so common in representational systems are simply self-specifications stating that one description should be considered as having certain components if other descriptions have those components as well.[37] Likewise, Minsky's "K-lines" can be viewed as self-specifications stating that the state of mind should contain one subset of (K-node) components if it also contains the corresponding enabling (K-node) component.[38] In fact, much of what goes by the name of "self-description" in artificial intelligence is not merely descriptive but instead normative, and so properly viewed as self-specification rather than self-description.[39] Self-specifications have also begun to make appearances in computer science more generally, the best examples being the "integrity constraints" of database theory[40] and N. Minsky's approach to program design based on formally expressed and automatically maintained "laws" of the system.[41]

## 3.4   The Concept of Mind

### 3.4.1   Convergence of the Theories

We can now not help but see a convergence of ideas between philosophy of mind and artificial intelligence. Philosophy began with the idea that psychological theories describe the mind in ecological terms, but abandoned that view in favor of the idea of narrow psychological theories since ecological facts offer little predictive power about behavior, even when they are accurate descriptions of mental states. On the other hand, the theory of machines arrived somewhat earlier at the notion of effectiveness, a stronger notion entailing narrowness. Early on, descriptions of machines (either

---

[36] See for example, Weyhrauch 1980 and Sussman and Steele 1980.
[37] See, for example, Fahlman 1979 and Doyle 1983c.
[38] Minsky 1980.
[39] See Doyle 1983d for a semantic approach to self-specifications, and Doyle 1988 for a treatment of self-specifications as "mental constitutions."
[40] Reiter 1988.
[41] Minsky 1988.

abstract or programmed) were effective, hence narrow, theories of machines states and behavior. But effectiveness was so strong as to obscure matters. Effectiveness of machine description implies rather direct physical realizability: this fact lies at the heart of the practice of programming. Because of their privileged status in these direct realizations, programs became identified with the machines realizing them. Considerable effort was required to regain the perspective of abstract, general, and multiple theoretical specifications of machines, as opposed to unique or privileged machine descriptions. In computer science, the recovered perspective proved crucial in ecological specifications of machines in their environment of application. In artificial intelligence, the recovered perspective proved crucial in the design of adaptive machines reconstructing themselves by means of narrow self-specifications. We attribute narrowness rather than effectiveness to the self-specifications of artificial intelligence because often these specifications were introduced as ideal (but narrow) specifications only approximated in their interpretation by an accompanying effective algorithm. While philosophy came to narrowness seeking predictive power, artificial intelligence came to narrowness seeking adaptive power.

### 3.4.2   Possible Minds Defined

The two paths to narrowness of psychological theories suggest the importance of the idea for rational psychology. It might seem that the motivation for adaptiveness subsumes the motivation of predictive power, since the rationality of a particular adaptation involves the agent's expectations about the effects of the changes. But in fact the motivations are separate, since many of the adaptation applications leading to the idea of narrow self-specification need not be deliberate or considered adaptations, but may be automatic reorganizations choosing some possible adaptation without regard to comparative advantages or disadvantages. These converging motivations mean that while any psychological theory, narrow or not, may be of interest in ecological studies of minds in their environments, only narrowly realized psychological theories need matter to rational psychology. We draw on the apparent significance of this idea to turn it around and say that *all* narrowly realized psychological theories matter to rational psychology, that the set of such realizations forms the set of possible minds.

Defining the set of possible minds as the set of narrowly realized theories has several advantages for rational psychology, advantages of neutrality on several important questions. This neutrality permits the use of these questions as dimensions for classification rather than as presuppositions of the science. Specifically, the definition is neutral on questions of psychological ontology, complexity, effectiveness, and determinateness.

The definition is neutral on psychological ontology because as long as the theory has some realization, we may posit any mental entities we desire. For example, one can express narrow stimulus-response psychologies in terms of relations between sensors and effectors; attitudinal psychologies in terms of relationships between beliefs and desires (or whatever attitudes one chooses); Freudian psychologies in terms of ego, superego, id, energy, and flows; and even the monolithic states of finite state machines. Thus the first dimension of classification of minds is by the mental components, by psychological ontology.

The definition is neutral on psychological complexity for reasons similar to its neutrality on psychological ontology. As long as the theory is narrowly realizable, it is a possible psychology no matter how trivial or complex it is. Possible minds may be as simple as a soda machine, or as complex as Lev Tolstoy. Thus the second dimension of classification of minds is by their structural complexity, by the variety of ways their components may be combined to form mental states.

The definition's neutrality on effectiveness follows since effectiveness is a stronger notion than narrowness. The range of possible minds includes both mechanically realized psychologies as well as physically realized psychologies which might not admit mechanized realizations. The definition allows for universes in which the notions of narrowness and effectiveness coincide, and for universes like our own in which narrowness subsumes effectiveness. Moreover, it allows for universes in which effectiveness is even more restricted than in our own. This neutrality opens a whole range of new questions for physical theorists. One might conjecture from the amazing coincidence of effective calculability and recursive computability in our universe that other universes might offer analogous coincidences of effectiveness with the degrees of recursive unsolvability or with the degrees of computational complexity.[42] What form would the physics of such universes take? Need they have different laws, or might they differ from ours only in the values of the fundamental constants?

Finally, the definition of possible minds is neutral on the question of determinism, admitting both theories in which a mental state may have at

[42] Rogers 1967, Aho, Hopcroft, and Ullman 1974, Garey and Johnson 1979.

most one possible successor state and theories in which a mental state might be followed by any of several others. Deterministic and nondeterministic Turing machines are examples of these. Of course, even nondeterministic psychologies can have deterministic realizations, and the existence of non-deterministic realizations is a question of physics.

Defining possible minds to be narrowly realized theories has a seemingly unavoidable and perhaps unwelcome consequence in addition to the pre-viously discussed advantages. The neutralities on psychological ontology, complexity, effectiveness, and determinateness add up to a neutrality on realizations. According to the definition, any satisfiable theory is a possible psychology, and by taking the entire domain of the model to be an agent, any realized theory is a possible mind. This makes the idea of narrowness of theoretical realizations analogous to the idea of closed systems in phy-sics, and with similar importance, the laws of physics being taken to describe all and only closed systems. The generality of the definition means that any object and an accurate internal description of it constitute a possible mind. For example, supposing the known laws of physics correct, the universe is a possible mind, with the laws of physics as its psychology. Similarly, the U.S. economy and a correct economic theory constitute a possible mind, as does *Hamlet* together with a correct descriptive analysis, as do the natural numbers together with Peano's axioms (assuming their correctness). If the aim of rational psychology is to classify all possible minds, then it includes as subdisciplines not just psychology and artificial intelligence, but also physics, theology, model theory, sociology; the list goes on. If rational psychology is so all-embracing, what endeavor is *not* rational psychology?

My own feelings are mixed about this problem. On the one hand, I find the seeming intellectual imperialism of this view distasteful, but on the other hand I can offer some perspectives from which it seems less so, even natural. First, the generality of the definition does no real harm, for the point of the science is to introduce distinctions, and the first action of anyone interested in thinking would be to introduce distinctions of domains so as to reinstate the disciplines in their traditional fiefs. Indeed, most disciplines have ways of viewing the whole world from their perspective, but modesty and com-mon sense keep them from overstepping their most fruitful bounds.

Second, the generality seems unavoidable if one wants the field to en-compass both the trivial mind (e.g., the soda machine) and physically realized but not effectively realizable minds. Bizarre and pointless minds need not be very interesting to anyone, but the scope of the science must include them precisely so that terms like "bizarre" and "pointless" can be substantively applied. Group theory has its "monster" groups: rational psychology needs its "psychopaths." It is worth emphasizing that rational psychology *requires* this generality of domain, lest restrictions on its freedom to consider possible psychological structures prevent it from discovering the best mathematical forms of psychological concepts. This intended neutrality on questions of what constitutes human thinking sharply distinguishes the notions of possible mind appropriate for rational psychology from the notions of human understanding and mental states involved in Searle's critique of the "strong AI" view that minds are programs.[43] From the perspective presented here, artificial intelligence is not about programs, but about theories of machines, about narrowly realized psychological theories of machines, whether human or otherwise, and about whether humans are indeed machines.

Third, and finally, there is a hidden, underlying rightness to the definition. All possible minds must incorporate all possible mental structures, of that there can be no doubt. Yet what are the mathematical structures of physics, the logical theories of model theory, the programs of computer science, the constitutions of governments, and the articles of the faiths if not ideas in the minds of men?

## 3.5  Conclusion

Cognitive psychology and artificial intelligence currently dominate cognitive science, and with them come the dominant methodologies of experimental data collection and speculative construction. If the arguments of this paper are understood, practitioners of these fields will at least have been introduced and perhaps converted to a methodological viewpoint that begins with the set of all possible minds and proceeds by formulating distinctions and classifying minds. The new viewpoint does not reject but subsumes the previous viewpoints, since experiment and speculation remain useful in the problems of formulation and classification.

Even if one remains attached to one's familiar methodology and hesitant before the general conception of mind introduced above, I think important practical benefits follow from approaching the study of mind in the pro-

---

[43] Searle 1980.

posed way. I am not familiar enough with the literature of cognitive psychology to promise cognitive psychologists these benefits, but I am familiar with artificial intelligence and feel the intelligibility of its literature might be increased by adoption of the proposed viewpoint: not just intelligibility to outsiders, but to insiders as well. One of the commonly acknowledged problems in artificial intelligence is the difficulty of telling what someone else has done. Almost every researcher has his own vocabulary and viewpoint, and while the gist of papers is usually intelligible, the details present more difficulties because one person's omitted explanatory trivialities may be someone else's stumbling blocks. While the classificatory viewpoint cannot by itself reconcile vocabularies or world-views, consciousness of the task of classification might strengthen incentives for scholarly analysis of comparable works. Moreover, the classificatory viewpoint also makes it possible to state and infer what results are scientific results and what results are engineering advances. The scientific aim of artificial intelligence is a question of formulation and existence: whether or not there are interesting psychologies realizable in Turing-equivalent machines. The answer to this question will likely involve an actual realization. The details of this realization are not scientifically interesting, but instead are matters of engineering. This is not meant to belittle engineering problems, merely to distinguish two endeavors. The situation is similar to that in mathematics, where in the context of a particular theory, an individual proof is without mathematical significance except for its conclusion. Of course in a wider context the proof will have importance as an example of a method for discovering analogous proofs. Likewise, the details of an intelligent machine's construction will be answers to important engineering questions, perhaps useful in constructing realizations of other psychologies, but scientifically insignificant as far the answered existential question is concerned. This distinction between scientific and engineering questions allows clearer explanations of the problems and results reported in artificial intelligence. Is the purpose of a paper to show how to realize feature $f$ of the psychology $\psi$ currently being worked toward (a scientific advance)? Or is it to show ways in which feature $f$ of the machine $M$ might be utilized independently of any particular psychology (an engineering advance)? Is the paper's purpose to modify the target psychology in light of changing estimates of feasibility of realizations? Or is it to modify the underlying machine so as to enhance feasibility of realization? The first two of these questions serve to mitigate the apparent scientific irrelevance of papers on programming techniques and programming systems by viewing them as engineering advances rather than psychological theories. Likewise, the second two questions serve to clarify the revolutionary claims often made in the literature. Papers changing the target psychology or underlying machine change particular scientific aims. Papers inventing a new programming technique do not, but they advance the progress of the scientific or engineering investigation of a particular set of scientific aims. Artificial intelligence may well be yet a field most concerned with problems of formulation, but let us at least make clear what is being formulated and studied, namely pairs of psychologies and machines.

The proposed perspective on the aims of artificial intelligence can benefit the clarity and ease of construction of programs as well as the clarity and construction of their exegeses. The advantages of initial specification and subsequent implementation are well known from programming methodology in computer science, even if intermediate specifications and verifications of implementations rarely matter in artificial intelligence's problems of formulation. But the proposed perspective can have a far more substantial impact on the construction of artificial agents than simply as an explanatory aid. Earlier, we introduced the idea that intelligent machines can interpret narrow self-specifications to guide their adaptations. If we take this suggestion seriously, then designing machines to continually construct and interpret sets of self-specifications becomes a powerful aid to programming. In this methodology, intelligent machines are always designed to construct and update their mental states by interpreting their self-specifications. Reason maintenance systems were mentioned earlier as an example of this idea, but so are the constraint-based programming systems currently enjoying interest. Constraints are nothing more than self-specifications, and in programming systems based on them one simply describes the psychology of the program as a set of narrowly interpreted logical statements, which the programming system examines to maintain the current mental state. Of course, in artificial intelligence there must be not just narrow, but effective and feasible ways of interpreting the specifications, so that one repeatedly reformulates the specifications of the psychology as one's store of feasible interpretation techniques changes. For example, the extant constraint-based programming systems fantastically restrict the complexity of psychological specifications because they incorporate means for interpreting only a few of the very simplest specifications. But these restrictions are not essential, and future systems might allow incremental addition of interpretation techniques for specifications of more complex logical form.

The proposed methodology can be expressed as the thesis of self-interpretation: *Thinking is a process of narrow self-specification and self-interpretation.*[44] That is, mental actions are all described and realized by means of self-interpretive psychological theories that augment themselves with new self-specifications, purge themselves of unwanted self-specifications, or reinterpret their existing self-specifications. In this way mental actions are understood in terms of the psychology itself (e.g., reasons, beliefs, and desires), rather than in terms of the realization of the psychology (e.g., Con's, Rplaca's, etc.).

## Acknowledgments

I owe much to Joseph Schatz for advice on this paper. I also benefited from discussions with Ned Block, Johan de Kleer, Merrick Furst, Allen Newell, Dana Scott, and Richmond Thomason. Preparation of this paper was supported by National Institutes of Health Grant No. R01 LM04493 from the National Library of Medicine.

## References

Aho, A. V., J. E. Hopcroft, and J. D. Ullman. 1974. *The Design and Analysis of Computer Algorithms.* Reading, Massachusetts: Addison-Wesley.

Backus, J. 1978. Can programming be liberated from the von Neumann style? A functional style and its algebra of programs, *Communications of the Association for Computing Machinery* 21, 613–641.

Barendregt, H. P. 1981. *The Lambda Calculus: Its Syntax and Semantics.* Amsterdam: North-Holland.

Boring, E. G. 1950. *A History of Experimental Psychology.* Second edition. New York: Appleton Century Crofts.

Brentano, F. 1874. *Psychologie vom empirischen Standpunkte.* Leipzig.

Chomsky, N. A. 1965. *Aspects of the Theory of Syntax,* Cambridge: MIT Press.

de Kleer, J. 1986. An assumption-based TMS. *Artificial Intelligence* 28, 127–162.

Descartes, R. 1637. Discourse on the method of rightly conducting the reason and seeking for truth in the sciences. In *The Philosophical Works of Descartes,* Vol. I. (E. S. Haldane and G. R. T. Ross, trans.). Cambridge: Cambridge University Press, 1931.

---

[44] This thesis is a descendant of the comparable thesis about reasoning proposed in Doyle 1979.

Dennett, D. C. 1978. Intentional systems. In *Brainstorms*. Montgomery, Vermont: Bradford Books, 3–22.

Doyle, J. 1979. A truth maintenance system. *Artificial Intelligence* 12, 231–272.

Doyle, J. 1983a. Some theories of reasoned assumptions: an essay in rational psychology. Pittsburgh: Carnegie-Mellon University, Department of Computer Science report 83–125.

Doyle, J. 1983b. What is Rational Psychology? Toward a modern mental philosophy. *AI Magazine*. Vol. 4, No. 3, 50–53.

Doyle, J. 1983c. A society of mind: multiple perspectives, reasoned assumptions, and virtual copies. *Eighth International Joint Conference on Artificial Intelligence*. William Kaufmann, Inc., Los Altos, California 309–314.

Doyle, J. 1983d. Admissible state semantics for representational system. *IEEE Computer*. Vol. 16, No. 10, 119–123.

Doyle, J., 1988. Artificial intelligence and rational self-government, Pittsburgh: Carnegie-Mellon University, Department of Computer Science TR CMU–CS–88–124.

Elgot, C. C., and A. Robinson. 1964. Random access stored program machines. *Journal of the Association for Computing Machinery* 11, 365–399.

Fahlman, S. E. 1979. NETL: *A System for Representing and Using Real-World Knowledge*, Cambridge, Massachusetts: MIT Press.

Feigl, H. 1958. The "mental" and the "physical." In *Minnesota Studies in the Philosophy of Science* Vol. II, 370–497. H. Feigl, M. Scriven, and H. Grover, eds. Minneapolis: University of Minnesota Press.

Fodor, J. A. 1968. *Psychological Explanation: An Introduction to the Philosophy of Psychology*. New York: Random House.

Fodor, J. A. 1975. *The Language of Thought*. New York: Crowell.

Fodor, J. A. 1981. Methodological solipsism considered as a research strategy in cognitive psychology. In *Representations: Philosophical Essays on the Foundations of Cognitive Science*, 225–253. Cambridge, Massachusetts: MIT Press.

Frege, G. 1884. *Die Grundlagen der Arithmetic*. Breslau: Verlag von Wilhelm Koebner, translated by J. L. Austin as *The Foundations of Arithmetic*. Second revised edition. Evanston: Northwestern University Press, 1968.

Frege, G. 1892. Über Sinn und Bedeutung. *Zeitschrift für Philosophie und philosophische Kritik* 100, 25–50.

Freud, S. 1895. Project for a scientific psychology. *Standard Edition of the Complete Psychological Works of Sigmund Freud*, Vol. I, 281–397. J. Strachey, tr. and ed. London: Hogarth Press, 1966.

Gandy, R. 1980. Church's thesis and principles for mechanism. In *The Kleene Symposium*. J. Barwise, H. J. Keisler, and K. Kunen, eds. Amsterdam: North-Holland, 123–148.

Garey, M. R., and D. S. Johnson. 1979. *Computers and Intractability: A Guide to the Theory of NP-Completeness*. San Francisco: W. H. Freeman.

Goldstein, H. H. 1972. *The Computer from Pascal to von Neumann*. Princeton: Princeton University Press.

Hilbert, D. 1900. Mathematical Problems. Lecture Delivered Before the International Congress of Mathematicians at Paris. M. W. Newson, trans. *Bulletin of the American Mathematical Society* 8 (1902), 437–479.

Hintikka, J. 1971. Semantics for propositional attitudes. In *Reference and Modality*. L. Linsky, ed. Oxford: Oxford University Press, 145–167.

Kaplan, D. 1977. *Demonstratives*. Unpublished manuscript.

London, P. E. 1978. Dependency networks as a representation for modelling in general problem solvers. University of Maryland, Department of Computer Science TR–698.

McAllester, D. A. 1980. An outlook on truth maintenance. MIT Artificial Intelligence Laboratory, Memo 551.

Minsky, M., 1967. *Computation: Finite and Infinite Machines*. Englewood Cliffs, New Jersey: Prentice-Hall.

Minsky, M. 1980. K-lines: a theory of memory. *Cognitive Science* 4, 117–133.

Minsky, N. H. 1988. Law-governed systems. Unpublished manuscript. Rutgers University Computer Science Department.

Peters, R. S., and C. A. Mace. 1967. Psychology. In *Encyclopedia of Philosophy*, Vol. 7, 1–27. P. Edwards, ed. New York: Macmillan and Free Press.

Place, U. T. 1956. Is consciousness a brain process? *British Journal of Psychology* 47, 44–50.

Plotkin, G. 1972. A set-theoretical definition of application. University of Edinburgh School of Artificial Intelligence, Memo MIP–R–95.

Putnam, H. 1975a. The meaning of "meaning." In *Mind, Language, and Reality*, Cambridge: Cambridge University Press, 215–271.

Putnam, H. 1975b. Minds and machines. In *Mind, Language, and Reality*. Cambridge: Cambridge University Press, 362–385.

Putnam, H. 1975c. Philosophy and our mental life. In *Mind, Language, and Reality*, Cambridge: Cambridge University Press, 291–303.

Quine, W. V. 1970. *Philosophy of Logic*, Englewood Cliffs, New Jersey: Prentice-Hall.

Randell, B., ed. 1975. *The Origins of Digital Computers: Selected Papers*. Berlin: Springer-Verlag.

Reiter, R., 1988. On integrity constraints, *Proceedings of the Second Conference on Theoretical Aspects of Reasoning about Knowledge* (M. Y. Vardi, ed.), Los Altos, California: Morgan Kaufmann, 97–111.

Rogers, H. Jr. 1967. *Theory of Recursive Functions and Effective Computability*. New York: McGraw-Hill.

Ryle, G. 1949. *The Concept of Mind*. London: Hutchinson.

Scott, D. 1973. Models for various type-free calculi. In *Logic, Methodology and Philosophy of Science IV*. P. Suppes, L. Henkin, A. Joja, Gr. C. Moisil, eds. Amsterdam: North-Holland, 157–187.

Searle, J. R. 1980. Minds, brains, and programs. *Behavioral and Brain Sciences* 3, 417–424.

Shepherdson, J. C., and H. E. Sturgis. 1963. Computability of recursive functions. *Journal of the Association for Computing Machinery* 10, 217–255.

Skinner, B. F. 1957. *Verbal Behavior*. New York: Appleton Century Crofts.

Smart, J. C. C. 1959. Sensations and brain processes. *Philosophical Review* 68, 141–156.

Stallman, R. M., and Sussman, G. J., 1977. Forward reasoning and dependency-directed backtracking in a system for computer-aided circuit analysis. *Artificial Intelligence* 9, 135–196.

Sussman, G. J., and G. L. Steele Jr. 1980. CONSTRAINTS—A language for expressing almost-hierarchical descriptions. *Artificial Intelligence* 14, 1–39.

Thomason, R. H. 1979. Some limitations to the psychological orientation in semantic theory. Unpublished manuscript. University of Pittsburgh.

Truesdell, C. 1966. *Six Lectures on Modern Natural Philosophy*. Berlin: Springer-Verlag.

Turing, A. M. 1936. On computable numbers with an application to the entscheidungs-problem. *Proceedings of the London Mathematical Society* (Ser. 2) 42, 230–265.

Watson, J. B. 1914. *Behavior: An Introduction to Comparative Psychology*. New York: Holt.

Weyhrauch, R. W. 1980. Prolegomena to a theory of mechanized formal reasoning. *Artificial Intelligence* 13, 133–170.

Whitehead, A. N., and B. Russell. 1910. *Principia Mathematica*. Cambridge: Cambridge University Press.

W. Wundt. 1874. *Grundzüge der physiologischen Psychologie*. Leipzig: W. Englemann.

# 4 Memory, Reason, and Time: The Step-Logic Approach

**Jennifer J. Elgot-Drapkin, Michael Miller, and Donald Perlis**

## 4.1 Motivation

Traditional theoretical treatments of reasoning do not, in our view, address reasoning per se at all. Rather they seek to characterize the *end results* of reasoning. We have four complaints with this. First, it is not clear that reasoning has clearly identifiable end results, but rather goes on and on as part of the active history of an individual reasoner. Second, reasoning is a process or activity, and this is simply ignored in traditional studies. Third, as a consequence, crucial issues of temporal and spatial resources are not taken into account. Fourth, if we are going to understand realizable intelligent systems, we must look at what they actually do, that is, we must accept at least a certain amount of cognitive plausibility (whether human or computer).

The paradigm for such a reasoning agent would seem to be that suggested by Nilsson (1983), namely, a computer individual with a lifetime of its own. What is of interest is not its "ultimate" set of conclusions, but rather its changing set of conclusions over time. Indeed, there will be, in general, no ultimate or limiting set of conclusions.

The notion of time enters the reasoning process in two ways. Not only does reasoning take time, but it often deals with time as an object of reasoning. The latter has of course been extensively studied, in so-called temporal and tense logics. But there, once again, it is the *end results* and not the *process* of drawing conclusions that is studied. We seek to do both, in one model of reasoning. This pointedly includes the case of reasoning going on in time (of course, as it must) while the system is focused on (reasoning about) that very passage of time as it reasons. This, we will argue, is no mere curiosity, but rather a central feature of intelligent thought.

Similarly, space enters in two ways. On the one hand there is spatial reasoning, again well studied. On the other hand there is the fact that reasoning takes up space in the form of memeory. Again we are interested in modeling both. Moreover, we want both forms of temporal reasoning and both forms of spatial reasoning to go on together in the same system.

To this end we initiated a project some years ago, toward the development of an automatic reasoner. This work is summarized in section 4.2. Later we came to realize that in it there lurked certain features that suggested formalization, and so we embarked on the development of a

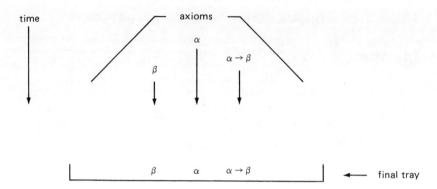

**Figure 4.1**
Final-tray logical studies

suitable logic. The logic retains much of the traditional approach and yet also breaks loose from that in several key respects; in particular, the new formalization—which we call *step-logic*—does not focus on end results. This will be explained in section 4.3. So far, we have concentrated on time rather than space (memory) in this formalization. Section 4.4 suggests future directions including the incorporation of space concerns.

To illustrate what we called the end-result character of traditional approaches to formalizing commonsense reasoning, note that the traditional approaches suffer from the problem of logical omniscience: if an agent has $\alpha_1, \ldots, \alpha_n$ in its belief set, and if $\gamma$ follows from $\alpha_1, \ldots, \alpha_n$ according to the agent's rules of inference, then the agent also believes $\gamma$ (i.e., $\gamma$ is also in the belief set). As a specific example, if a typical omniscient agent believes $\alpha$, and also believes $\alpha \to \beta$, then the agent believes $\beta$. As an illustration, refer to figure 4.1. The reasoner begins with a set of axioms, and the deductive mechanism generates theorems along the way, e.g., $\alpha$, later $\alpha \to \beta$, still later $\beta$. Such mechanisms have usually been studied in terms of the set of all theorems deducible therein, what we call the "final tray of conclusions" into which individually proven theorems are represented as dropping, thereby ignoring their time and means of deduction. One asks, for instance, whether a wff $\alpha$ is a theorem (i.e., is in the final tray), *not* whether $\alpha$ is a theorem proven in $i$ steps.

A particularly vexing aspect of this type of reasoning is what we call the "swamping problem"—namely that from a contradiction all wffs are concluded. For this reason most formal studies of reasoning deliberately avoid contradictions; those that do not (e.g., Doyle 1979), provide a separate device for noting contradictions and revising beliefs while the "main" reasoning engine sits quiescent. In general, however, this will not do, since the knowledge needed to resolve conflicts will depend on the same wealth of world knowledge used in any other reasoning. Thus reasoning about birds involves inference rules applied to beliefs about birds, whether used to resolve a conflict or simply to produce nonconflicting conclusions. We contend, then, that one and the same ongoing process of reasoning should be responsible both for keeping itself apprised of contradictions and their resolution, and for other forms of reasoning.

We seek potentially inconsistent, but nevertheless useful, logics where a real-time self-referential feature allows a direct contradiction to be spotted and corrective action taken, as part of the same system of reasoning. We will suggest some specific inference mechanisms for real-time default reasoning, notably a form of introspection relevant to default reasoning. This facilitates the study of *fallible* agents reasoning over time. A fallible agent may derive or encounter an inconsistency, identify it as such, and then proceed to remedy it. Contradictions then need not be bad; indeed, they can be good, in that they allow sources of error to be isolated (see Perlis 1986).

The agent should be able to reason *about* its own ongoing reasoning efforts, and, in particular, reason whether it has or has not yet reached a given conclusion. One of our main focuses here is the problem of an agent's determining that in fact it does *not* (currently) know something. This *negative introspection* will be a key feature of the deduction, and subsequent resolution, of contradictions in our later examples of default reasoning in section 4.3.2.4. It turns out that negative introspection presents certain temporal constraints that will strongly influence the formal development.

The literature contains a number of approaches to limited (non-omniscient) reasoning, apparently with similar motivation to our own. However, with very little exception, the idealization of a "final" state of reasoning is maintained, and the limitation amounts to a reduced set of consequences rather than an ever-changing set of tentative conclusions. Thus Konolige (1983) studies agents with fairly arbitrary rules of inference, but assumes logical closure for the agents with respect to those rules, ignoring the effort involved in performing the deductions. Similarly, Levesque (1984) and Fagin and Halpern (1988) provide formal treatments of limited reasoning, so that, for instance, a contradiction may go unnoticed; but the conclusions that *are* drawn are done so instantaneously, i.e., the steps of reasoning involved are not explicit. Fagin and Halpern in particular postulate a notion of awareness, so that if $\alpha$ and $\alpha \rightarrow \beta$ are known, still $\beta$ will not be concluded unless the agent is aware of $\beta$; just how it is that $\beta$ fails to be in the awareness set in unclear. Goodwin (1987) comes a little closer to meeting our desiderata but still maintains a largely final-traylike perspective.

This next section describes the automatic reasoner.

## 4.2  A Pragmatic Approach

### 4.2.1  Background

Most of the AI systems built today are designed to solve one problem only. That is, the system is turned on, labors away for some period of time, then spits out the (hopefully correct) answer. It is then turned off, or works on another problem with no knowledge of its past. In contrast, consider a system with a "life-time of its own," one whose behavior significantly depends on its continued dealings with a variety of issues.

In the current section, we imagine a robot (i.e., some kind of reasoning agent) situated on a desert island (i.e., some kind of robust world) left to its own devices. It has been endowed with a database of information that it can use in order to get along in this world.

It is clear that an autonomous robot will have to deal with a world about which it will have only partial knowledge. Conclusions will frequently be drawn without full justification. As a consequence, some facts will have to be retracted in the face of further information. An underlying premise is that a real-world reasoner is limited, at least in terms of the scope and accuracy of the information to which it has access. We must back off a bit from the more traditional topic of idealized reasoning agents that are infallible and omniscient. Additionally, if we limit the computing resources of the robot (much as people are limited), then some of the difficulties of formal representation of commonsense reasoning become more tractable. That is, greater limitations serve to constrain solutions to the point that answers may be more easily seen.

A centerpiece, and bugbear, of formal research in commonsense reasoning has been that of (global and derivational) consistency tests. Even when, as in the case of circumscription (see McCarthy 1980), direct testing of consistency is avoided by clever syntactic manipulations, there is still implicit reference to global properties of the reasoning system (i.e., its set of axioms). Time is then taken to assess logical consequences of these properties before a commonsense conclusion is drawn. Thus a strong flavor of idealized reasoning has persisted.

Suppose we would like to have a reasoning system use a rule such as $\alpha \to \beta$ to conclude $\beta$, given $\alpha$, and later, in the face of new evidence, be able to retract its belief in $\beta$. A somewhat standard (idealized) way of dealing with this to use a rule such as, "If $\alpha$, and it is consistent to believe $\beta$, then conclude $\beta$." This is called a default rule, and is the source of the aforementioned consistency tests. The point of the "it is consistent to believe $\beta$" is to see whether there *already* is evidence to disbelieve $\beta$, that is, to prevent the conclusion $\beta$ in the first place. Instead of holding up the system's conclusion until such a test can be made, our approach allows the system to jump directly to the conclusion $\beta$, and *then* decide whether it was rash.

In the robot's world, it seems, nearly all rules are actually defaults, since we can rarely be sure of anything. It is then tempting to use a "brute force" method of encoding these defaults: simply encode the rule as "If $\alpha$, then conclude $\beta$," with no "unless it is not consistent to do so" condition. One would then proceed as normal in the inference process until a direct contradiction is somehow brought to the reasoner's attention (a process which will be explained shortly). At this point something would have to be done to resolve the inconsistency. It is important to note that a contradiction should not be something that will incapacitate our system. Rather, it is something that is to be expected, recognized (but only when relevant to the current focus of attention), and resolved by the system as part of its normal operation. In particular this allows the use of a rule such as $\alpha \to \beta$, even though it may be recognized as not strictly true. (Though this is not a trivial point, we will leave further discussion for a future paper. See Glymour and Thomason 1984 for a related idea.)

We can now think of our robot as a real-world, resource-limited reasoner acting, albeit somewhat slowly, over time. It uses defaults to allow itself a short-cut to quick deductions, correcting fallacy when it is recognized.

### 4.2.2   Details of Model

Our robot is essentially a *memory model* that is controlled by an *inference cycle* mechanism. The model's components hold data in various forms so that as time evolves the inference mechanism is able to simulate reasoning.

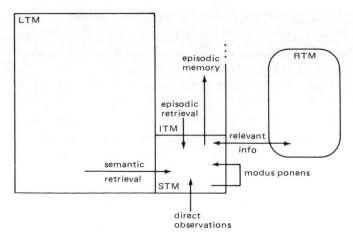

**Figure 4.2**
Architecture of the memory model

The model has been implemented, and the examples later in this section are from actual computer trials.

**4.2.2.1 Architercture.** The memory model contains five key elements: STM, LTM, ITM, QTM, and RTM. The first three of these are standard parts of cognitively based models of memory. See figure 4.2.

STM is meant to represent the reasoner's current focus of attention. Its chief purpose is to allow access to a very large database (LTM), yet not suffer an exponential explosion of inferences. STM is a small set of beliefs that are currently "active." These beliefs are represented as logical formulae and are used to help establish STM's next state, a process which will be described in the next section. STM is structured as a FIFO queue. Since STM's size is limited,[1] as new facts are brought into STM, old facts must be discarded. That is, the older, discarded facts are no longer in focus.

It is convenient to conceive of STM as a theorem prover to which LTM supplies axioms. LTM may then be thought of as a database of information to which the robot has access. LTM is implemented as a series of tuples of the form:

---

[1] In our implementation, STM's size is fixed, yet easily changed for experimental purposes. An interesting sidelight is that an STM size of eight is the smallest that has led to effective task-oriented behavior over several domains, and that larger sizes have offered no advantage. This is in surprising accord with psychological data which measure human short-term memory to hold seven plus-or-minus two "chunks" of data at one time (Miller 1956).

$$\langle T_1, \ldots, T_n, B \rangle$$

where the $T_i$ and $B$ represent logical formulae. The idea behind LTM is that beliefs are held as a series of associations. Thinking about certain triggers (i.e., the $T_i$'s) causes possibly many past associations (i.e., the $B$'s) to be brought into focus.

ITM is of unbounded size and holds all information which is discarded from STM in chronological order, that is, in order of entry. Thus, ITM is implemented similarly to a stack, in that the most recently entered facts are the most easily accessed, although they are never removed.

QTM is a technical device that controls the flow of information into STM.

RTM is the repository of default resolution and relevance. RTM is implemented as a list of facts that have most recently been is STM. Facts are coded with a time decay variable so that they can decay out of RTM as they are no longer relevant, that is, not found in STM for a specified number of inference cycles.

**4.2.2.2 Inference.**  An *inference cycle* can be thought of as the process of updating the system's current focus of attention. Given some state of STM, four different mechanisms work simultaneously to produce a new state. These four mechanisms are direct observation, modus ponens (MP), semantic retrieval from LTM, and episodic retrieval from ITM.

To model this simultaneity, our implementation uses a temporary waiting queue (QTM) which holds the next cycle's STM facts until all four mechanisms have finished working on the old STM facts. Once they have finished, elements of QTM are placed into STM one at a time, disallowing repetition of facts in STM. Throughout this process, older items in STM are moved into ITM as needed to maintain STM's size. Note that if QTM is very large, other means will be required to select elements reasonably to go into STM.[2]

Currently, direct observation is modeled by allowing outsiders to simply assert a fact to the system. This allows us the pretense of an autonomous system noting events in a dynamic environment.

MP is applied in the following form: from $Ac$ and $(Ax \to Bx)$, $Bc$ is inferred. That is, $Bc$ is brought into QTM if $Ac$ and $(Ax \to Bx)$ are already contained in STM. Consequently, at the end of such a cycle, $Bc$ is a candidate for STM.

---

[2] In part this is handled by RTM.

Facts from LTM are brought into STM by association. When facts in STM unify with the first $n$ elements of some $\langle T_1, \ldots, T_n, \beta \rangle$, in LTM, then $\beta$ will be brought into QTM (and subsequently into STM), with its variables properly bound.

Information retrieved from ITM into STM can take several forms. For example, since ITM is a chronological listing of all past STM facts, its structure allows for the retrieval of goal statements that are not yet satisfied, but that have already been pushed out of STM. This allows the system to work through a goal–subgoal process.

**4.2.2.3  General Features.**    Before illustrating the memeory model with an example, it is worthwhile making brief mention of several of its features.

First, in most of our work we have limited the size of STM to eight elements. That is, eight formulae can be held in STM at any one time. We have had a fair amount of success solving problems with an STM of that size. However, adjustments can easily be made to STM's size and, indeed, our examples will use a size of four.

Second, LTM can hold inconsistent data without the usual disastrous consequences of customary inference systems. In fact as long as a direct contradiction does not occur in STM, no inconsistency is even detected.

Third, the system is capable of meta-inference or "introspection" very simply by searching its list of STM elements. For example, it can determine whether a given formula and its negation are both currently in STM. This activity occurs via inference steps no different in principle from any of its other inferences. If effect, the system may look at snapshots of itself as it runs, rather than extrapolating to some final state.

Fourth, the utility of RTM is to allow for such things as prohibiting faulty default conclusions. That is, since STM is so small, it is likely that information that would typically block a default conclusion from being drawn has recently left STM, but it still remains in RTM. Being in RTM is sufficient to prohibit a faulty default, as we consider RTM's entries as relevant enough to have a bearing on reasoning, yet not central enough to be the catalyst of further inference.

Finally, information stored in ITM and in RTM is at times accessible to STM. Thus, information from the past can be brought back into focus when appropriate. This allows the system to use such information in working through goal–subgoal behavior as well as using past information as a default when the frame problem arises.

**4.2.2.4 An Example.**    As an example of this mechanism in action, consider
the following state of affairs. STM contains the fact that Tweety is a bird.
LTM contains two pieces of information: the presence of bird(x) in STM
is to trigger the fact that birds fly; the presence of flies(x) in STM is to trigger
the fact that flying things have wings. ITM is initially empty. To simplify
the example, the size of STM is fixed at a maximum size of four. A star, *,
indicates a newly placed item in STM.

*ITM*:  ∅
*STM*:  *bird(Tweety)*
*LTM*:  $\langle bird(x), bird(x) \rightarrow flies(x) \rangle$
        $\langle flies(x), flies(x) \rightarrow winged(x) \rangle$

The fact that Tweety is a bird will trigger the rule that birds fly, resulting in:

*STM*:  *bird(Tweety)*
  \*   $bird(x) \rightarrow flies(x)$

An application of MP would then leave:

*STM*:  *bird(Tweety)*
       $bird(x) \rightarrow flies(x)$
  \*   *flies(Tweety)*

Again, a new association will be triggered from LTM, resulting in:

*STM*:  *bird(Tweety)*
       $bird(x) \rightarrow flies(x)$
       *flies(Tweety)*
  \*   $flies(x) \rightarrow winged(x)$

This new fact would then trigger MP again (and have the side-effect of
pushing *bird(Tweety)* into ITM).

*ITM*:  *bird(Tweety)*
*STM*:  $bird(x) \rightarrow flies(x)$
       *flies(Tweety)*
       $flies(x) \rightarrow winged(x)$
  \*   *winged(Tweety)*

**4.2.3   Real-Time Nonmonotonicity**

It does not take an especially large effort to produce a rudimentary form
of nonmonotonic reasoning using our architecture. As an illustration we

present the following example. This time we start the system in the following state, where the second entry in LTM is different from before:

*ITM:*    ∅
*STM:*    *bird(Tweety)*
*LTM:*    $\langle bird(x), bird(x) \rightarrow flies(x) \rangle$
          $\langle ostrich(x), ostrich(x) \rightarrow \neg flies(x) \rangle$

As before, the fact that Tweety is a bird will trigger the rule that birds fly, resulting in:

*STM:*    *bird(Tweety)*
  *        $bird(x) \rightarrow flies(x)$

An application of MP would result in:

*STM:*    *bird(Tweety)*
          $bird(x) \rightarrow flies(x)$
  *        *flies(Tweety)*

Now suppose the system discovers (through direct observation, or some other means) that Tweety is an ostrich. We would then have:

*STM:*    *bird(Tweety)*
          $bird(x) \rightarrow flies(x)$
          *flies(Tweety)*
  *        *ostrich(Tweety)*

This new fact would then trigger the rule from LTM that ostriches do not fly (with the side-effect of pushing *bird(Tweety)* into ITM).

*ITM:*    *bird(Tweety)*
*STM:*    $bird(x) \rightarrow flies(x)$
          *flies(Tweety)*
          *ostrich(Tweety)*
  *        $ostrich(x) \rightarrow \neg flies(x)$

Again MP is applied, resulting in:

*ITM:*    *bird(Tweety)*
          $bird(x) \rightarrow flies(x)$
*STM:*    *flies(Tweety)*
          *ostrich(Tweety)*

$$ostrich(x) \rightarrow \neg flies(x)$$
\*     $\neg flies(Tweety)$

At this point STM contains both the belief that Tweety does not fly, as well as the belief that Tweety does fly. Is this a problem? We think not. We would like to be able to say that the fact that Tweety flies was concluded *by default*; through the use of a rule of typicality. Now given the additional information that, in fact, Tweety is an ostrich, we would like the system to be able to retract the belief that Tweety flies, and instead conclude that Tweety, in fact, does not fly.

Our approach then is first to let an inconsistency arise, and then once both $\alpha$ and $\neg \alpha$ are together in STM, we want to be able to decide which (if either) of the two should be kept as a belief. Since STM is small, we will always be able to determine quickly and easily whether such a direct contradiction exists.

Several methods of conflict resolution are available to us, each requiring little more than providing an extra term to facts in STM which indicates the justification for bringing that fact into focus. For example, something that is brought into STM as a result of direct observation can be tagged with the term "OBS," while a fact deduced through modus ponens can be tagged with "MP" and so forth. These tags then allow the system to favor, say, an observed fact over a deduced fact, and a more recent observation over an earlier one.

All information about Tweety may soon leave STM, but will remain in RTM for some number of inference cycles (and thus still remain relevant). If at a later time (not too late, as decay out of RTM may eventually occur), Tweety is in focus again, RTM's record of Tweety's inability to fly will block the statement *flies(Tweety)* from reappearing in STM. Thus the default rule is no longer applicable. That is, once a contradiction arises in STM and we have resolved the contradiction in favor of one of the contradictory facts, we can simply remove the other fact from STM.[3] Furthermore, we can just as easily remove this fact from RTM so that it no longer bears any relevance to the reasoning from that point on.

---

[3] In our implementation we actually retain the fact that has been determined to be incorrect, but we tag this fact in such a way that its incorrect nature is evident. This is done so that ITM can maintain a complete chronological listing of STM facts. We suspect this will be important in the future as we implement a learning device that scans ITM, attempting to identify patterns of reasoning.

Any number of conflict resolution heuristics of this sort can be implemented rather easily. This is not to say that resolution of such contradictions is trivial; on the contrary, it is in general very hard, but at the very least we have a model in which to test different approaches.

With the above model of commonsense reasoning in the place it is natural to try to formalize the behavior and properties exhibited by such a reasoner. We discuss this theory in the following section.

## 4.3   A Theoretical Approach

### 4.3.1   Background

We have argued that we do not want to characterize the *end results* of reasoning; rather we seek to understand reasoning as an *ongoing process*. This requires that the formalism be capable of dealing with time as an object of reasoning. This can be done in ordinary logic, if the representation is in the metatheory, through the use of a time argument to a predicate representing the agent's proof process. However, in order for the agent to reason about the passage of time that occurs *as* it reasons, time arguments must be put into the agent's own language. But now since time goes on as the agent reasons, and since this phenomenon is part of what is to be reasoned about, the agent will need to take note of facts that come and go, for example, "It is now 3 PM and I am just starting this task.... Now it is no longer 3 PM, but rather it is 3:15 PM, and I still have not finished the task I began at 3 PM." This immediately puts us in a nontraditional setting, for we lose monotonicity: as the history evolves, conclusions may be lost. Because of this, the formalism cannot in general retain or inherit all conclusions from one step to the next. The formalism must be augmented with a notion of "now," which appropriately changes as deducions are performed. It turns out that this is not an easy task.

We propose step-logic then as a model of reasoning that focuses on the ongoing process of deduction. As a simple example, refer to figure 4.3. The reasoner starts out with an empty set of beliefs at time 0. Certain "conclusions" or "observations" may arise at discrete time steps. At some time, $i$, it may have belief $\alpha$, concluded based on carlier beliefs, or as an observation arising at step $i$. At some later time, $j$, it comes up with $\alpha \rightarrow \beta$. Later still, the agent might deduce $\beta$. Of course, much the same might be said of any deductive logic. However, in step-logic these time parameters can figure

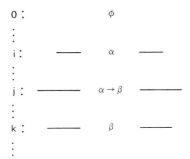

**Figure 4.3**
Step-like logical studies

in the ongoing reasoning itself. Note that we are focusing on the *ongoing* reasoning process and *not* on the end results of reasoning.

The memory model (section 4.2) of course proceeds in a steplike fashion, and indeed it was what motivated the effort toward the theoretical approach in this section. The memory model can even record the times at which its conclusions are drawn, in further steplike fashion. However, that model does not serve well as a theoretically concise set of principles for understanding broad issues of reasoning behavior at an abstract level. For that purpose we need something more like a step-logic.

### 4.3.2 Details of Step-Logic

**4.3.2.1 The Basics.** A step-logic is characterized by a language, observations, and inference rules. At each step $i$ *all* immediate consequences of the rules of inference applied to the previous step are drawn (and therefore are among the wffs at step $i$). However, for real-time effectiveness and cognitive plausibility, at each step we want only a finite number of conclusions to be drawn.[4]

In order for a reasoner to be able to deal appropriately with the common-sense world, three major mechanisms are necessary: introspection, awareness of time, and retraction. Since the agent must be able to reason about its own processes, a belief, or knowledge, predicate is needed. We employ

---

[4] Indeed it should not be just finite, but small. Our current idealization does not go this far; we intend, however, to eventually make broad use of a "retraction" mechanism to keep things to a reasonable size. Specifically, we anticipate the introduction of a notion of relevance along the lines of RTM in our memory model.

a predicate symbol, $K$, for this purpose: $K(i, \text{'}\alpha\text{'})$ is intended to mean that the agent knows wff $\alpha$ at time $i$.[5] We drop the quotes in $K(i, \text{'}\alpha\text{'})$ in the remainder of the paper.

The agent needs information as to how the $i$ in $K(i, \alpha)$ relates to the ongoing time as deductions are performed. This requires the agent to have information as to what time it is now. We achieve this through the use of the predicate expression $Now(i)$, which is intended to mean the time currently is $i$. Therefore, this is a belief which must change as deductions are performed.

Default reasoning is an integral part of a commonsense reasoner's thought processes. By default reasoning we mean the process of believing a particular fact when there is no evidence to suspect the contrary; however, later, in the face of new evidence, the former belief may be retracted. We allow default reasoning through the use of a retraction mechanism. Retraction is facilitated by focusing on the dual: inheritance. We do *not* assume that all deductions at time $i$ are inherited (retained) at time $i + 1$. Thus by carefully restricting inheritance we achieve a rudimentary kind of retraction. The most obvious case is that of $Now(i)$. If at a given step the agent knows the time to be $i$, by having the belief $Now(i)$, then that belief is not inherited to the next time-step.

We have developed two distinct types of formalisms, that occur in pairs: the metatheory $SL^n$ *about* an agent, and the agent-theory $SL_n$ itself. $n$ is an index serving to distinguish different versions of step-logics. It is the latter, $SL_n$, that is to be step-like; the former, $SL^n$, is simply our assurance that we have been honest in describing what we mean by a particular agent's reasoning. The two theories together form a step-logic *pair*. In [Drapkin and Perlis 1986] we proposed eight such step-logic pairs, arranged in increasing sophistication, with respect to the three mechanisms above (introspection, awareness of time, and retraction), $\langle SL_0, SL^0 \rangle$, ..., $\langle SL_7, SL^7 \rangle$. $SL_0$ has none of the three mechanisms, and $SL_7$ has all.

The metatheories all are consistent, first-order theories, and therefore complete with respect to standard first-order semantics. However, their associated agent-theories are another matter. These we do not even *want* in general to be consistent, for they are (largely) intended as formal counterparts of the reasoning of fallible agents.

---

[5] We are not distinguishing here between belief and knowledge. See Gettier 1963 for a discussion of belief vs knowledge.

**4.3.2.2 Definitions.** In this section we present several definitions, most of which are analogous to standard definitions from first-order logic. Consequently certain results follow trivially from their first-order counterparts.

Intuitively, we view an agent as an inference mechanism that may be given external inputs or observations. Inferred wffs are called beliefs; these may include certain observations.

Let $\mathscr{L}$ be a first-order language, and let $\mathscr{W}$ be the set of wffs of $\mathscr{L}$.

*Definition 1   An* observation-function *is a function* $OBS: \mathbf{N} \to \mathscr{P}(\mathscr{W})$, *where* $\mathscr{P}(\mathscr{W})$ *is the powerset of* $\mathscr{W}$, *and where for each* $i \in \mathbf{N}$, *the set* $OBS(i)$ *is finite. If* $\alpha \in OBS(i)$, *then* $\alpha$ *is called an* $i$-observation.

*Definition 2   A* history *is a finite tuple of pairs of finite subsets of* $\mathscr{W}$. $\mathscr{H}$ *is the set of histories.*

*Definition 3   An* inference-function *is a function* $INF: \mathscr{H} \to \mathscr{P}(W)$, *where for each* $h \in \mathscr{H}$, $INF(h)$ *is finite.*

Intuitively, a history is a conceivable temporal sequence of belief-set/observation-set pairs. The history is a *finite* tuple; it represents the temporal sequence up to a certain point in time. The inference-function extends the temporal sequence of belief sets by one more step beyond the history. In the example in figure 4.4 we see how these ideas are used to generate an

Let

- $OBS(i) = \begin{cases} \{bird(x) \to flies(x)\} & \text{if } i = 1 \\ \{bird(tweety)\} & \text{if } i = 3 \\ \varnothing & \text{otherwise} \end{cases}$

- $Thm_i \subseteq W, 0 \le i < n; Thm_0 = \varnothing;$

- $INF(\langle\langle Thm_0, OBS(1)\rangle, \ldots, \langle Thm_{n-1}, OBS(n)\rangle\rangle) =$
  $Thm_{n-1} \cup OBS(n) \cup \{\alpha(t) | (\exists \beta)(\beta(t), \beta(x) \to \alpha(x) \in (Thm_{n-1} \cup OBS(n)))\}.$

The history $h$ of the first five steps then would be:

$h = \langle\langle \qquad\qquad\qquad \varnothing \qquad\qquad\qquad ,\{bird(x) \to flies(x)\}\rangle,$
$\qquad \langle \qquad \{bird(x) \to flies(x)\} \qquad , \qquad\quad \varnothing \qquad\rangle,$
$\qquad \langle \qquad \{bird(x) \to flies(x)\} \qquad , \quad \{bird(tweety)\} \quad\rangle,$
$\qquad \langle \{bird(x) \to flies(x), bird(tweety), flies(tweety)\}, \qquad \varnothing \qquad\rangle,$
$\qquad \langle \{bird(x) \to flies(x), bird(tweety), flies(tweety)\}, \qquad \varnothing \qquad\rangle\rangle$

**Figure 4.4**
Example of *OBS* and *INF*

actual history based on an inference-function and an observation-function. Definitions 4 and 5 formalize this in terms of a step-logic $SL_n$.

*Definition 4    An $SL_n$-theory over a language $\mathscr{L}$ is a triple, $\langle \mathscr{L}, OBS, INF \rangle$, where $\mathscr{L}$ is a first-order language, $OBS$ is an observation-function, and $INF$ is an inference-function. We use the notation, $SL_n(OBS, INF)$, for such a theory (the language $\mathscr{L}$ is implicit in the definitions of $OBS$ and $INF$). If we wish to consider a fixed $INF$ but varied $OBS$, we write $SL_n(\cdot, INF)$.*

Let $SL_n(OBS, INF)$ be an $SL_n$-theory over $\mathscr{L}$.

*Definition 5    Let the set of 0-theorems, denoted $Thm_0$, be empty. For $i > 0$, let the set of $i$-theorems, denoted $Thm_i$, be $INF(\langle \langle Thm_0, OBS(1) \rangle, \langle Thm_1, OBS(2) \rangle, \dots, \langle Thm_{i-1}, OBS(i) \rangle \rangle)$. We write $SL_n(OBS, INF) \vdash_i \alpha$ to mean $\alpha$ is an $i$-theorem of $SL_n(OBS, INF)$.*[6]

*Definition 6    Given a theory $SL_n(OBS, INF)$, a corresponding $SL^n$-theory, written $SL^n(OBS, INF)$, is a first-order theory having binary predicate symbol $K$,[7] numerals, and names for the wffs in $\mathscr{L}$, such that*

$$SL^n(OBS, INF) \vdash K(i, \alpha) \quad iff \quad SL_n(OBS, INF) \vdash_i \alpha.$$

Thus in $SL^n(OBS, INF)$, $K(i, \alpha)$ is intended to express that $\alpha$ is an $i$-theorem of $SL_n(OBS, INF)$.[8]

**4.3.2.3 $SL_7$.** $SL_7$ is the most ambitious step-logic: it has all three mechanisms which we claim are necessary for a commonsense reasoner. We use the notation $SL_7$ for any of a family of step-logics whose $OBS$ and $INF$ involve the predicates *Now* and $K$ and contain a retraction mechanism. Choosing $OBS$ and $INF$ therefore fixes the theory within the family.

$SL_7$ is *not* intended in general to be consistent. If $SL_7$ is supplied *only* with logically valid wffs that do not syntactically contain the predicate *Now*, then indeed $SL_7$ will remain consistent over time: there will be no step $i$ at which the conclusion set is inconsistent, for its rules of inference are sound (see [Eigot-Drapkin 1988]). However, virtually all the interesting applications of $SL_7$ involve providing the agent with some nonlogical and potentially false axioms, thus opening the way to derivation of contradic-

---

[6] Note the nonstandard use of the turnstile here.
[7] We see that the predicate letter $K$ has two roles: in $SL^n$ and in $SL_n$. The context will make the role clear.
[8] In Drapkin and Perlis 1986a, b, we used $^i\alpha$ for $K(i, \alpha)$.

tions. This behavior is what we are interested in studying, in a way that avoids the swamping problem. The controlled growth of deductions in step-logic provides a convenient tool for this, as we will see.

The language of $SL_7$ is first-order, having unary predicate symbol $Now$, binary predicate symbol $K$, and ternary predicate symbol $Contra$, for time, introspection, and contradiction, respectively. We write $Now(i)$ to mean the time is now $i$; $K(i, \alpha)$ means that $\alpha$ is known[9] at step $i$; and $Contra(i, \alpha, \beta)$ means that $\alpha$ and $\beta$ are in direct contradiction (one is the negation of the other) and both are $i$-theorems.

The formulae that the agent has at step $i$ (the $i$-theorems) are precisely all those that can be deduced from step $i - 1$ using the applicable rules of inference. As previously stated, the agent is to have only a finite number of theorems (conclusions, beliefs, or simply wffs) at any given step. We write:

$i: \ldots, \alpha$

$i + 1: \ldots, \beta$

to mean that $\alpha$ is an $i$-theorem, and $\beta$ is an $i + 1$-theorem. There is no implicit assumption that $\alpha$ (or any other wff other than $\beta$) is present (or not present) at step $i + 1$. The ellipsis indicates that there might be other wffs present. Wffs are not assumed to be inherited or retained in passing from one step to the next, unless explicity stated in an inference rule. In figure 4.5 we illustrate one possible inference function, denoted $INF_B$, involving a rule for special types of inheritance; see rule 7.

For *time*, we envision a clock which is ticking as the agent is reasoning. At each step in its reasoning, the agent looks at this clock to obtain the time.[10] The wff $Now(i)$ is an $i$-theorem. $Now(i)$ corresponds intuitively to the statement "The time is now i."

*Introspection* involves the predicate $K$, and (in $INF_B$) a new rule of inference; see rule 5 in figure 4.5. This rule allows that agent to introspect negatively, that is, to reason at step $i + 1$ that it did not know $\beta$ at step $i$.[11] To keep things cognitively plausible, and also to keep the number of

---

[9] Known, believed, or concluded. As already stated, we are not distinguishing between these terms. See Gettier 1963, Perlis 1986, and Perlis 1988 for discussion of these.
[10] Richard Weyhrauch analyzed this idea in a rather different way in his talk at the 1986 Sardinia Workshop on Metal-level Architectures and Reflection. See Weyhrauch 1986.
[11] For a discussion of why the agent can't reason at step $i$ about its beliefs at that same step, see Elgot-Drapkin and Perlis 1988.

The inference rules given here correspond to an inference-function. $INF_B$. For any given history, $INF_B$ returns the set of all immediate consequences of Rules 1–7 applied to the last step in that history. Note that Rule 5 is the only default rule.

**Rule 1:**
$$\frac{i: \ldots}{i+1: \ldots, Now(i+1)}$$
Corresponds to looking at clock

**Rule 2:**
$$\frac{i: \ldots}{i+1: \ldots, \alpha}$$
If $\alpha \in OBS(i+1)$—Observations become beliefs

**Rule 3:**
$$\frac{i: \ldots, \alpha, \alpha \to \beta}{i+1: \ldots, \beta}$$
Modus ponens

**Rule 4:**
$$\frac{i: \ldots, P_1 a, \ldots, P_n a, (\forall x)[P_1 x \wedge \ldots \wedge P_n x) \to Qx]}{i+1: \ldots, Qa}$$
Another veriosn of modus ponens

**Rule 5:**
$$\frac{i: \ldots}{i+1: \ldots, \neg K(i, \beta)}$$
Negative introspection[a]

**Rule 6:**
$$\frac{i: \ldots, \alpha, \neg\alpha}{i+1: \ldots, Contra(i, \alpha, \neg\alpha)}$$
Presence of (direct) contradiction

**Rule 7:**
$$\frac{i: \ldots, \alpha}{i+1: \ldots, \alpha}$$
Inheritance[b]

a. where $\beta$ is not a theorem at step $i$, but is a closed sub-formula at step $i$.
b. where nothing of the form $Contra(i-1, \alpha, \beta)$ nor $Contra(i-1, \beta, \alpha)$ is an $i$-theorem, and where $\alpha$ is not of the form $Now(\beta)$. That is, contradictions and time are not inherited. The intuitive reason time is not inherited is that time changes at each step. The intuitive reason contradicting wffs $\alpha$ and $\beta$ are not inherited is that not both can be true, and so the agent should, for that reason, be unwilling to simply assume either to be the case without further justification. This does not mean, however, that neither will appear at the next step, for either or both may appear for other reasons, as will be seen. Note also that the wff $Contra(i, \alpha, \neg\alpha)$ will be inherited, since it is not itself either time or a contradiction, and (intuitively) it expresses a fact (that there was a contradiction at step $i$) that remains true.

**Figure 4.5**
Rules of inference corresponding to $INF_B$

conclusions at any given step finite, we allow the agent to introspect negatively only on those wffs of which it is aware. We say the agent is aware of a wff $\alpha$ at step $i$ if $\alpha$ appears as a closed subformula at step $i$.[12] Therefore, $\neg K(i, \alpha)$ is to be deduced at step $i + 1$ if $\alpha$ is not an $i$-theorem, but does appear as a closed sub-formula at step $i$. See Fagin and Halpern 1988 for another treatment of awareness.

*Retractions* are used to facilitate removal of certain conflicting data. Currently we handle contradictions by simply not inheriting the formulae directly involved.[13] In $SL_7(\cdot, INF_B)$, a conclusion in a given step, $i$, is inherited to step $i + 1$ if it is not contradicted at step $i$ and it is not the predicate $Now(j)$, for some $j$; see Rule 7 in figure 4.5.

$SL_7(\cdot, INF_B)$ was formulated with applications such as the *Brother Problem* (see section 4.3.2.4) in mind. This led us to the rules of inference listed in figure 4.5. Rule 3 states, for instance, that if $\alpha$ and $\alpha \rightarrow \beta$ are $i$-theorems, then $\beta$ will be an $i + 1$-theorem. Rule 3 make no claim about whether or not $\alpha$ and/or $\alpha \rightarrow \beta$ are $i + 1$-theorems.

**4.3.2.4 An Example: The Brother Problem.** In this section we show how $SL_7(\cdot, INF_B)$ can be formulated to provide a real-time solution to Moore's Brother Problem (see Moore 1983). One reasons, "Since I don't know I have I have a brother, I must not." This problem can be broken down into two: the first requires that the reasoner be able to decide he doesn't know he has a brother; the second that, on that basis, he, in fact, does not have a brother (from *modus ponens* and the assumption that "If I had a brother, I'd know it.") The first of these seems to lend itslef readily to step-logic, in that the negative reflection problem (determining when something is not known) reduces to a simple look-up.

We present synopses of computer-generated results for three different scenarios where the agent determines whether or not a brother exists. Let $B$ be a 0-argument predicate letter representing the proposition that a brother exists. Let $P$ be a 0-argument predicate letter (other than $B$) that represents a proposition that implies that a brother exists.[14] In each case, at some step $i$ the agent has the axiom $P \rightarrow B$, and also the following

---

[12] A sub-formula of a wff is any consecutive portion of the wff that itself is a wff. Note that there are only finitely many such sub-formulae at any given step.

[13] In future work we hope to have a mechanism for tracing the antecedents and consequents of a formula $\alpha$ when $\alpha$ is suspect, à la Doyle and deKleer (see Doyle 1982, de Kleer 1986), though in the context of a real-time reasoner.

[14] $P$ might be something like "My parents have two sons," together with appropriate axioms.

$i$:      $\underline{Now(i)}$, $P \to B$, $(\forall x)[(Now(x) \wedge \neg K(x-1, B)) \to \neg B]$

$i+1$:   $\underline{Now(i+1)}$, $P \to B$, $(\forall x)[(Now(x) \wedge \neg K(x-1, B)) \to \neg B]$, $\underline{\neg K(i, B)}$, $\underline{\neg K(i, \neg B)}$, $\underline{\neg K(i, P)}$

$i+2$:   $\underline{Now(i+2)}$, $P \to B$, $(\forall x)[(Now(x) \wedge \neg K(x-1, B)) \to \neg B]$, $\neg K(i, B)$, $\neg K(i, \neg B)$, $\neg K(i, P)$, $\underline{\neg B}$, $\underline{\neg K(i+1, B)}$, $\underline{\neg K(i+1, \neg B)}$, $\underline{\neg K(i+1, P)}$

**Figure 4.6**
Negative introspection succeeds

autoepistemic axiom which represents the belief that not knowing $B$ "now" implies $\neg B$.

AXIOM 1    $(\forall x)[(Now(x) \wedge \neg K(x-1, B)) \to \neg B]$

The following behaviors are illustrated:

• If $B$ is among the wffs of which the agent is aware at step $i$, but not one that is believed at step $i$, then agent will come to know this fact ($\neg K(i, B)$, that is was not believed at step $i$) at step $i+1$. As a consequence of this, other information may be deduced. In this case, the agent concludes $\neg B$ from the autoepistemic axiom (Axiom 1). Clearly the *Now* predicate plays a critical role.

• The agent must refrain from such negative introspection when in fact $B$ is already known.

• A conflict may occur if something is coming to be known while negative introspection is simultaneously leading to its negation. The third illustration shows this being resolved in an intuitive manner (though not one that will generalize as much as we would like; this is an area we are currently exploring).

*Simple negative introspection succeeds.*   In this example the agent is not able to deduce the proposition $B$, that he has a brother, and hence is able to deduce $\neg B$, that he does *not* have a brother (see figure 4.6.). For ease of reading we underline in each step those wffs which are new (i.e., which appear through other than inheritance). For the purposes of illustration, let $i$ be arbitrary and let

$$OBS_{B_1}(j) = \begin{cases} \{P \to B, (\forall x)[(Now(x) \wedge \neg K(x-1, B)) \to \neg B]\} & \text{if } j = i \\ \varnothing & \text{otherwise} \end{cases}$$

Since $B$ is not an $i$-observation (and thus is not an $i$-theorem), the agent

$i$:      $Now(i), P \rightarrow B, (\forall x)[(Now(x) \wedge \neg K(x-1, B)) \rightarrow \neg B], B$

$i+1$:   $Now(i+1), P \rightarrow B, (\forall x)[(Now(x) \wedge \neg K(x-1, B)) \rightarrow \neg B], B, \underline{\neg K(i, \neg B)}, \underline{\neg K(i, P)}$

**Figure 4.7**
Negative introspection fails appropriately

uses rule 5, the negative introspection rule, to conclude $\neg K(i, B)$ at step $i+1$. At step $i+2$ the agent concludes $\neg B$ from the autoepistemic knowledge stated above (Axiom 1) and the use of the alternate version of *modus ponens*, rule 4.

*Simple negative introspection fails (appropriately).*   In this example, let

$OBS_{B_2}(j)$

$$= \begin{cases} \{P \rightarrow B, (\forall x)[(Now(x) \wedge \neg K(x-1, B)) \rightarrow \neg B], B\} & \text{if } j = i \\ \varnothing & \text{otherwise} \end{cases}$$

Thus the agent has $B$ at step $i$, and is blocked (appropriately for this example) from deducing at step $i+1$ the wffs $\neg K(i, B)$ and $\neg B$. See figure 4.7.

Note that a traditional final-tray-like approach could produce quite similar behavior to that seen in figures 4.6 and 4.7 if it is endowed with a suitable introspection device, although it would not have the real-time step-like character we are trying to achieve.

*Introspection contradicts other deduction.*   In this example, let

$OBS_{B_3}(j)$

$$= \begin{cases} \{P \rightarrow B, (\forall x)[(Now(x) \wedge \neg K(x-1, B)) \rightarrow \neg B], P\} & \text{if } j = i \\ \varnothing & \text{otherwise} \end{cases}$$

In figure 4.8 we see then that the agent does not have $B$ at step $i$, but is able to *deduce* $B$ at step $i+1$ from $P \rightarrow B$ and $P$ at step $i$. Since the agent is *aware* (in our sense) of $B$ at step $i$, and yet does not have $B$ as a *conclusion* at $i$, it will deduce $\neg K(i, B)$ at step $i+1$. Thus both $B$ and $\neg K(i, B)$ are concluded at step $i+1$. At step $i+2$ Axiom 1 (the autoepistemic axiom), together with $Now(i+1)$ and $\neg K(i, B)$ and Rule 4, will produce $\neg B$. A conflict results, which is noted at step $i+3$. This then inhibits inheritance of both $B$ and $\neg B$ at step $i+4$. Although neither $B$ nor $\neg B$ is inherited to step $i+4$, $B$ is re-deduced at step $i+4$ via *modus ponens* from step $i+3$.

$i$:　$\underline{Now(i)}, P \to B, (\forall x)[(Now(x) \wedge \neg K(x-1,B)) \to \neg B], \underline{P}$

$i+1$:　$\underline{Now(i+1)}, P \to B, (\forall x)[(Now(x) \wedge \neg K(x-1,B)) \to \neg B], P, \underline{B}, \neg K(i,B), \neg K(i, \neg B)$

$i+2$:　$\underline{Now(i+2)}, P \to B, (\forall x)[(Now(x) \wedge \neg K(x-1,B)) \to \neg B], P, B, \neg K(i,B), \neg K(i, \neg B),$
　　　　$\neg B, \underline{\neg K(i+1, \neg B)}$

$i+3$:　$\underline{Now(i+3)}, P \to B, (\forall x)[(Now(x) \wedge \neg K(x-1,B)) \to \neg B], P, B, \neg K(i,B), \neg K(i, \neg B),$
　　　　$\neg B, \neg K(i+1, \neg B), \underline{Contra(i+2, B, \neg B)}$

$i+4$:　$\underline{Now(i+4)}, P \to B, (\forall x)[(Now(x) \wedge \neg K(x-1,B)) \to \neg B], P, \neg K(i,B), \neg K(i, \neg B)$
　　　　$\neg K(i+1, \neg B), Contra(i+2, B, \neg B), \underline{B}, \underline{Contra(i+3, B, \neg B)}$

**Figure 4.8**
Introspection conflicts with other deduction and resolves

Thus $B$ "wins out" over $\neg B$ due to its existing justification in other wffs, while $\neg B$'s justification is "too old": $\neg K(i+2, B)$, rather than $\neg K(i, B)$, would be needed. We see then that the conflict resolves due to the special nature of the time-bound "now" feature of introspection.

A traditional final-tray-like approach would encounter difficulties with this third example, for at step $i+2$ there is a contradiction. This means that the final tray for a tray-like model of a reasoning agent would simply be filled with all wffs in the language—and no basis for a resolution is possible within such a logic.

## 4.4 Future Work

We have presented a brief overview of a model of memory that is motivated by a psychological approach to reasoning. Combining that model with the idea that reasoning occurs in time has led us to build a computational model of reasoning; one that isn't bound to a final state, conclusion, or goal. It turns out that the foundational theory that we have developed to study this model has the nice property of being grounded in first-order logic without suffering the unpleasantries typically associated with contradiction.

This, however, is only the beginning of our work. We have identified at least three major categories of research that is yet to be undertaken. First there is a need to extend and refine the memory model's implementation. Similarly, step-logic can be extended to further conjoin it to the memory model. Finally, we have identified problems in reasoning research that the memory model and step-logic seem well suited to handle. Below is a short list of endeavors that fall into one or more of these categories. The list is certainly not exhaustive of related research, nor do we expect that the items on it are exclusive of one another. We do, however, feel that it illustrates the breadth of ideas that are relevant to this work.

**Parallel retrieval.**   If LTM is really intended to represent long term memory, then it makes sense to retrieve associations concurrently. There is certainly no benefit to be had from serial retrieval, and it may, in fact, impose orderings on STM that are undesirable. We seek a model of concurrent retrieval that may (or may not) require a different implementation representation of LTM, but doesn't infringe on the general model.

**Restricting STM.**   We need a robust mechanism that will restrict the size of STM. LTM is likely to be very, very large. Lots of associations can be expected at each inference cycle. Yet it seems that context ought to be able to prevent some of these associations from actually entering STM. After all, it isn't necessary, nor would it be desirable, to recall each time the concept of bird is encountered that male birds are generally more colorful than females. But, if the task is to identify a particular bird, this fact is indeed relevant. We hope to extend the power of RTM to handle this task.

**Formalize LTM in step-logic.**   To understand the memory model better, it is necessary to make precise more of its components. Step-logic is the formalism we would like to use to do this. There is currently no notion of association or retrieval in step-logic, though there doesn't seem to be anything that would prohibit this addition to the theory.

**Make LTM dynamic.**   The utility of LTM is severely limited unless it can be updated with both additions and deletions. This ability is part of any psychological model of intelligence and will add a necessary flexibility to the memory model. Our hope is that a dynamic LTM is one way to model learning in the memory model. (It is too early to make any claim about sufficiency.) An interesting addendum to this would be to formalize the dynamic LTM in step-logic.

**Plan generation in step-logic.**   Here time is explicitly part of the problem solving process, the paradigmatic case involves forming *and* enacting a plan before a deadline time is reached. Although time is explicit in step-logic, it has only recently been used in a real-time problem solving setting.

## Acknowledgments

We would like to thank the following organizations for financial support:
the IBM Corporation, and the U.S. Army Research Office (DAAL03-88-
K0087).

## References

de Kleer, J. 1986. An assumption-based TMS. *Artificial Intelligence* 28:127–162.

Doyle, J. 1979. A truth maintenance system. *Artificial Intelligence* 12(3):231–272.

Doyle, J. 1982. *Some Theories of Reasoned Assumptions: An Essay in Rational Psychology.*
Carnegie-Mellon University Department of Computer Science, Technical Report.

Drapkin, J., and D. Perlis. 1986a. A preliminary excursion into step-logics. In *Proceedings of
the SIGART International Symposium on Methodologies for Intelligent Systems.* Knoxville,
Tennessee: ACM, 262–269.

Drapkin, J., and D. Perlis. 1986b. Step-logics: an alternative approach to limited reasoning.
In *Proceedings of the European Conference on Artificial Intelligence,* pp. 160–163.

Elgot-Drapkin, J. 1988. Step-logic: Reasoning Situated in Time. Ph.D. dissertation, University
of Maryland.

Elgot-Drapkin, J., and D. Perlis. 1988. *Reasoning Situated in Time I: Basic Concepts.* University of Maryland Department of Computer Science, Technical Report CS–TR–2016.

Fagin, R., and J. Halpern. 1988. Belief, awareness, and limited reasoning. *Artificial Intelligence*
34(1):39–76.

Gettier, E. 1963. Is justified true belief knowledge? *Analysis* 23:121–123.

Glymour, C., and R. Thomason. 1984. Default reasoning and the logic of theory perturbation.
In *Proceedings of the Workshop on Non-monotonic Reasoning.* New Paltz, New York: AAAI,
93–102.

Goodwin, J. 1987. A Theory and System for Non-monotonic reasoning. Ph.D. dissertation,
Linköping University, Sweden.

Konolige, K. 1983. A deductive model of belief. In *Proceedings of the Eighth International Joint
Conference on Artificial Intelligence.* Karlsruhe: Kaufmann, 377–381.

Levesque, H. 1984. A logic of implicit and explicit belief. In *Proceedings of the Third National
Conference on Artificial Intelligence.* Austin: Kaufmann, 198–202.

McCarthy, J. 1980. Circumscription—a form of non-monotonic reasoning. *Artificial Intelligence* 13(1, 2):27–39.

Miller, G. 1956. The magical number seven plus or minus two. *The Psychological Review*
63:81–97.

Moore, R. 1983. Semantic considerations on nomonotonic logic. In *Proceedings of the
Eighth International Joint Conference on Artificial Intelligence.* Karlsruhe: Kaufmann, 272–
279.

Nilsson, N. 1983. Artificial intelligence prepares for 2001. *AI Magazine* 4(4):7–14.

Perlis, D. 1986. On the consistency of commonsense reasoning. *Computational Intelligence* 2:180–190.

Perlis, D. 1988. Languages with self reference II: knowledge, belief, and modality. *Artificial Intelligence* 34:179–212.

Weyhrauch, R. 1986. The building of mind. In *1986 Workshop on Meta-level Architectures and Reflection*. Alghero, Sardinia: unpublished manuscript.

# 5 Artificial Intelligence and Hard Problems: The Expected Complexity of Problem Solving

**Clark Glymour, Kevin Kelly, and Peter Spirtes**

## 5.1 Introduction

A great deal of cognitive psychology has developed around analyses of human problem solving, and a considerable part of artificial intelligence work has been devoted to designing programs that solve problems at least as rapidly and accurately as humans do. Consider a few examples:

• An instance of the Tower of Hanoi problem consists of three posts in a line, with three plates (with center holes) of different sizes placed on the left most post, the smallest plate on the middle-sized plate and the latter on the largest plate. The task is arrange all of the plates in the same order on the rightmost post by moving plates one at a time to any post but in such a way that a larger plate never rests on a smaller post. Other instances of the problem can be obtained by varying the number of posts, the number of platters and the initial distribution of the platters.

• An instance of the alphabet-arithmetic problem is: find a mapping, $f$, from letters to digits from 0 to 9 such that $f(D) = 5$ and DONALD + ROBERT = GERALD is transformed by $f$ into a valid sum. Other instances are obtained by varying the words and the constrained values of the transformation.

• An instance of the function-maximum problem consists of some definite but unknown function $F$, defined on the set of strings $\{111, 110, 101, 011, 100, 010, 001, 000\}$ and taking rational numbers as values. The problem solver has the power to call for the value of $F$ for any particular member of the set, and to make as many such calls as is desired. The task is to find a member of the set for which $F$ takes a maximum value. Other instances of the problem vary the string length, which is 3 in this instance, and the unknown function.

There are endless problems of these kinds in the cognitive-psychology literature, and many of them have been addressed by aritificial-intelligence programs. It is clearly trivial to write a program that solves any one instance of a problem of these kinds instantly: simply program the answer. Interesting programs have the capacity not only to solve a particular instance of such a problem, but also to solve at least all instances of a particular problem. When a procedure is capable of solving not just a few instances of a problem but every instance, is it therefore capable of doing something hard? Since there are in general many different ways to solve such problems, the question of evaluation naturally arises: are some ways of solving a problem better than others? In computation theory the common way to approach answering such questions is in terms of some complexity measure imposed on the procedure: how do the computational requirements of the procedure grow with some intuitive or useful measure of the size of a problem instance? Does the problem admit of alternative solution procedures that are more efficient by such measures than is the procedure in question? Is there an "easy" solution to the problem?

In common cognitive science and artificial intelligence practice, comparisons and evaluations are instead made by exhibiting the performance of a procedure on a few instances of the problem. Theorists may (and do) complain of such failures to give theoretical analyses of the properties of a procedure or the problem it addresses, but we wish to point out a difficulty that is perhaps more fundamental: It is generally not possible to tell whether a problem-solving procedure in the artificial intelligence and cognitive science literature has solved an easy problem or a hard problem because for the application of the relevant senses of "easy" and "hard," the problem is not fully specified. The reason is that the complexity properties that separate algorithms often have to do with the average or expected computational requirements, and these measures are only determinate once there is a probability distribution specified on the instances of a problem. Typically, every algorithm that solves the problems of interest requires exponentially increasing computational sources to solve the most difficult problems of each size. The "worst case" does not distinguish among procedures; the expected or average case may. The force of this otherwise banal observation lies in the realization that under "natural" uniform probability distributions on their instances, various classical problem solving tasks are trivial; there are algorithms that will solve them, on the average, using computational resources that are always less than some (often small) constant value, no matter how large the size of the instances may be.

Newell and Simon's *Human Problem Solving* (1972) provided the framework for much of contemporary cognitive psychology and artificial intelligence. In one representation of problem-solving, they consider "set-predicate" problems. A set-predicate problem instance consists of a set of entities, a subset having a particular property, a method of enumerating or naming the entities, and some method (an oracle) that determines for each particular entity whether or not it has the property in question. The problem solving task is to find an entity in the set that has the property. The interpretation of the representation is that the entities in the set represent sequences of "operators" or actions of some finite number of kinds, and the goal subset is understood to consist of those sequences of operators that produce a desired result. Another representation of problem solving is not explicit in *Human Problem Solving* but is certainly implicit, and is widely used in the artificial-intelligence literature. This second, or finite automaton representation, takes an instance of a problem to be given by a finite automaton whose arc labels signify actions available to the agent, whose nodes signify states of the world resulting from actions, whose final states represent goal states, and whose initial state represents the initial world state in which the problem solver is situated. Some mechanism provides the problem solver with a description of the node, or world state, that results from any sequence of actions the problem solver undertakes. The task is to find a path through the automaton from the initial state to a final state.

A key idea of Newell and Simon's approach is that problem solving is computationally difficult and typically requires recourse to *heuristic* search procedures, and, of course, that real human problem solvers do indeed use heuristic problem solving techniques. It is clear that the obvious algorithms for problem solving in either the set-predicate or the finite automaton representations are indeed *worst-case* exponential in natural measures of the size of a problem instance. Although the enumeration algorithm for problem solving that Newell and Simon describe (the "British Museum" algorithm), and other enumeration algorithms, are worst-case exponential, the interesting question of the *expected complexity* of enumeration procedures for problem solving remains open and relevant. Indeed, cognitive scientists sometimes argue that the worst cases are rare, and expected complexity measures are more relevant to questions of feasibility.[1] In discussing the learning of procedures, John Anderson (1976:502) considers algorithms that identify finite state machines, observes that enumeration algorithms will be worst-case exponential and asks us to consider the possibility

---

[1] We have heard this defense, for example, to objections to artificial intelligence programs that implement procedures that are worst-case exponential.

...that target machines may not be equally likely and that the learner's hypotheses progress from the more likely machines to the less likely. For instance, suppose the machines were ordered, such that the $n$th machine had probability $a(1 - a)^{n-1}$ of being the correct machine. That is, there was a geometric probability density across the possible machines. Then the mean number of machines that need to be considered before the correct machine would be $1/a$. Even if the probability of a particular machine being correct is very small, the mean time to success would avoid astronomical values.

In the usual analysis of expected complexity, a problem is taken to be a collection of *instances*. Instances are viewed as having *sizes*, and there are at most finitely many instances of any given size. For each possible instance size, a probability measure, usually the uniform distribution, is assumed over all instances of that size. For any algorithm that solves the problem the expected number of steps the algorithm requires to solve a randomly selected instance of size $n$ is then a well defined function of $n$. This function, the expected complexity function, can have a very different structure from the worst case complexity function for the same algorithm. Recently, for example, Wilf (1986) has shown that for a well-known NP complete problem, the graph 3-coloring problem, there is an algorithm that has an expected complexity function that is bounded, for all $n$, by 192. Thus every known algorithm that decides whether or not the vertices of a graph can be assigned three colors, in such a way that no two adjacent nodes receive the same color, requires a number of computational steps that in the worst case increases at least exponentially with the number of vertices of the graph, but some algorithm requires an *average* of 192 steps, for each instance size. What happens is that as the size measure—the number of vertices in a graph—increases, the proportion of graphs that are "easy" to decide also increases in such a way as to keep the average number of computational steps less than a constant.

Essentially the same mathematical phenomenon can occur in problem solving. We will show, using any of several natural measures, that an algorithm for the general case of problem solving in Newell and Simon's set-predicate formulation has a *constant expected complexity*. Further, we will show that there is a constant upper bound on the expected number of operators that must be applied in obtaining a solution to a problem instance of any finite size. Similarly, we will show that if a uniform probability measure is used, there is an algorithm that solves the finite automaton representation that also has a constant expected complexity, although the bound is different.

## 5.2    The Expected Complexity of Problems in the Set-Predicate Formulation

Newell and Simon present the "set-predicate" formulation of problem solving this way (95–96):

To be given a problem in this formulation means to be given, somehow, a set, $U$, and the goal of finding, producing or determining a member of a subset $G$ of that set—this latter identified most generally by a test that can be performed on the elements of $U$.

In Newell and Simon's problem solving framework, the elements of $U$ can be regarded as finite sequences of operators. If each operator is identified by a letter in a set $\Sigma$, then $U$ and $G$ can be regarded as sets of words over the alphabet $\Sigma$, or as subsets of $\Sigma^*$, the set of all finite strings of elements of the alphabet.

Newell and Simon describe an algorithm that solves all problem instances of this kind. They illustrate it for the case of theorem proving, where it is called the "British Museum Algorithm."

• Measure the length of a word in $\Sigma^*$ by the number of letters it contains, and enumerate all words, shorter words before longer words.

• Test each word in turn for membership in $G$.

• Stop when a word in $G$ is found.

The procedure is guaranteed to find a member of $G$ if there is one. Moreover, it is guaranteed to satisfy a side constraint that is often imposed on problem solving tasks, namely a preference for the shortest sequence of operations that solves the problem instance.

If $G$ is empty the Newell-Simon algorithm will continue forever. In the cases Newell and Simon consider, however, there is generally[2] a feature of any problem instance that can be used to bound the search and to modify the algorithm so that the procedure stops if no word in $G$ is found within that bound.

Newell and Simon themselves suggest that problem instances come with size bounds:

The initial space in which the solver encodes the problem already provides some measure of how big a world he has to consider.

[2] But not always, for example not in the case of theorem proving.

The size bound on a set-predicate problem instance could be taken to be $n$, where $n$ is an upper bound on the length of words in $G$. The size $n$ is an upper bound on the number of operations necessary to solve the problem instance. Size bounds of this kind are important because they guarantee that a problem instance is finite and can be solved by an exhaustive search of the words of length less than or equal to the bound. If a bound of this kind is assumed to be implicit in the problems addressed, we can without loss of generality take both $U$ and $G$ always to be finite sets, ignoring any sequences of operators longer than the length given by the value of the size measure.

Let $\Sigma$ be an alphabet. Let $\Sigma^n$ denote the set of all strings of length no greater than $n$ drawn from symbols in $\Sigma$. Now, we take a set-predicate *problem instance* to be an alphabet $\Sigma$, a size limit $n$, a finite subset $G$ of $\Sigma^n$, and an oracle for $G$ that given a word in $\Sigma^n$ returns "yes" or "no" accordingly as the word is or is not in $G$. A *problem* is the set of all problem instances for a fixed alphabet.

A *deterministic problem solver* is an effective procedure that given $\Sigma$ and a size bound determines at each step what word to query the oracle about, and conjectures a word after making queries to the oracle. A deterministic problem solver *solves a problem instance* iff it conjectures a word in $G$ and then immediately halts. A problem solver *solves a problem* iff it solves every instance of the problem.

In this paper we examine two different measures of problem solving complexity. The *oracle call* complexity of a deterministic problem solver on a particular problem instance is the number of calls to the oracle the problem solver makes before halting. The *operator application* complexity of a problem solver on a problem instance is the sum of the lengths of the words queried before the problem solver halts on that instance. Clearly, the operator application complexity of a problem solver is never smaller than its oracle call complexity.

For a given problem and complexity measure, the number of problem instances of any given size is finite and there is a worst value for the complexity of a deterministic problem solver for instances of that size (assuming that the problem solver never queries the oracle about the same hypothesis twice). For a deterministic problem solver and problem, the worst-case complexity is a function of the size of problem instances. It is straightforward to show that there are problems no algorithm can solve with only polynomially many oracle calls (see Propositions 1 and 2 of the appendix). But does the worst-case analysis imply that problem-solving is infeasible in an intuitive sense? We will show that for a variety of probability distributions over problem instances, the answer is no.

First, we assume for any problem, in the sense of "problem" defined above, and for any value of the size measure for problem instances, a uniform probability distribution on the problem instances of that size. An enumeration algorithm then has, for every instance size, an expected complexity for instances of that size.

THEOREM 1:    For any set-predicate problem, the expected number of oracle calls of any enumeration algorithm is bounded above by 2.

Each member of $U$ is a finite sequence of operators, and also a word in the language $\Sigma^*$. Theorem 1 says that on the average, for problem instances of any given size, we have to query no more than 2 words before we find a word in $G$. The result is intuitive on a little reflection. Denote the universe set $U$ for instances of size $n$ by $U(n)$. Let $S(n)$ be the cardinality of $U(n)$; it is equal to

$$\sum_{i=1}^{n} |\Sigma|^i$$

where $|\Sigma|$ is the cardinality of $\Sigma$.

The problem instances of size $n$ correspond to all ways of choosing solution sets $G$ from $U(n)$. The number of such subsets is $2^{S(n)}$, and under the uniform measure each is as probable as any other. The number of such instances that contain the first word in the enumeration is $2^{S(n)-1}$, and so $2^{S(n)-1}/2^{S(n)} = 1/2$ is the probability that the *very first* conjecture is correct. The number of instances that do not contain the first word conjectured but do contain the second is $2^{S(n)-2}$, and so the probability that the second word in the enumeration is the first word in $G$ to be conjectured is $1/4$. In general, the probability that the $k$th word is the first in $G$ to be conjectured is $1/2^k$. The expected number of conjectures is therefore

$$\sum_{i=1}^{S(n)} \frac{i}{2^i}$$

Since the sum of this series from 1 to infinity is 2, the result follows, and in fact it follows that 2 is the smallest bound that holds for all $n$.

Now let us consider the expected operator application complexity of problem solving—that is, how many "actions" must be taken, on the average, by the problem solver before it succeeds.

THEOREM 2:    For any set-predicate problem with an alphabet of two or more letters, the expected number of occurrences of letters in words that the oracle is queried about by any enumeration algorithm that enumerates shorter words before longer words is bounded above by 10.

A proof of this result is given in the appendix. We do not claim that the bound given here is the best possible.

To illustrate these results, imagine problem instances of the following kind: A door with a combination lock must be opened. In actual safes, one sequence of numbers (the combination) opens the safe. Suppose that in this case *sets* of sequences of numbers open the safe, that is, it is possible that more than one combination opens the safe. With a problem instance of this kind, we consider a letter to be a dial setting, and a word to be a sequence of dial settings. For a problem instance of size $n$, we know that a sequence of no more than $n$ dial settings is required to open the door, so we need not consider words on the alphabet of lock settings of length greater than $n$. In this case $U$ is the set of all such sequences, and $G$ is any subset of $U$. The first theorem tells us that for *every* positive $n$, if we consider all problem instances of size $n$, the average number of sequences tried before the safe is successfully opened is never greater than 2; the second theorem tells us that in the same circumstance the average number of separate dial twists performed before the door opens is no greater than 10.

Problems that consist of compositions of set-predicate problems may be analyzed straightforwardly using these results. For example, consider a safe with $n$ dials that is opened by $n$-tuples of sequences, where each sequence in an $n$-tuple corresponds to a sequence entered on a different dial. If for each dial all subsets of combinations are equally likely to be chosen to be the combinations for that dial that contribute to an open-door state, and the probability of contributing to an open-door state is, for each dial, independent of any other dial, then the expected complexity of the enumeration algorithm is bounded by a linear function of $n$.

Our results show that an arbitrary enumeration can solve the safe dial problem quickly on the average because a preponderance of the problem instances of a given size are solved on the first few guesses. The difficulty of particular problem instances is, however, sometimes implicitly judged by the number of steps a random hypothesis generator would require to solve the particular instance. Our results do not imply that *each* instance of the safe dial problem is easy in this sense. If a random generator produces only hypotheses that are members of $U$, then the expected number of steps, and the number of steps required to have any given confidence in finding a word in $G$, can be calculated from a binomial distribution in which the probability of success on any trial is given by $(G/U)$. Thus if there is a single setting of a safe dial that opens the vault, for a random hypothesis generator it is intuitively a very hard problem. In contrast, expected complexity measures locate the probability in the problem instances, not in the hypothesis generators. Our results mean this: If there are a vast collection of vault doors each with a single dial, and if for any two *sets* of combinations there are as many doors that open with any combination in the one set as with any combination in the other set, then if you select vault doors at random from the collection, on the average no more than 2 guesses will be needed to find a combination that unlocks the vault door.

A more realistic application is to recent work by Ackley (1987). Ackley studied the behavior of a number of algorithms designed to determine any maximum value of real valued functions defined on the space, $B^n$, of $n$-place bit vectors. $B^n$ is the space of all strings of length $n$ on the vocabulary $\{0, 1\}$. Since $B^n$ is finite, every real valued function on this space has a maximum. Ackley's algorithms included familiar hillclimbing procedures and a procedure Ackley called stochastic iterated genetic hillclimbing that integrates connectionist and genetic algorithms (Ackley 1985, Holland 1975). The procedures were allowed to ask for the value of the target function for any element of $B^n$. Comparison of the performance of the various algorithms was based on the number of queries of this kind the procedure made before finding the maximum value. The procedures were not required to recognize that a value *was* the maximum (that is, in the terminology of learning theory [Osherson and Weinstein 1986] they were not self-monitoring), nor were they required to continue to output the maximum value once it was found. His study applied seven algorithms to each of six functions for various values of $n$. The functions were chosen to differentiate properties of alternative hillclimbing procedures.

With three qualifications, Ackley's arrangements form a set-predicate problem of the kind we have described. $G$ is the set elements of $B^n$ for which the target function assumes its maximal value; $U(n)$ is $B^n$. The measure of complexity is exactly as in Theorem 1. The qualifications are that there is no test for membership in $G$, that in this application $U(n)$ is all strings exactly of length $n$, not all strings of length $n$ or less, and, finally, Ackley's algorithms are not exclusively deterministic.

If we put a uniform probability distribution on the (nonempty) subsets of $G$, we can ask for the expected number of queries that any enumeration algorithm will make before finding a member of $G$. The answer is given by Theorem 1. The difference in $U(n)$ affects only the value of $S(n)$ in the proof of that theorem, which is irrelevant to the result.

### 5.3   Alternative Probability Distributions

These results quite naturally raise questions about the expected complexity of problem solving when it is not assumed that all instances of a given size are equally probable. We will show that even when nonuniform probability distributions are assumed there are still algorithms with constant expected complexity that solve set-predicate problems.

Suppose that not all instances of size $n$ are equiprobable, but that all instances of the size $n$ having the same cardinality of $G$ are equiprobable, and each subset of instances of size $n$ containing all and only instances with the same cardinality of $G$ is as probable as any other such subset. Then the probability that a randomly selected instance of size $n$ will have any specified value for the cardinality of $G$ is $1/S(n)$, where $S(n)$ is the cardinality of $U$.

Given these probability distributions over instances, there is a problem solver whose expected number of oracle calls is bounded above by 2, for all instance sizes. Since the problem solver with this property is stochastic we must first introduce some definitions.

A *stochastic problem solver* is a stochastic procedure that given $\Sigma$ and a size bound stochastically determines at each step which word to query the oracle about, and either runs forever or conjectures a word after making queries to the oracle. A stochastic problem solver *solves a problem instance* iff with probability 1 it conjectures a word in $G$ and then halts. A stochastic problem solver *solves a problem* iff it solves every instance of a problem.

We measure the complexity of a stochastic problem solver on a problem instance of a given size by the *expected* number of calls made to the oracle by the problem solver.

We consider a Bernoulli trial algorithm that determines its queries to the oracle by sampling randomly with replacement from a population in which there is a uniform distribution on $\Sigma^n$.

We note the following well-known result:

If independent Bernoulli trials are performed, each with probability $p$ of success, and $X$ is the random variable representing the number of trials until the first success, then

$$\text{prob}(X = k) = p(1 - p)^{k-1}$$

and

$$\text{Exp}(X) = 1/p$$

and

$$\text{Exp}(X^2) = (1 - p)/p^2$$

The Bernoulli trial algorithm will, for each instance of size $n$, have an expected number of oracle calls determined entirely by the cardinality of $G$, namely $S(n)$ divided by the cardinality of $G$. The cardinality of $G$ can range from 1 to $n$. Let $g$ denote the cardinality of $G$. The probability of success on any given trial is the probability that some randomly chosen word $x$ in $\Sigma^n$ is in $G$.

$$P(x \,\varepsilon\, G \,||\, G| = g) = \frac{g}{S(n)}$$

$$P(x \,\varepsilon\, G) = \sum_{g=1}^{S(n)} P(x \,\varepsilon\, G \,||\, G| = g)P(|G| = g) = \sum_{g=1}^{S(n)} \frac{g}{S(n)} \frac{1}{S(n)}$$

$$= \frac{\sum_{g=1}^{S(n)} g}{S(n)^2} = \frac{\frac{S(n)(S(n) + 1)}{2}}{S(n)^2} = \frac{S(n) + 1}{2S(n)}$$

$$\text{Exp}(X) = \frac{1}{P(x \,\varepsilon\, G)} = \frac{2S(n)}{S(n) + 1}$$

Hence the expected number of calls to the oracle is bounded above by 2 for all $n$.

Suppose again that we do not assume that all problem instances of the same size are equally probable. Suppose instead it is known that the cardinality of $G$ is always a fixed (non-zero) proportion of the cardinality of $U$, but otherwise make no assumption about the probability distribution on instances of a given size. Consider again a problem solving procedure that randomly selects (with replacement) a word from $U$ and conjectures it, until a word in $G$ is found. Whatever the instance considered, application of the procedure produces a sequence of independent Bernoulli trials each with probability $p$ of success, and so it follows from the results just cited that the expected number of steps in the procedure is bounded by $1/p$ for all $n$, and that the variance of the number of steps required is $(1 - p)/p^2$. Clearly this is not the "best" problem solving algorithm, and it could be improved by sampling from $U$ *without* replacement. Equally clearly, the result can provide an upper bound on the expected complexity in cases in which it is only known that for every instance the ratio of the cardinality of $G$ to the cardinality of $U$ is *at least p*.

On the other hand, suppose the cardinality of $G$ has a fixed upper bound. In that case the algorithm that samples with replacement can for any instance of any size still be viewed as a sequence of independent Bernoulli trials, but $p$, the probability of success on any trial, approaches zero as the size measure, $n$, increases without bound. Thus the expected complexity function is in these cases unbounded for this algorithm, and indeed one expects for any enumeration algorithm.

One can challenge the convention that defines a distinct probability measure for each instance size but no single probability measure over the set of all instances. There are many ways to define a measure on the set of all instances of a problem solving task. For example, many artificial-intelligence system designers seem to believe that in the environments in which their systems operate, small problem instances are much more probable than large problem instances. One can put measures on all of the problem instances over an alphabet $\Sigma$ that satisfy this restriction; for example, one can give the set of all instances of size $n$ the probability $(1/2)^n$, and divide the probability for the class of instances of size $n$ equally among the instances of that size. With this measure the expected number of oracle calls for a deterministic enumeration algorithm diverges. On the other hand, if one imposes a geometric distribution, as Anderson suggests, the expected number of oracle calls required of a deterministic enumeration algorithm is finite.

## 5.4  The Complexity of the Finite Automaton Formulation of Problem Solving

Following Newell and Simon, most problem solving research assumes problem instances to have more structure than the set-predicate formulation presents. It specifies that the world can assume a set of discrete states describable by a finite collection of unary predicates. The application of an operator may (or may not) change the state of the world, but an operator always gives the same resulting state from the same prior state. Some state is designated as the *initial* or *starting* state. Other states, possibly including the initial state, are designated as *goal* or *accepting* states. So construed, a problem instance is determined by a finite state automaton whose number of states is known to the problem solver, but whose graph and set of accepting states are not known. The task is to halt after producing an accepting path in the automaton, that is, a path from the initial state to an accepting state. The problem solver is not told which states are accepting states, so to recognize when to halt, it must query the oracle. Some of the standard illustrations of problem solving such as safe cracking have this form. The state of the combination lock as the cracker finds it is the initial state, and any state that opens the door is an accepting state. The opening of the door or its failure to open counts as the response from the oracle. Theorem proving, natural language parsing, and many other interesting tasks do not fit into the finite automaton framework since the number of possible world states is infinite, and hence cannot be described with a finite set of unary predicates.

Whenever problems can be represented by finite state automata whose nodes are state descriptions, the number of predicates, $n$, required for a state description determines the number of automaton states, $2^n$, and we are guaranteed that if there is an accepting path, that is, a word in $G$, there is one containing no more than $2^n - 1$ operators. Hence when the automaton assumption is made, it is natural to measure the size of a problem instance by the number of states of the problem instance. This size bound does *not* correspond to the size bound we considered above, for the following reason. Not every set of words containing words of at most length $n - 1$ letters over an alphabet $\Sigma$ is exactly the set accepted by some finite state automaton with $n$ states. The smallest automaton accepting all and only the words in a set $G$ of words, all of length $n$ or shorter, has a set of states that may be exponential in $n$. Thus the bank vault door problem, for example, has in the previous measure a size given by the maximum number of dial twists required to open the door, and all problem instances—all sets of door opening values—with the same maximum number of dial twists have the same size. But if the size of a problem instance is measured by the number of states of the smallest automaton that accepts all and only the words in G for that instance, then different specifications of the combinations of dial settings that open the bank vault will give problem instances of different sizes, and some of these sizes will be much larger than the maximum number of dial twists required to open the safe.

If it is assumed that the problem instances are all generated by finite automata, then in many cases it is quite natural to take the number of states of the automaton to measure the size of the problem. In that case we can put a uniform measure on all labeled finite automata with a common initial state, arc labels from an alphabet $\Sigma$, and having $n$ states.

What is the expected complexity of problem solving with the Newell-Simon enumeration algorithm for problem instances generated by finite state automata?

THEOREM 3: The expected complexity function of the Newell-Simon enumeration algorithm for the finite state automaton problem over any nonempty alphabet, $\Sigma$, has a finite bound determined by the cardinality of $\Sigma$.

The proof is given in the appendix. The bound in this case may be much larger than 2, but in typical cases is not "astronomical." In Theorem 3 all automata count, including those with inaccesible states; in many cases this is realistic, since the states of the automaton are descriptions of *logically possible* situations, and some logically possible situations are nonetheless impossible in the sense that no actions will bring about their realization. We conjecture, however, that an analogue of Theorem 3 holds even if one counts only automata all of whose states are accessible.

## 5.5  Conclusion

In this paper, we have examined a class of problems that could not be effectively or stochastically solved without queries to an oracle. We have measured the complexity of an algorithm by the number of queries it made to an oracle. However, results similar to those we have described can be produced for other problems and other measures of complexity.

For example, consider the class of problems which require finding an accepting path through a finite state automaton, but in which the accepting states are known. Some of the standard illustrations in the problem-solving literature, such as Christians and Cannibals or Towers of Hanoi are problems of this kind. If such a problem has a solution, then it is trivial that there are algorithms that solve the problem with zero queries to an oracle. Some other measure of complexity is needed. One way to solve these problems is through a "testing" enumeration algorithm that rather than using oracle calls to determine the accepting states, uses an effective test of some kind. One natural measure of the complexity of a "testing" enumeration algorithm is the number of tests it makes. For example, the Towers of Hanoi problem consists of three pegs $A$, $B$, and $C$, and $n$ rings of varying size, initially stacked on peg $A$ in order of decreasing size. The problem is to move all of the rings one at a time from $A$ onto $B$ (using $C$ as temporary storage) in such a way that no ring is ever placed on a smaller ring. An accepting state can be effectively tested for, since it is simply one in which all of the rings are stacked on peg $B$. (Of course, what counts as a "testing" enumeration algorithm, and what counts as a test in such an algorithm cannot always be determined, but is perfectly clear in some particular cases.) Under this measure of complexity, a proof parallel to the one given for Theorem 3 shows that there are "testing" enumeration algorithms that have a finite upper bound determined by the cardinality of $\Sigma$, regardless of the order of enumeration and the instance size.

Similarly, it is natural to consider "testing" enumeration algorithms that solve set-predicate problems in which an effective test for membership in $G$ can be constructed. A proof analogous to Theorem 1 shows that there are "testing" enumeration algorithms for which the expected number of tests performed is bounded above by 2, regardless of the order of enumeration and the instance size.

Our results also parallel, for a setting of psychological interest, results about expected complexity that have been obtained independently for NP complete problems. A celebrated NP complete problem concerns the determination of the simultaneous satisfiability of a set of clauses. Goldberg (1979) has shown that an algorithm for this problem, the Davis-Putnam Procedure, requires a number of steps which with probability approaching one is approximately quadratic in the number of clauses, provided a reasonably natural probability distribution is assumed for the instances of any size. More recently, Franco and Pauli (1983) showed that a procedure that simply enumerates truth assignments and checks whether they satisfy a set of clauses has, with probability approaching 1, a constant time bound if the same probability distribution for instances is used. They also show that under a different distribution, the Davis-Putnam procedure will with probability 1 require a number of computational steps that is exponential in the instance size. Hofri (1987:4) concludes from these results that, "The moral is that we need robust procedures. Or that we need to know how to tailor an algorithm to a given situation."

Some other conclusions may be broached. One is that "stupid" enumeration procedures, which are often compared unfavorably to "intelligent" heuristic procedures, are not always so stupid. If the computational tractability of a procedure is any indication of intelligence, then enumeration sometimes does quite well. These expected complexity results complement other work that shows, for example, that in a worst case the "version space" learning heuristic requires more computational resources than does simple enumeration. Algorithms that seem "clever," as do the Davis-Putnam procedure for satisfiability, or version space learning algorithms, or various problem solving heuristic procedures, may in various circumstances be less efficient and less powerful than enumeration algorithms that seem "inane."

Whether a problem solving or learning situation requires recourse to heuristic procedures depends on what is known, or believed, about the situation, and in a variety of cases knowledge about the situation can straightforwardly be turned into complexity analyses that are directly relevant to the design of intelligent systems, or that show the computational admissability of various hypotheses about how natural intelligent systems are able to do what they do. The demonstration that a problem solving procedure is reliable and efficient on a few selected instances of a problem is no evidence at all that it is more reliable or more efficient than other procedures on other instances of that same problem. The question of the difficulty of a problem or the optimality or even "satisficity" of a procedure require some knowledge of the distribution of instances that procedure will encounter.

The analyses given here are rather simple, and assume that the probability of occurrence of instances of any kind is unaffected by the evidence obtained in attempting to solve a particular problem instance. A more thoroughly Bayesian analysis would relax this assumption and interpret the probability distribution over instances of a given size as degrees of belief to be changed by forming a sequence of conditional probability distributions as evidence accrues. Indeed, the sorts of problems considered here are rather close to the problem originally treated by Reverend Bayes.[3]

## Appendix

Consider the following problem. Let $\Sigma$ be a finite alphabet with cardinality $s > 1$. Let $n > 0$, and let $S$ be an arbitrary subset of $W = U_n\Sigma^n$, the set of all strings from the alphabet of length $y$, $0 \le y < n$. You are given $n$, and an oracle for $S$. The oracle will respond "yes" to the question "Is $\pi$ in $S$?" if $\pi$ is in $S$, "no" if $\pi$ is not in $S$, and will make no other responses. After asking as many questions as you please of the oracle, you are to output a string in $S$ if there is one, and the words "no solution" if there is not one. Call the triple $\langle \Sigma, n, S \rangle$ a *set predicate problem instance*. A *set predicate problem* is the set of all set predicate problem instances with a common alphabet. A *problem solver* is a procedure that, given $\Sigma$ and $n$, makes a finite number of queries to the oracle and outputs a string. The sequence of queries, and the output of the procedure, must be a function of $\Sigma$, $n$, and the sequence of oracle responses. A problem solver succeeds on a problem instance $\langle \Sigma, n, S \rangle$ if it ouputs a string in $S$ if there is one when the input to the procedure is $\langle S, n \rangle$ and the oracle is for $S$, and outputs "no solution" if $S$ is empty. A problem solver succeeds on a problem if it succeeds on every instance of the problem.

There are some easy observations to be made about the computational difficulty of this problem. We will measure complexity by the number of calls made to the oracle. For clarity, we denote $\Sigma^k$ by $s^k$.

PROPOSITION 1:    There is a procedure that solves the set predicate problem with at most $\Sigma_{k=1}^{n} s^k$ queries.

*Proof:*    The cardinality of $W$ is $\Sigma_{k=1}^{n} s^k$. Consider the following simple enumeration procedure where $\mu$ is an enumeration of $\Sigma^n$ such that no longer string occurs before any shorter string, and strings of the same length are in lexical order:

---

[3] We thank Jay Kadane, Teddy Seidenfeld, and Bas Van Fraassen for very helpful suggestions.

SIMP(n):
begin
   until either the oracle answers "yes" concerning string $\pi$
     or each string in $\mu$ has been queried
  do
     query concerning the first unexamined string in $\mu$ and
     if the oracle answers "yes" for string $\pi$ then output this string;
     if the oracle answers "no" for the last string in $\pi$ then output
     "no solution"
end.

Clearly this algorithm expends $k$ queries iff the first string in the target language is in position $k$ of $\mu$. So in the worst case the entire sequence is traversed and $\Sigma_{k=1}^{n} s^k$ queries are made. QED.

It is easy to see that the worst case upper bound on the set predicate problem given by SIMP cannot be improved.

PROPOSITION 2:    For each $n$, in the worst case any solution to the set predicate problem makes at least $\Sigma_{k=1}^{n} s^k$ queries.

*Proof:*    Suppose that for some $n > m$, learner $f$ can solve each instance of size $n$ with fewer than $\Sigma_{k=1}^{n} s^k$ queries. Then if the target language is the empty language, $f$ will stop after some $k < \Sigma_{k=1}^{n} s^k$ queries. Let $\pi$ be some string not queried by $f$. Then when the target language is $\{\pi\}$, the sequence of queries made by $f$ will be the same as for the empty language, and the series of responses by the oracle will be the same as for the empty language, and $f$ will halt after $k$ queries with the same output as for the empty language. Hence $f$ will not succeed on $\{\pi\}$, which is a contradiction. QED.

Clearly a result completely analogous to Proposition 2 holds if the set of strings is required to be regular. If an $n$ state automaton accepts a string, it accepts a string of length no longer than $n - 1$. So suppose we are to guess a string in a regular set given the number of states in an acceptor of that set. We know we needn't check any strings longer than $n$ to find one if it exists. Viewed this way, our upper bound on the set predicate problem is an upper bound for finding a string in a regular set using an oracle.

In applications, the number of states, $n$, in the finite state acceptor of a regular target language is usually some quantity exponential in another large parameter. For example, if automaton states are constructed as state descriptions in a language with $p$ monadic predicates, then $n = 2^p$, so the overall number of queries by SIMP is in the worst case $\Sigma_{k=1}^{2(p)} s^k$, where $2(p)$ denotes $2^p$.

THEOREM 1: For all $\Sigma$, the expected complexity of the set predicate problem is bounded by 2.

*Proof:* Let $P$ be a uniform probability measure on the power set of $W$. That is, for each subset $S$ of $W$, $P$ assigns $\{S\}$ probability $(1/2)^r$, where $r = \Sigma_{k=1}^n s^k$. Recall that SIMP asks $k$ questions of the oracle when the first string in $\mu$ that is in the target language occurs in position $k$ in $\mu$. Therefore the probability that SIMP uses $k$ queries is the probability that the $k$th string to occur in $\mu$ is the first string in $\mu$ that is a member of the target language. In other words, the probability $P(k)$ that SIMP uses $k$ queries is the sum of all $P(S)$ such that $S$ is a subset of $W$ and string $\pi$ is in $S$, and no string prior to $\pi$ in $\mu$ occurs in $S$. Each subset $S$ of $W$ that contains $\pi$ but no $\pi'$ prior to $\pi$ in $\mu$ can be expressed as the union $\{\pi\} \cup S'$, where $S'$ is in the power set of $K = W - \{\pi' : \pi' = \pi$ or $\pi'$ is prior to $\pi$ in $\mu\}$. Since $\pi$ is in position $k$, the cardinality of $K$ is $\Sigma_{k=1}^n s^k - k = r - k$. Hence there are $2^{(r-k)}$ subsets of $W$ that contain $\pi$ but do not contain any $\pi'$ prior to $\pi$ in $\mu$. Hence $P(k) = 2^{(r-k)}/2^r = 2^{-k}$.

The expected number $E(n)$ of queries of SIMP for all instances of size $n$ and alphabet $\Sigma$ is the sum from one to $\Sigma_{k=1}^n s^k = r$ of $k$ times $P(k)$. So $E(n) = \Sigma_{k=1}^r (k/2^k)$. The infinite series $\Sigma_{k=1}^\infty (k/2^k)$ is greater than $E(n)$, for every $n$, and converges to 2, since

$$\sum_{k=1}^\infty k/2^k = 1/2 + \sum_{k=1}^\infty (k+1)/2^{(k+1)} = 1/2 + \sum_{k=1}^\infty k/2^{(k+1)} + \sum_{k=1}^\infty 1/2^{(k+1)}$$

$$= 1/2 + 1/2 \sum_{k=1}^\infty k/2^k + 1/2,$$

and hence $1/2 \Sigma_{k=1}^\infty k/2^k = 1$. QED.

THEOREM 2: The expected number of letters in queries in any set predicate problem is bounded by 10.

*Proof:* Let $Pki$ be the probability that the first word in the enumeration SIMP that is in the target language is the $i$th word of length $k$. $s$ is the cardinality of $\Sigma$. There are $ik$ letters in the first $i$ words of length $k$ and there are $\Sigma_{u=1}^{(k-1)} s^u u$ letters in all strings of length less than $k$. Therefore

$$\left[ ik + \sum_{u=1}^{(k-1)} s^u u \right]$$

gives the number of letters in the enumeration $\mu$ of SIMP($n$) up to and including letters in the $i$th word of length $k$. There are $s^k$ (denoted by $s(k)$ in upper limits of summation) words of length $k$. Hence the expected number of letters in queries by SIMP($n$) is

$$E(n) = \sum_{k=1}^{n} \sum_{i=1}^{s(k)} Pki \left[ ik + \sum_{u=1}^{(k-1)} s^u u \right]. \tag{1}$$

Reasoning as in the proof of Theorem 1, there are $2^r$ equiprobable subsets of $W$. The number of such sets containing the $i$th word of length $k > 0$ and no preceeding word in $\mu$ is $2^{[r-(i+U)]}$, (where $U = \Sigma_{u=1}^{k-1} s^u$, and we understand that if $k = 1$, $U$ is zero), because the $i$th word of length $k$ is the $(i + U)$th word in $\mu$. Hence $Pki = 1/2^{[i+U]}$ and substituting in (1) we have:

$$E(n) = \sum_{k=1}^{n} \sum_{i=1}^{s(k)} \left[ ik + \sum_{u=1}^{k-1} s^u u \right] / 2^{[i+U]}. \tag{2}$$

The right hand side of (2) is the sum of two terms:

$$T1 = \sum_{k=1}^{n} \sum_{i=1}^{s(k)} ik/2^{[i+U]}$$

$$T2 = \sum_{k=1}^{n} \sum_{i=1}^{s(k)} \left[ \sum_{u=1}^{k-1} s^u u \right] / 2^{[i+U]}$$

We first derive a bound on $T1$ for all $n$.

$$T1 = \sum_{k=1}^{n} \sum_{i=1}^{s(k)} ik/2^{[i+U]} = \sum_{k=1}^{n} \left( \sum_{i=1}^{s(k)} i/2^i \right) k/2^U < \sum_{k=1}^{n} 2k/2^U,$$

where the inequality follows from the argument of Theorem 1. Rearranging the right hand side of the inequality we have $T1 < 2\Sigma_{k=1}^{n} k/2^U$. Now for all $s > 1$ and all $k$, $U = \Sigma_{u=1}^{(k-1)} s^u$ is greater than or equal to $k$, and hence $2^U$ is greater than or equal to $2^k$. Therefore:

$$T1 < 2\sum_{k=1}^{n} k/2^U \le 2\sum_{k=1}^{n} k/2^k < 2\sum_{k=1}^{\infty} k/2^k = 4.$$

Finally, we derive a bound on $T2$. We define $Uu = \Sigma_{u=1}^{(k-1)} s^u u$. With that abbreviation:

$$T2 = \sum_{k=1}^{n} \sum_{i=1}^{s(k)} Uu/2^{[i+U]} = \sum_{k=1}^{n} \left( \sum_{i=1}^{s(k)} 1/2^i \right) Uu/2^U < \sum_{k=1}^{n} Uu/2^U$$

Now $U^2 \geq \Sigma_{u=1}^{(k-1)} s^{2u} > \Sigma_{u=1}^{(k-1)} s^u u = Uu$ because $s^u > u$ for all values of $u$. Hence $T2 < \Sigma_{k=1}^{n} Uu/2^U < \Sigma_{k=1}^{n} U^2/2^U$. The quantity $U = \Sigma_{u=1}^{(k-1)} s^u$ is a distinct number for every value of $k$. Therefore $T2 < \Sigma_{j=1}^{\infty} j^2/2^j = 1/2 + \Sigma_{j=1}^{\infty} (j+1)^2/2^{(j+1)}$.

Expanding the righthand side of the second equality we obtain

$$\sum_{j=1}^{\infty} j^2/2^j = (1/2) \sum_{j=1}^{\infty} j^2/2^{(j+1)} + 2 \sum_{j=1}^{\infty} j/2^{(j+1)} + \sum_{j=1}^{\infty} 1/2^{(j+1)} + 1/2.$$

Now

$$\sum_{j=1}^{\infty} j^2/2^{(j+1)}(1/2) \sum_{j=1}^{\infty} j^2/2^j; 2 \sum_{j=1}^{\infty} j/2^{(j+1)} = \sum_{j=1}^{\infty} j/2^j = 2; \text{and } \sum_{j=1}^{\infty} 1/2^{(j+1)} = 1/2.$$

Hence

$$\sum_{j=1}^{\infty} j^2/2^j = 1/2 + (1/2) \sum_{j=1}^{\infty} j^2/2^j + 2 + 1/2$$

and there $T2 < \Sigma_{j=1}^{\infty} j^2/2^j = 6$. QED.

Take an automaton problem instance to be quadruple $\langle \Sigma, L, A, n \rangle$ where $L$ is the set of strings from alphabet $\Sigma$ accepted by $A$, and $A$ has $n$ states. Assume as before an oracle for $L$, and understand automaton problem and automaton problem solver by analogy with the set predicate case. The number of states, $n$, of $A$ will measure the size of any problem instance, and a problem solver is given $\Sigma$, $n$ and of course the responses of the oracle to any queries the problem solver makes. As in the set predicate case, we can investigate bounds on the average, over all problem instances of size $n$ for a fixed alphabet, of the number of queries a problem solver, and SIMP($n$) in particular, makes before ouputting a word in $L$ if there is one, or "no solution" if $L$ is empty. Since in applications the automaton states are usually given as state descriptions in a monadic predicate language, we take the states of the automaton to be labeled, and distinguish otherwise isomorphic automata with distinct labelings.

Counting finite automata meeting conditions on the existence of an accepting path of a specified length but having no shorter path is difficult. The following theorem avoids the difficulty by finding easily counted properties that bound the expected number of queries for automaton problem instances of a given size.

THEOREM 3:   For every finite $\Sigma$ there exists a number $N$ such that for all $n$, the expected number of queries for the SIMP algorithm over all instances of automata problems based on $\Sigma$ and of size $n$ is less than $N$.

*Proof:*   We assume that the initial state is fixed. Any subset of the $n$ labeled states may be chosen to be the set of accepting states, so there are $2^n$ specifications of accepting states. Each of the $n$ states has $s$ (the cardinality of $\Sigma$) arcs out of it, and for each arc there are $n$ choices of sink. So there are

$$n \times n \ldots \times n \times n \times n \ldots \times n \times \ldots\ldots\ldots \times n \times n \times \ldots n$$

$[s \text{ factors}] \; [s \text{ factors}] \ldots\ldots\ldots [s \text{ factors}\}$

$\{\ldots\ldots\ldots n \text{ factors} \ldots\ldots\ldots\}$

or $(n^s)^n$ graphs. Hence there are $2^n n^{ns}$ automata for $\Sigma$ having $n$ states. (If the initial state is not fixed, the number is $2^n n^{(ns+1)}$, which would make no significant difference in the argument that follows.) It is easy to show that the number of finite automata with $n$ states accepting word $i$ of length $l(i)$ on a path without circuits is $2^{(n-1)} n^{(ns-l(i))}$. For let $p$ be the sequence of arcs whose labels in sequence form the string $i$. The terminus of $p$ must be an accepting state. Any subset of the remaining $n - 1$ states may be accepting, hence there are $2^{(n-1)}$ choices of sets of accepting states. All of the arcs out of any state not touched by $p$ may be freely chosen, and so may the arcs out of the terminal node of $p$. There are $l(i) + 1$ states touched by $p$. Hence there are $(n^s)^{(n-l(i))}$ choices for the collections of arcs. All but one of the arcs out of each of the states touched by $p$ (save the terminal state of $p$) may be chosen freely. There are $n^{(s-1)l(i)}$ such choices. Hence there are $n^{(s-1)l(i)} 2^{(n-1)} n^{s(n-l(i))} = 2^{(n-1)} n^{(ns-l(i))}$ automata that accept word $i$ without circuits. If a word is accepted by a path with a circuit then the word cannot be the shortest accepted by the automaton. Thus the number of automata accepting a given word by a path without a circuit is at least as large as the number of automata for which that word is the first word in the enumeration $\mu$ that is accepted. Hence the probability, $Pi$, that $i$ is the first word of $\mu$ accepted by a randomly chosen $n$ state automaton is less than $2^{(n-1)} n^{(ns-l(i))}/2^n n^{ns} = 1/(2n^{l(i)})$.

Now the expected number of queries for instances of size $n$, $E(n)$, satisfies

$$E(n) < \sum_{i=1}^{r} i/2n^{l(i)} \text{ where } r = \sum_{j=1}^{(n-1)} s^j. \tag{1}$$

Note that

$$\sum_{i=m}^{(m+k)} i \le (k + m + mk + k^2/2). \tag{2}$$

The expression on the right hand side of (1) can be expressed as a sum of "chunks":

$$\sum_{l=1}^{(n-1)} [1/2^{l(i)}] \sum_{j=L(i)}^{M(i)} j$$

where $L(i)$ abbreviates the number of words in the enumeration of length less than $l(i)$, and $M(i)$ abbreviates $s^{l(i)}$. Applying (2) to this expression we obtain

$$E(n) < \sum_{l(i)=1}^{(n-1)} [1/2n^{l(i)})][(s^{l(i)} - 1) + L(i) + 1 + (L(i) + 1)(s^{l(i)} - 1)$$

$$+ (s^{l(i)} - 1)^2/2]. \tag{3}$$

On simplifying (3) by multiplying through, the largest terms obtained are $L(i)s^{l(i)}/(2n^{l(i)})$ and $s^{2l(i)}/(2n^{l(i)})$. We show by induction that for all $s > 1$ and all $l(i) > 0$, $L(i)s^{l(i)}/(2n^{l(i)}) < s^{2l(i)}/(2n^{l(i)})$ because $s^{l(i)} > L(i)$. The base case is immediate since $1 > 0$. Assume for $l(i) = k$ that $L(i) = \sum_{j=1}^{(k-1)} s^j < s^k$. We must show that $\sum_{j=1}^{(k,j)} < s^{(k+1)}$. Now $\sum_{j=1}^{k} s^j = \sum_{j=1}^{k-1} s^j + s^k < s^k + s^k$ by the assumption. Hence $\sum_{j=1}^{k} s^j < 2s^k \le s^{(k+1)}$, which proves the claim.

Returning to (3), we know that the largest term on the right hand side is $\sum_{l(i)=1}^{n-1} (s^2/n)^{l(i)}$. For every $n > s^2$, $\sum_{l(i)=1}^{n-1} (s^2/n)^{l(i)} < \sum_{k=1}^{\infty} (s^2/n)^k$. Since $s^2/n < 1$ for $n > s^2$, this series converges with some limit $R$. For every $n \le s^2$, $\sum_{l(i)=1}^{n-1} (s^2/n)^{l(i)}$ is finite, and since $s$ is fixed, there is a finite set of such quantities. Let $Q$ be the largest of them. Then for every $n$, $\sum_{l(i)=1}^{(n-1)} (s^2/n)^{l(i)} \le \max\{R, Q\}$. So there is a bound on the largest term in the right hand side of (3), for all $n$. Hence there is a $K$ such that for all $n$, $E(n) < K \max\{R, Q\}$. QED.

## References

Ackley, D. 1985. A Connectionist Genetic Algorithm. In *Proceedings of an International Conference on Genetic Algorithms and Their Applications*, 121–135. J. Grefenstette, ed. Pittsburgh: Carnegie-Mellon University.

Ackley, D. 1987. Stochastic Iterated Genetic Hillclimbing. Ph.D. thesis, Carnegie-Mellon University Department of Computer Science.

Anderson, J. 1976. *Language, Memory, and Thought.* New York: Erlbaum.

Angluin, D. 1981. A Note on the Number of Queries Required to Identify Regular Languages. *Information and Control* 51:76–87.

Franco, H., and M. Pauli. 1983. Probablistic Analysis of the Davis-Putnam Procedure for Solving the Satisfiablity Problem. *Disc. Appl. Math.* 5, 77–87.

Goldberg, A. 1979. Average Case Complexity of the Satisfiability Problem. In *Proceedings of the Fourth Workshop on Automatic Deduction,* Austin.

Holland, H. 1975. *Adaptation in Natural and Artificial Systems.* Ann Arbor: University of Michigan Press.

Hofri, M. 1987. *Probabilistic Analysis of Algorithms.* New York: Springer-Verlag.

Kelly, K. 1988. Version Spaces, Structural Descriptions and NP-Completeness. Carnegie-Mellon University Laboratory for Computational Linguistics, Technical Report.

Mitchell, T. 1982. Generalization as Search. *Artificial Intelligence* 18:203–226.

Newell, A., and H. Simon. 1972. *Human Problem Solving.* Englewood Cliffs, New Jersey: Prentice-Hall.

Osherson, D., M. Stob, and S. Weinstein. 1986. *Systems That Learn.* Cambridge, Massachusetts: MIT Press.

Wilf, H. 1986. *Algorithms and Complexity.* Englewood Cliffs, New Jersey: Prentice-Hall.

# 6 Normative and Descriptive Ideals

Henry Kyburg

## 6.1 The Normative and the Descriptive

There are a number of areas of inquiry that can be looked at either from a normative point of view or a descriptive point of view. David Hume, in the *Treatise on Human Nature*, remarked forcefully on the distinction between "is" and "ought." He took to task those authors who imperceptibly slip from asserting propositions about what *is* the case to asserting propositions about what *ought* to be the case. This distinction, and the fallacy of ignoring it, have become basic features of our scientific outlook. It is a proper part of science to *describe* the behavior of people in their relations to other people, to *describe* the events of the marketplace. The normative characterization of what people may or should do in their relations with other people, of how the marketplace should operate, is no part of science, but left for philosophers and preachers. The sociologist or anthropologist is warned, "Don't make value judgments!" It is true that scientists make value judgments pertaining to the conduct of personal and public life; but they do so as citizens and moral beings, not as scientists.

We can look at decision theory, to take one of the most complicated cases, either as a theory of how human beings do actually make decisions, or as a theory of how human beings ought ideally to make decisions. The former is descriptive; the latter normative. In the former case we are offering a theory of how people act. In the latter case we are offering a theory of how they ought to act. This seems simple enough on the face of it, but closer examination renders the distinction less clear.

The theory of how people ought to act is likely to have, for many, ethical or even moralistic overtones. (One ought to begin to eat only after the hostess has invited one to begin, or has herself started to eat.) On the face of it, decision theory is not of a piece with manners. Decision theory is purely practical: a question of how to choose in such a way as to maximize one's satisfactions, or expected satisfactions. It is a matter, as philosophers have been wont to put it, of practical reason.

Normative, no doubt. But we slid disjunctively over an important distinction: "in such a way as to maximize one's satisfactions" or "in such a way as to maximize one's expected satisfactions." The ideal goal of a theory of decision, one would think, would be to provide rules that would maximize one's actual satisfactions, not one's expected satisfactions. (We leave to one side the question, perfectly valid and at least as important as these other questions, of what satisfactions: present? future? actual? ideal?) Why is this not the goal of a normative decision theory?

To maximize satisfactions is not the goal of a normative decision theory, because we take it for granted that no theory can do this. In a similar vein, we take it for granted that no normative epistemological theory can insure both that our bodies of knowledge have content and that they eschew all error. These constraints on possible decision theories or on possible theories of knowledge are constraints that derive from our knowledge of human limitations. It is a part of the human condition that we cannot predict the future perfectly, and therefore cannot choose the course that will in fact maximize our satisfactions. It is part of the way in which we can, at best, learn about the world, that we cannot always avoid error.

In principle, this is a somewhat slippery slope. For just as I cannot avoid sometimes getting misleading samples when I sample from the world, however conscientiously I try to do my sampling in the best way, so I cannot avoid sometimes getting the wrong answer when I add up a column of figures.

Yet we take the ideal, in the former case, to be getting samples that are no more misleading than would be expected statistically (at the 5 percent significance level, we expect to make false rejections of hypotheses no more than 5 percent of the time), while the ideal in the latter case is *never* to make a mistake.

What we take as a normative theory, as the ideal, depends on what we take to be possible for human agents, but it depends on it in no simple way. It nevertheless requires input reflecting the abilities, potentialities, and perhaps interests, of human beings—all matters of descriptive rather than normative character.

On the other hand, a descriptive theory of human decision making appears to require a normative element. Thus, for example, although a man may choose $A$ over $B$, he may recognize that he has made an error when he is reminded of his own probabilities and utilities. It is very difficult to draw a distinction between this case and that in which a man adds seven and six to get fifteen. There seems to be an implicit underlying normative theory behind the description of how people make decisions and what they take to be errors in their decisions.

Let us illustrate these ideas in three domains: deductive logic, defeasible reasoning, and decision theory.

## 6.2   Deduction

Deductive logic seems quite straightforward: If you believe that all men are mortal and that Socrates is a man, then you should believe that Socrates is mortal.

Humbug. In the first place it is not at all clear that standard first-order logic is the appropriate representational discipline for beliefs—even such simple beliefs as this, leaving entirely aside beliefs about necessities, obligations, and unicorns. Supposing that this is an appropriate representation for some beliefs, it isn't clear that this is one of those beliefs. Is the universal quantifier the right quantifier? Is the truth-functional conditional the right connective? Should we be expressing the belief by some relation, rather than by a connective? If so, should we think of it as a relation between sentences, between propositional functions, or between properties, or classes, or sets?

It could be argued that in fact it is the intuitive validity of this argument that constrains the way in which we express the component ingredients of the argument. This in turn could be defended as a descriptive generalization of human habits of inference of the better sort. "The better sort," of course, could be unpacked in terms of success: in point of fact, such habits of inference will lead from truths only to truths.

An even better sort would be a habit of inference that will lead to a lot of truths, and only truths, from any premises, true or false. But that is not for us.

Let us leave to one side the problem of translating our body of knowledge into some standard notation, and let us suppose that the standard notation is that of first-order logic. Given the ideality of the translation, we still should not expect the resulting theory to constitute a description of anybody's actual body of knowledge. Mere finitude precludes that. This applies as well to our AI systems: they, too, are finite, and thus cannot contain (for example) all the logical truths.

We might make our demand weaker: we might ask for consistency, rather than closure. Thus instead of saying that you should believe that Socrates is mortal, perhaps all we should ask is that you *not* believe that he is *immortal*. Even consistency admits of grades, though. Strong consistency would demand that the set of one's beliefs be consistent in the sense that no contradiction is contained in its deductive closure. But this is surely not a description of any realistic body of belief. Surely among the beliefs of the best of us there lurks a set of propositions that entails a contradiction.

So one might weaken the demand even more: we might ask only for
$k$-consistency: that is, that there be no set of $k$ or less statements in the body
of knowledge that entail a contradiction. (See Kyburg 1970.)

Now we could turn back to the question of what logic we should
adopt—three valued? One with some form of strict implication or some
form of subjunctive conditional? Should we decide on the basis of descriptive facts about the way people think? Or on the basis of the way we take
ideal people to reason? Or on the basis of the way we think people *ought*
to reason? Or on the basis of the way we want our ideal constructions in
AI to operate?

There are genuine disputes about logic. They fall into two categories.
Some people think that the standard first-order predicate calculus is seriously in error: we should adopt a logic that embodies a number of truth
values beyond "true" and "false," or that is not committed to bivalence, or
that does not have the distribution principle as a theorem. There are more
people who think that standard logic is too weak to do justice to real human
inference, and who therefore want to extend first-order logic to deal with
modal, deontic, epistemic, and similar arguments.

However we decide what logic is the best for our purposes, it will surely
not be the case that our formal and explicit logic will accurately reflect how
people do in fact reason or think; and it will surely not be the case that our
formal and explicit logic will reflect the divine norm of achieving all and
only truths.

## 6.3   Probabilistic Inference

There is a lot of concern now in artificial intelligence for systems of defeasible reasoning, or default reasoning, or nonmonotonic reasoning, or (a
special case) inheritance hierarchies. In the classical philosophical tradition,
this is the same as the traditional philosophical concern with inductive
reasoning, nondeductive inference, ampliative inference, scientific reasoning, and so on. We may also think of it as the problem of probabilistic
inference.

By "probabilistic inference" I do not mean manipulations of probabilities
in accord with the probability calculus. I mean real *inference*—that is,
arguments that proceed from premises taken as evidence, to a categorical
(not a probabilistic) conclusion supported by but not entailed by that
evidence.

A paradigm case is that of statistical inference. If we obtain a large sample of $A$s, and find that the proportion in the sample that are $B$s is $r$, then a natural thing to do is to conclude that the proportion of $B$s among $A$s is *close* to $r$. This is not the same as concluding that it is *probable* that the proportion of $B$s among $A$s is close to $r$, though that, too, is true.

Whether or not it is best to allow probabilistic inference in this sense is open to question and argument. Some writers—those who find the Bayesian paradigm attractive (Cheeseman 1988)—think that a probabilistic rule of acceptance is awkward, unreasonable, and unwarranted. Others think that the only way to make substantive reasoning tractible is to allow for defeasible inference, and to permit the acceptance of statements that may in due course come to be rejected. Here again intuitions differ. And here again, it seems likely that only the construction and comparison of actual systems is going to lead to a resolution of the question. My own view is that, even technical questions of intractability aside, a purely Bayesian approach that eschews acceptance is doomed to be practically unmanageable. But this is a question that deserves to be tested.

## 6.4   Decision Theory

If deductive logic represents a mixture of normative and descriptive elements, decision theory is even more of a muddy mixture. The Bayesian principle that one ought to maximize one's expected utility seems on the surface to be both a description of what people, however inefficiently and awkwardly, try to do, and such a pervasive and intuitive principle of rationality that no one could deny it. The principle has come very close to being regarded as a tautology in recent decades, since Frank Ramsey (1931), Richard Jeffrey (1965), Jimmy Savage (1954), Ward Edwards (1962), and others have taken preferences to reveal what there is to be revealed about probabilities and utilities.

Again, however, people's preferences are not consistent with the Bayesian axioms concerning probabilities and utilities. The theory is not, at first glance, an adequate descriptive theory of the preferences people have or the way in which they make decisions.

Should we treat this as a matter of weak flesh (or neurons)? Savage thought so. He recognized that his own preferences could well be inconsistent with the Bayesian axioms, and argued that the import of this was merely that he would be inclined to make adjustments in his beliefs (and utilities) at any point at which such an inconsistency might be pointed out to him. That is: the Bayesian axioms are to be taken as a normative standard of revision, rather than as a description of normal human preference structures.

But there are difficulties even with this somewhat attenuated normative view. First of all, people do not always modify their beliefs to conform to the calculus of probability, even when disparities are pointed out, as Kahneman and Tversky (1982) and others have shown. Second, there are some cases, described by Allais (1952) and Ellsberg (1961) where very smart people have argued that the classic rules are wrong. Third, there are psychological studies, such as those conducted and referred to by Lola Lopes (1983), that indicate that a number of central moments of distributions, rather than just the expectation, or even the expectation and variance, are relevant to the way people make decisions.

Our concern is not to try to argue one way or the other about these matters, but rather to point out that it is not at all clear how normative and descriptive aspects of decision theory are supposed to interact. We do not agree on what to take as normative—even within the Bayesian framework—and we take the descriptive, when it is quite universal, as it is in the case of the "paradoxes" of Allais and of Ellsberg, to be no more than an influential guide in our normative quest.

This is a nontrivial matter in philosophy, where, after all, we would like to understand what is right and what is wrong in theories of decision under uncertainty. But it is an absolutely crucial matter in artificial intelligence, where we are going to build into our systems some decision procedure. What our system is going to do will depend on what decision procedure we build into it. We had better give this question some serious thought if our systems are to be taken seriously.

This coin has another side: it may well be that the artificial systems can give us a testbed for our philosophical ideas about decision theory. We can see how one approach or another turns out. This can be done in several ways. The traditional philosophical way is to see if there are natural or anomalous consequences of the assumptions we make. An artificial system can generate a lot more consequences than a piece of paper and a pencil. There is also the possibility, not available to the traditional philosopher, of running such a system on a range of problems, or in a range of possible circumstances, and seeing how well it does. Perhaps we should measure a decision theory by its success!

This leads to another problem: We surely do not mean to measure the appropriateness of a decision theory by its short-term success. Even if Madam DuBois correctly picks the winner in the next horse race, we do not install her as our fundamental principle of decision theory. What we want is not an instance of success, but a reasonable indication of long-run success. And this is a matter of induction or defeasible inference, which we already considered in section 6.3. Have we thereby succumbed to terminal circularity? Or are we applying our intuitions to a collection of related criteria?

## 6.5   Probabilities

Even if everybody's preferences and choices could be bent into a shape that could be accounted for by a subjective probability function and a subjective utility function, there are normative considerations that would lead us to be critical of some of those functions. For present purposes we shall leave utility functions to one side, but there are surely probability functions that we would regard as crazy. This judgment has empirical and descriptive roots: most people don't believe preposterous things for no reason (except in matters of religion). There are, some of us believe, norms for probability judgment that go beyond conformity to the probability calculus.

According to Frank Ramsey, my degrees of belief should satisfy the probability calculus "on pain of inconsistency." This makes it sound as if (some of) the norms of probability judgment can rest on principles of deductive logic. But it is misleading. The alleged "inconsistency" consists in laying oneself open to having a book made against one. Someone whose beliefs were deductively sound would not have a book made against him regardless of his degrees of belief.

For example, if I have a degree of belief equal to one-third in heads, and a degree of belief equal to one-third in tails, I am, on Ramsey's view, expressing my willingness to bet at 2:1 against heads and my willingness to bet at 2:1 against tails. But I am not, by any stretch of the imagination, expressing my willingness to bet *simultaneously* at 2:1 against heads and at 2:1 against tails. First come, first served, I say.

Furthermore, observe that I am not bound to lose with these degrees of belief. Every bet I make at these crazy odds, on a sequence of occasions, *may* turn out in my favor.

I take it to be a descriptive fact that most reasonable people would regard these odds as odd. I take it to be a normative fact that they *should* be regarded as odd—that is, that there is a standard to which degrees of belief should conform that goes beyond conformity to the probability calculus.

Interval-valued evidential probability provides one normative view according to which some degrees of belief, given the evidence that we have, are prohibited as irrational and unacceptable. It is a gratifying feature of that view of probability that one can show there exists a classical belief function conforming to the intervals of evidential probability (Kyburg 1983).

Here again we see a balance between descriptive and normative considerations playing a role in the development of our theory. And while we may and should take descriptive facts concerning the degrees of belief that people have as a clue to the normative standards we wish to embody in our machines and in ourselves, and just as intuition concerning basic principles and intuition concerning particular cases can also play a role, the ultimate test of the cooking is in the pudding.

## 6.6   Updating Probabilities

There are Dutch Book arguments that concern the updating of degrees of belief, just as there are Dutch Book arguments concerning static degrees of belief. Again, there is no question of "inconsistency" in having one's beliefs violate the dynamic condition of updating by temporal conditionalization. But this time it turns out that temporal conditionalization is inconsistent with interval valued evidential probability as we have defined it.

This provides a real, down-to-earth, illustration of the theoretical dynamics of normative and descriptive considerations. People tend, other things being equal, to conform to temporal conditionalization. People tend, other things being equal, to base their probability assessments on reference classes that yield relatively sharp probabilities. These two tendencies come into conflict in certain rather special situations, and intuitions conflict about what is the right way to go in these situations.

Here is a case where it seems quite likely that artificial intelligence systems, run on a collection of sensible cases, may enable us to make a philosophical judgment about the best way to go. It is also a case where, without an initial philosophical guess, there would be no way for an AI system to get off the ground.

## 6.7   Testing

We have looked at a number of issues that constitute only a fraction of those that come up in either the philosophical or the computational analysis of cognition. It has been suggested that in some sense we should judge these issues by reference to the performance of systems that embody one or another of the possible sets of commitments one might make.

We have already noticed that this is more complicated than it appears, since short-run "success" can't be our standard. What we need as a basis for choice is evidence concerning the long run success of one set of commitments as opposed to another. But this is a matter of defeasible inference, or induction, or probabilistic inference, or probability: that is, it is a matter of the very kind of thing that is at issue.

One possible basis for choice among the principles that satisfy our intuitions and that seem to be reflected in actual human behavior would be the frankly pragmatic basis of content. Assume that there is some plausible way to measure the predictive empirical content of the consequences of a finite set of sentences (axioms). For very simple languages, it might be the cardinality of the set of predictive empirical consequences. For languages with quantitative functions, it might depend on the precision of the assertions embodied in the sentences.

Given such a measure of content of a finite set of sentences, we might compare two logical/linguistic frameworks according to the content of their predictive assertions. This takes probability for granted, and thus may beg the question concerning the choice of probabilities. On the other hand, perhaps it takes for granted only what is common to any plausible view of probability. The object of the present exersize is only to indicate that it is an area that should be explored.

A view that has attracted considerable attention in AI is the view that we can elucidate defeasible reasoning in terms of *specificity*. In its simplest form the specificity principle directs us to formulate our (defeasible) opinions about an object according to the smallest set of which we know that it is a member. The classical illustration is that of Tweety the penguin: we infer that Tweety does not fly, even though Tweety is a bird, because penguins are a subset of birds, and penguins don't fly.

So far so good. But this does not take care of all cases, as has been widely recognized. The next development of the principle has to do with logical

strength: base your defeasible inference on the logically strongest knowledge you have of the object in question.

If this is construed merely as a principle of total evidence it seems
uncontroversial, but it does not guide us in the choice of a set of objects to
which we should refer the object in question, or anything like that. It
provides no concrete guidance. On the other hand, there are two cases
about which our intuitions seem to be pretty strong, that do not seem to
be accounted for by any kind of specificity (Kyburg 1991).

## 6.8   Conclusion

Subject to this last conjecture, we can claim both that logic (and probability,
and decision theory) is conventional, and at the same time that there are
rational ways of choosing among the available conventions. The choice
reflects the interplay among the facts of human cognition and especially
human limitations, our intuitions concerning the principles to be found in
simple cases, and pragmatic considerations of the sort last mentioned.
Probability gives us a handle on these things, but of course probability is
one of them itself. Is it more fundamental? Sure. Does that cut much ice?
Not much. To the extent that we can limit our considerations to what is
common to a number of views of probability, we may find that we have a
basis for choice.

What we need is an account of defeasible reasoning—that is, of a kind
of reasoning that will give us practical certainties, but that is not monotonic.
It will be a kind of reasoning that allows us to change our minds in response
to new evidence. The principle of specificity seems to work well in a limited
domain of cases—namely the cases in which we should be looking at
subsets. Construed broadly, as logical strength, the principle seems un-
controvertible, but it also seems devoid of useful content. Construed as
something in between the recommendation to choose a subset over a
superset as a reference class, and the general heuristic recommendation to
use all the evidence you have, it is not clear how to apply the principle.

One lesson we learn is that while the basic distinction between normative
and descriptive principles seems as solidly grounded as ever, the principles
from among which we must select, both in constructing normative philosophical frameworks for knowledge and inference, and in constructing
artificial systems for both pure and applied purposes, must include both

sorts. We must look to what people do, to what they are capable of doing, and to what they ought to do, in order to gather the materials for epistemic reconstruction and self-improvement.

## References

Allais, M. 1952. The Foundations of a Positive Theory of Choice Involving Risk and a Criticism of the Postulates and Axioms of the American School. In *Expected Utility Hypotheses and the Allais Paradox*. M. Allais and O. Hagen, eds. Dordrecht: Reidel.

Cheeseman, P. 1988. Inquiry Into Computer Understanding. *Computational Intelligence* 4:58–66.

Edwards, W. 1962. Subjective Probabilities Inferred from Decisions. *Psychological Review* 69:109–135.

Ellsberg, D. 1961. Risk, Ambiguity, and the Savage Axioms. *Quarterly Journal of Economics* 75:528–557.

Hume, D. 1740 [1949]. *An Enquiry Concerning Human Understanding: Selections from a Treatise on Human Nature*. La Salle, Illinois: Open Court.

Jeffrey, R. 1965. *The Logic of Decision*. New York: McGraw-Hill.

Kahneman, D., P. Slovic, and A. Tversky, eds. 1982. *Judgment Under Uncertainty: Heuristics and Biases*. Cambridge: Cambridge University Press.

Kyburg, H. 1970. Conjunctivitis, in M. Swain (ed.) *Induction, Acceptance, and Rational Belief*, Reidel pp. 55–82.

Kyburg, H. 1983. The Reference Class. *Philosophy of Science* 50:374–397.

Kyburg, H. 1991. Beyond Specificity. Proceedings of IPMU, Paris.

Lopes, L. 1983. Some Thoughts on the Psychological Concept of Risk. *Journal of Experimental Psychology* 9:137–144.

Ramsey, F. 1931. *The Foundations of Mathematics and Other Essays*. New York: Humanities Press.

Savage, L. 1954. *Foundations of Statistics*. New York: John Wiley.

# 7 Ampliative Inference, Computation, and Dialectic

## R. P. Loui

## 7.1

What makes inference ampliative?[1] Traditionally, deductive inference has been considered nonampliative, while induction and analogy have been ampliative. This distinction is threatened by AI's view of representation and reasoning.

Representing knowledge in a language is a peculiar responsibility. Inference rules applied to what is explicitly represented in a language reveal what is implicitly represented. This terminology (etched in AI minds by H. Levesque)[2] is no accident. In the AI view, the representer of knowledge is responsible for both the explicit and the implicit. That is, in representing a set of sentences explicitly in a language, it must be the intention to represent the implicit knowledge too. Inept use of language is discounted as a possibility. All language users are assumed facile.

Against this backdrop, two anima conspire against the ampliative-nonampliative distinction. They are the advent of logics of defeasible reasoning (or nonmonotonic reasoning), and the extreme formality with which AI requires that inference systems be viewed. The rise of defeasibility in the formalization of inference derides the distinction between ampliative and nonampliative because defeasible reasoning combines inductive and deductive inference. If indeed nonmonotonic reasoning is a bit like non-ampliative deduction, especially in form, but also a lot like ampliative induction, then which is it: ampliative or not? Like induction, it makes guesses that allegedly go beyond the evidence. Like deduction, the license to produce its conclusions is written plainly for all to see.

AI views inference with extreme formality. A system of inference is a programming language. One language is as good as another, though some are more expressive, and there are unmistakable differences in convenience. Change the logical language and one simply changes the sentences used to represent particular situations. Choice of inference system is by convention;

---

[1] I am indebted to D. Israel for bringing this question to my attention. Apparently, we should thank early philosophers for raising it in the first place.

[2] Levesque used the explicit/implicit distinction for different purposes. Doyle's use of the distinction between constructive and manifest belief is closer to what I have in mind, but I prefer the phrase "implicit commitment" to the phrase "constructible commitment." Could history be altered, "manifest" would be a better term for Levesque, and "explicit" would be the better term for Doyle.

it is clearly a pact between compiler-writer and programmer: that is, between logic-program developer and knowledge representer. There has never been the suspicion in AI that an epistemic situation could be described by an *ideal* set of sentences in an ideal language. Most of the day-to-day research involves freely altering existing axioms and languages. There are those who perceive deduction to be a privileged mode of inference, possessing attractive properties with respect to certain mathematical interpretations; they represent one faction among many.

At one point, I called this situation the "curse of Frege" (openly borrowing the phrase from I. Levi): that there should be an inkling of privilege among the contending factions, while an extremely formal view of representation and reasoning invalidates a priori claims about the superiority of one inference system over another. Of course, this is just the curse of conventionalism, and it might as well be attributed to any of a number of conventionalists. I held merely that unselfconscious faith in a Fregean kind of inference is what prevents more widespread understanding of the conventionalist view.

Something similar is afoot here. On this formal, conventionalist view of inference and language, no special status can be claimed for deduction, as nonampliative, as opposed to induction or analogy, which I think should also be called nonampliative. It would be simple enough to say that induction is ampliative *relative to deduction*, while deduction is not ampliative relative to deduction.[3] This would be separation by fiat.

There is a much better distinction to be made along the ampliative-nonampliative lines. But it is a distinction that can perhaps not be understood without explaining a wholly different kind of inference, which is based on dialectic. It certainly cannot be understood without appealing to computation.

There are three theses here. The first is that noncomputationally conceived inference merely expands notation. This includes induction as well as deduction, and thus both deserve the adjective nonampliative. Deriving entailments merely expands shorthand. All of the familiar formalisms for reasoning do just this. There now exist examples of formalisms for reasoning that do something else. They are deliberative, and to say in what way they are deliberative requires reference to the process through which they compute their entailments. I explain this, my second thesis, subsequently.

[3] A thought I owe to P. Hayes.

Perhaps I should call the familiar formalisms *rewriting*, as opposed to the latter, which are *dewriting*.[4] In this way, I could avoid debating the use of the term ampliative. But I claim, as my third thesis, that the original ampliative-nonampliative terminology best survives as referring to this new distinction. So I retain the older terms. Viewed formally, all other attempted distinctions either presume deduction to be privileged, or else fail to separate inference that actually tells us something new from inference that simply rehashes what has already been represented.

## 7.2

The first thing to note is that induction, once formalized, expands shorthand as shamefully as deduction. The shame is clear for deduction. Clearly, writing "$a$" and writing "$b$" commits one to writing "$a$ & $b$": that is, when the writing is done in $L_D$, a language with meaning postulates that encode patterns of deductive inference. In the case of induction, consider $L_I$, a language with meaning postulates that encode inductive patterns of inference. Write that one hundred ravens have been black, none have been white, and this raven is a random raven. In $L_I$, this would entail that the probability that the raven is black is high: in fact, sufficiently high for acceptance of the inductive inference that it is black.

This inference is supposed to go beyond what was represented. It surely goes beyond what could have been inferred from "those same sentences" had they been written in $L_D$. But it is not clear that the inference was not already contained in the premises. In fact, it was.

In writing that this raven is a random raven, in $L_I$, having already written down the sampling information, one might as well have written that the raven was black. Blackness is entailed of this raven in $L_I$. Part of what it means to be random in $L_I$ is that frequencies are inherited as probabilities. We know this is entailed because asserting now that this raven is not black would force a revision; some premise must go: either the tally of the sampling, or the claim that the raven was a random raven with respect to color.

The situation is analogous to writing "$b$" in $L_D$ after writing "$a$". Writing "$b$" in the presence of "$a$" commits the implicit assertion of "$a$ & $b$". That is

---

[4]"Dewriting," as in "de-adjectival," "derived from an adjective," or "decompound," "to compound further." I owe this to a Ph.D. student in English (who by no means condones my invention of words).

what "$b$" means in the presence of "$a$". If the epistemics of the situation were so as not to warrant asserting "$a$ & $b$", then do not assert "$b$" in the presence of "$a$". Similarly, if times and places are such that blackness of this raven is not plain to the eye, then do not assert that this raven is random in the class of ravens. Assert something else: that it *seems* to be random, which does not conspire with the sampling information to entail blackness.

Sometimes a language will not express subtleties of epistemic situations upon which we happen: we cannot assert "$a$" and assert "$b$" without asserting "$a$ & $b$", in $L_D$. $L_D$ may not be the perfect language. But it is clear enough that in those situations in which each of "$a$" and "$b$" is asserted, and those sentences in the language are used to depict the situation, then he who so uses the language depicts a situation in which "$a$ & $b$" is asserted.

This unhappy observation of implicit commitment is the result of asserting explicitly that the raven is random. There are inductive languages in which the implicit commitment is more roundabout.

In $L_{I2}$, assert just that one hundred ravens have been black and that this raven is a raven. If this is all that is asserted, $L_{I2}$ sanctions the inference that the raven is black ($L_I$ could be I. Levi's language, and $L_{I2}$ could be that of H. Kyburg). This appears ampliative; it seems to go beyond the premises. Asserting now that the raven is white, for instance, would require no retraction. In fact, add that the raven is albino, with no inconsistency, and its whiteness is entailed.

I will treat $L_{I2}$ by explaining first the nonampliative character of an AI nonmonotonic language. By analogy, $L_{I2}$ will be seen to be also nonampliative.

Consider Bob Moore's auto-epistemic nonmonotonic language, $L_{AE}$. Write in $L_{AE}$ that if I don't know I have a brother, then I don't have a brother. That is all that is asserted. In particular, do not write that I know I have a brother, nor that I know I don't have a brother. Apparently, I just haven't reflected on whether I have a brother. This sentence in $L_{AE}$ is supposed to represent this state of affairs. In fact, it does not. In $L_{AE}$, this sentence alone entails that I don't have a brother (see Moore for details). The description of the world by *just*

"$\neg KB \supset \neg B$"

in $L_{AE}$ entails "$\neg B$" as part of the description. So saying that the world is such that

"$\neg KB \supset \neg B$"

in $L_{AE}$ is tantamount to saying the world is equally well described by

"$(\neg KB \supset \neg B)$ & $\neg B$".

The sentence, "$\neg KB \supset \neg B$" in $L_{S5}$, a modal epistemic deductive language, does not entail "$\neg B$". So it would seem that "$\neg B$" is an inference of sorts, ampliative with respect to $L_{S5}$. But that is a ruse. Simply, $L_{AE}$ is selectively inexpressive. There is no way to express just

"$\neg KB \supset \neg B$"

in $L_{AE}$ without also expressing "$\neg B$". Similarly, there is no way to express

"$a$" and "$b$"

in $L_D$ without also expressing "$a$ & $b$".

Let me lampoon the situation to expose it starkly. Suppose a computer has a 32-bit word that is supposed to represent an integer. Ostensibly, it will represent $2^{32}$ integers. But imagine that there is no way to load a 32-bit word without enduring a computation that reduces the integer to its parity:

"00000...000" for even parity strings, and

"00000...001" for odd parity strings.

It may seem that this computer can represent $2^{32}$ integers: loading

"00000...110"

would represent the integer six (6) in a normal computer. But in fact, its expressiveness is limited to two states: all other strings of 0's and 1's are disingenuous shorthands. Users of the machine beware! Likewise it is with languages and their associated inference rules. Construing inference as an association between a set of sentences and the set of sentences that is their entailment simply reduces the range of language.

There is a further point about nonmonotonic languages which is customary to make. Adding "$B$" to "$\neg KB \supset \neg B$" does not invalidate a premise. The description

"$B$ & $(\neg KB \supset \neg B)$"

is a useable description in this language, unlike

"$a \ \& \ b \ \& \ \neg(a \ \& \ b)$"

in $L_D$ But this does not diminish "$\neg B$" in any way as an entailment of (just) "$\neg KB \supset \neg B$" in $L_{AE}$. It simply means that the useable description

"$B \ \& \ (\neg KB \supset \neg B)$",

one way the world could be described, can be formed by *adding* symbols without *subtracting*, starting with

"$\neg KB \supset \neg B$",

which is some other useable description in this language.

But this is not significant. The string "00000 ... 101" can be had from "00000 ... 100" by turning on bits without zeroing any. It remains the case that "$\neg B$" follows from just "$\neg KB \supset \neg B$" in as much as it remains the case that "00000 ... 1000" has odd parity; hence, our strange computer reduces it to "00000 ... 001." These are properties of the syntax: accidents of patterns of marks. Some shorthands are had by removing symbols. Some are had by removing symbols and adding others. Nonmontonicity of this kind merely defines a different kind of shorthand.

In AI, everyone had thought that this static, syntactic nonmonotonicity had something to do with revision of belief. Evidence mounts as time passes, apparently forcing sentences to be added to the previous description of the world. But the meaning of sentences in languages is as intimately tied to what is *not* in the description as to what is in the description. This has yet to be fully appreciated. So adding sentences representing new observation in these languages is as much a revision of the original apprehension of the situation as outright change: deleting and then adding.

What allowed the derivation of "$\neg B$" in $L_{AE}$ from "$\neg KB \supset \neg B$" was the fact that "$\neg KB \supset \neg B$" was *all* that was asserted. Technically, it is an artifact of the metalinguistic definition of the inference relation, which has as much access to the relation "Not-Asserted" as to the relation "Asserted" (if that makes no sense, take a quick look at how auto-epistemic and other nonmonotonic reasoning is defined).

Now return to the hundred ravens. Today's raven may not be random; it may or may not be albino. But the fact that nothing has been said about the raven that might interfere with its being random is significant in $L_{I2}$. Saying nothing about lack of randomness, saying nothing about properties that might interfere with the direct inference from the largely black class of ravens, is shorthand for saying that it is random. This is the nature of $L_{I2}$.

How can one say that one hundred ravens have been black, in $L_{I2}$, without saying that a raven about which nothing else is known, is in fact black? Perhaps it cannot be done, like trying to represent six in our strange computer. That is a limitation of the language, with which its users must cope.

Saying only that the hundred ravens have been black, and saying no more, in $L_{I2}$, amounts to saying that the raven is black. To call the inductive inference that it is black ampliative is a misnomer. It amplifies the premises in a weak sense: if these exact sentences had been transliterated in $L_D$, symbol for symbol, they would still be well-formed (an accident of syntax), and blackness would not have been implicit. But clearly, using $L_{I2}$ requires more dexterity than that.

One cannot use $L_{I2}$ thinking that one is using $L_D$. The same sentences in $L_D$ represent quite a different state of affairs. Translations from $L_D$ to $L_{I2}$ and back must be more sophisticated: they must pay closer attention to the entailments under each language. Translation is more than transliteration.

Perhaps inductive inference in $L_{I2}$ is an ex-post policy applied to sentences written by users of $L_D$. The sentences "One hundred ravens have been black" and "This is a raven" are sentences in $L_D$, implying what they do in $L_D$, not what they would in $L_{I2}$. Once written, as if in $L_D$, the meaning postulates of $L_{I2}$ are then applied. In this fashion, $L_{I2}$'s inductive patterns of inference amplify what was committed in $L_D$. A good analogy of this among nonmonotonic languages is circumscription. In circumscription, an assumption is made *after* sentences have been written in $L_D$: a predicate's extension is assumed to be limited to that which it is asserted to predicate.

This is self-deception, not inference. It is $L_{I2}$ that is being used, or $L_{Circumscr}$, but not $L_D$. Maybe language users are so constituted that the best way for them to use $L_{I2}$ is to pretend to be using $L_D$. The thought is perverse, but not unembraceable. It might be that for a certain community of programmers, the most efficient and error-free c++ programs result from telling the programmers that they are programming in c. In any case, pretending to be representing knowledge in $L_D$ while actually representing in $L_{I2}$ is still a use of $L_{I2}$. What is interesting is the reinterpretation of ostensible $L_D$-sentences as $L_{I2}$-sentences, *not* the rewriting of these sentences to produce their "inductive" entailments. This reinterpretation may be interesting, but is not a candidate for ampliative inference. There is no formal difference between reinterpreting sentences in some language as $L_{I2}$, and representing the knowledge in $L_{I2}$ in the first place.

## 7.3

Beware that sympathy for this view of inference, representation, and language produces a dilemma. As long as $L_X$ is formal, for any $X$ which is supposed to encode some interesting form of inference, computing entailments in $L_X$ seems non-ampliative. Entailment does not venture beyond the premises in an interesting epistemological way. All of the interesting epistemology occurs when a language's "admissible states" (J. Doyle's lovely phrase) are matched with apprehensions of world-situations.

Computing entailments can be surprising for resource-bounded or error-prone users of the language. The conclusions of long proofs are contained wholly in their premises, yet are not obvious. I do not want to suggest that inference in these languages is trivial. But neither surprise nor opacity makes inference ampliative, lest some deductive inferences qualify as ampliative. If deduction, as well as induction, should be called ampliative because there can be long, surprising proofs in both, or undecidable truths, that is a fine use of "ampliative." What I am disputing is the claim that there is an interesting sense in which induction is ampliative, while deduction is not. No deductions are ampliative. So induction, and other alleged ampliative inference, must not be ampliative either.

What, then, is ampliative about any *formal* system of inference?

Jon Doyle has identified a simple example of what would seem to qualify as inference going beyond what has been represented in a language: as genuine ampliative inference. Giving his example steals the thunder from a different example that I find more worthy. And Doyle's putative example is of dubious rationality; it may be ampliative inference, but maybe not *rational* ampliative inference. Nevertheless, the example shows immediately what would be required to escape the rewriting nature of all the inference considered above: to differ from all the inference systems defined in terms of entailments.

Doyle cites the example of credulous nonmonotonic reasoners. These are the nonmonotonic languages that make a nondeterministic choice among several potential conclusions. There are situations in which the sentences in a nonmonotonic language can have multiple extensions, or multiple fixed points. Whereas deductive closure is a function from sets of sentences to sets of sentences, nonmonotonic closure becomes a relation here.

Writing in $L_{AE}$ just

"$(\neg KB \supset \neg B) \,\&\, (\neg K \neg B \supset B)$"                                                          (1)

is ambiguous between

"$(\neg KB \supset \neg B) \,\&\, (\neg K \neg B \supset B) \,\&\, B$"                                             (1a)

and

"$(\neg KB \supset \neg B) \,\&\, (\neg K \neg B \supset B) \,\&\, \neg B$"                                       (1b)

This is different from the sense in which "$a$" in $L_D$ might be said to be ambiguous between "$a \,\&\, b$" and "$a \,\&\, \neg b$". "$a$" in $L_D$ is neither one nor the other. But (1) is supposed to be either the same as (1a) or else the same as (1b). $L_{AE}$ could have been defined so that (1) describes an admissible state; it could be a meaningful, useable description of a state of the world which is different from (1a) and also from (1b). On other definitions of $L_{AE}$, (1) could be inadmissible. Both kinds of definitions are by now familiar cases: in the former, the expressiveness of the language is augmented; in the latter, a shorthand has been disallowed. On the third, more interesting kinds of definitions of $L_{AE}$, (1) is defined to be a shorthand for (1a) or for (1b), but no one could tell which, prior to the nondeterministic computation.

That is, prior to inference—ampliative inference—it is not determined which state is admitted. The representer of knowledge is responsible for limiting the choice, but cannot be held responsible for the ultimate outcome. The inference "$B$" or "$\neg B$" is new; it amplifies what was originally represented. Of course, it is a lousy inference: no more than a guess.

So some kinds of bad inference are ampliative. Is any good inference ampliative?

Doyle thinks that certain decision-theoretic deliberations are ampliative. If the underlying decisionmaking is dialectical in the sense that I elaborate next, then I agree. If it merely expands represented preferences, implicit in an explicit utility function, in some decision-theoretic $L_{DT}$, then I believe they are merely rewriting, hence not examples of ampliative inference.

## 7.4

Something I call dialectic produces rational, ampliative inference: it is dewriting. Dialectic is based on new ideas in the formalization of personal, deliberative inference, and I believe it is the candidate most deserving to be called ampliative. Dialectic makes sense only for defeasible reasoning, and moreover, only for inference defined relative to a set of constructed arguments that may not exhaust all constructible arguments. That is, dialectical inference produces different conclusions, as more arguments are constructed.

Unlike $L_{AE}$ and other first-generation non-monotonic reasoning, defeasible reasoning is often based on the production of arguments. Arguments combine reasons to chain from premises to putative conclusions. They are like proofs, except that proofs (in $L_{AE}$, $L_{I2}$, or $L_D$) establish their conclusions once and for all. A proof is a proof, irrespective of what other proofs there may or may not be. In contrast, arguments justify their conclusions if there are no effective counterarguments or rebuttals. An argument can defeat another argument; an argument that defeats an argument that counters a third argument can reinstate that third argument. Formalisms for this kind of reasoning have been developed by recent authors (Poole, Loui, Pollock, Simari, etc.).

Generally, resource-bounded defeasible reasoners are governed by a process that constructs arguments over time and determines what is justified relative to what arguments have been constructed. Entailment in $L_D$ could likewise have been defined over time, relative to increasing sets of constructed proofs. This having been done, the difference would be that entailments grow monotonically in computation for $L_D$. For defeasible reasoners, sentences justified at a time bear no such relation to sentences justified at a later time. Conclusions are nonmonotonic in computation. This is what essentially frees them to reach beyond explicit and implicit representation.

Dialectic refers to a set of policies for constructing arguments, that is, permissible search strategies for deliberation. Given what is currently justified, dialectic mandates that attention be focused on constructing arguments for some propositions and not others. Dialectic defines one style of deliberation for resource-bounded defeasible reasoners.

Consider, for example, resource-bounded defeasible reasoning about action. Here is the qualitative case, which belies the merit of the quantitative case, but which is more perspicuous. The explicit commitment is that

driving quickly results in arriving sooner;

driving quickly results in endangering lives;

driving quickly results in having fun;

and so forth;

arriving sooner is desirable;

endangering lives is undesirable;

having fun is desirable;

(having fun) + (endangering lives) is undesirable;

   and so forth;

if $a$ results in $p$ and $a$ results in $q$ then $a$ results in $p + q$;

$a$ resulting in $p$ is reason for $a$ being as desirable as $p$;

do $a$ if $a$ is desirable;

do not do $a$ if $a$ is undesirable.

In a small amount of computation time, there may only be time to identify the argument to drive quickly based on the fact that driving quickly results in having fun. Since there are no other arguments that can be considered in this time (in particular, no counterarguments), driving quickly is warranted. In slightly more time, an effective counterargument might be constructed, which urges not to drive quickly because it results in endangering lives. At this time, neither driving quickly nor not driving quickly is warranted; the arguments interfere. Still later, the argument not to drive quickly might be constructed, based on the undesirability of the combined result: having fun and endangering lives. This defeats the less specific argument based solely on having fun. At this point, not driving quickly is warranted. And the process continues.

Distinguish between three kinds of nonmonotonicity. There is syntactic nonmonotonicity, discussed above, in which a notation does not always relate a growth of explicit knowledge with a growth of their entailments. It is a property of a representational language. Further, there are two varieties of temporal credal non-monotonicity.[5] Both are properties of actual beliefs of an agent situated in time, as represented in a language. The first is *external* temporal credal nonmonotonicity, when a belief is removed due to a revision forced by observation. This includes simple contractions of the corpus of beliefs and other epistemic shifts normally studied in belief revision.[6] External nonmonotonicity is not particularly interesting

---

[5] The terminology is taken from Levi's "temporal credal conditionalization."

[6] It was Doyle who showed me that outright contraction deserved to be considered a non-monotonic move.

because shifts of belief normally require contraction prior to expansion, and are therefore normally nonmonotonic. Finally, there is internal temporal credal nonmonotonicity, when a belief is removed due to deliberation on the entailments of explicit commitment. Nonmonotonicity in computation is internal temporal credal nonmonotonicity.

The point is that commitments come and go as the search for arguments becomes more complete. In finite systems, there may be a finite set of arguments, and it is meaningful to think of iterative approximation of the ideal state of deliberation. In the final iteration, the arguments constructed exhaust the space of constructible arguments, and warrant for conclusions is based thereupon. In these cases, under the classical view of commitment, there is a final set of implicit commitments for a set of explicit commitments. The agent committed to these explicit sentences is at all times committed to these implicit ideal commitments. Through computation over time, the agent is attempting to acknowledge just those commitments. My view is different. First it should be noted that there are not necessarily final commitments in infinite systems. Even in the finite systems, however, the nature of commitment is different. Specifying that sentences are defeasible reasons for other sentences is a commitment to their being used in resource-bounded defeasible reasoning that produces conclusions over time, which may be nonmonotonic in computation. It is not just another style of specifying ideal commitment. It is a commitment to all of the intermediate epistemic positions, devolved enroute to the ideal.

If facile users of the language were aware of the exact search strategy being used for the construction of arguments, that is, if this detailed control were a part of the language, then a user would be specifying a function from computation time to a set of entailments. Instead of one set of entailments per set of explicit sentences, there would be a set of entailments per computation step per set of explicit sentences. If this were the case, then inference might not seem ampliative. At a time, arguments would be constructed as envisioned, and those conclusions warranted with respect to those arguments would be drawn. Those conclusions would be a rewriting, for that time, of the sentences originally inscribed.

Time is an external variable which serves to index a particular rewriting of the sentences. We could argue at length whether this indexing alone results in inference that is *ampliative*.

Fortunately, there is another source of indeterminacy. The search strategy for arguments may have nondeterministic choices. Those choices are constrained, so that any particular sequence of choices instantiates rational search.

By hypothesis, in resource-bounded defeasible reasoning, dialectical search strategies are rational. Dialectical search implies that resources are at all times being expended to overturn currently warranted conclusions, or else to establish new ones. In the example of practical reasoning above, a dialectical reasoner could not have formed another argument to drive quickly, based on arriving sooner, prior to constructing the second argument, an argument for not driving quickly. Resources cannot be used to buttress arguments further, if there is no existing effective counterargument. Resources could be expended in that way in search strategies that are lobbying, that is, not dialectical. But to expend resources in that way does not guarantee the rationality of what results at every intermediate stage in the computation. Perhaps at a time, resources that could have been used to rebut a putative conclusion were used frivolously. All dialectical search strategies are rational, while not all lobbying search strategies are rational.

In writing sentences in a language of resource-bounded defeasible reasoning, the user commits to the results of any dialectical strategy, but does not know in advance the exact sequence of dialectical maneuvers. For example, an argument that could be challenged at any of a number of places will be challenged, though it is undetermined where the challenge will be made. The difference between this arbitrary resolution of indeterminacy and the resolution of multiple extensions by arbitrary choice of extension has to do with the claims of rationality of the process. Nondeterministic choice of maneuver is rational; nondeterministic choice of conclusion is not.

Dialectic produces more than just sentences that rewrite the commitment, but nevertheless, produces only sentences to which the agent has contracted to commit. It is as if there were reason to commit to the outcome of a coin toss between $p$ and $\neg p$. The coin is tossed: the inference made.

What we have been seeking is a language in which a prior commitment to the outcome of an indeterminate process can be specified. The process must itself be rational (this excludes guessing). And the indeterminacy cannot merely be the time at which the inevitable outcome is reached (this excludes nondeterministic use of deductive inference patterns). That is how inference can be more than the rewriting of commitment, but more than a stab in the dark. That is what constitutes ampliative inference.

*Ampliative inference is the result of rational nondeterministic nonmonotonic computation.*

Dialectic is the very best example of rational ampliative inference. We saw that nondeterministic choice of nonmonotonic extension is also an example. There are others. Abduction vaguely described as the inference to some causally sufficient condition might be ampliative. It has affinities to the multiple extension problem; there is an indeterminate specification of conclusion and a choice to be made with no formal guidance. Inference in connectionist networks is ampliative. There is a computational process that produces tentative conclusions through time. The time at which the network is inspected for its conclusions is often externally determined. Conclusions produced at one time may be overturned at a later time. There may be other approaches to ampliative defeasible reasoning, too.[7,8]

## 7.5

Nonmonotonic logics, by their form, suggest how internal credal nonmonotonicity might be achieved. But unless there is concern over resource-bounded computation, they exhibit only syntactic nonmonotonicity, which everyone agrees is a matter of style.

Traditional logicians deny interest in nonmonotonic logics because they disavow computation; they care only about the specification of an agent's commitment.[9] What we find here is that the reverse is true. In order to conceive of an inference that is not merely a rewriting of the agent's specified commitment, we have to turn our thoughts to computation.

### References

Doyle, J. 1989. Constructive belief and rational representation. *Computational Intelligence* 5.

Elgot-Drapkin, J. and Perlis, D. 1989. Reasoning situated in time. Submitted to *Artificial Intelligence*.

Geffner, H., and Pearl, J. 1990. A framework for reasoning with defaults. In H. Kyburg, R. Loui, and G. Carlson, eds., *Knowledge Representation and Defeasible Reasoning*. Kluwer.

Ginsberg, M. 1988. *Readings in Non-Monotonic Reasoning*. Morgan Kaufman.

Kyburg, H. 1974. *Logical Foundations of Statistical Inference*. Reidel.

[7] Consider nondeterministic versions of step-logics, e.g., Elgot-Drapkin and Perlis, or resource-bounded versions of irrelevance-introducing systems, e.g., Geffner and Pearl.
[8] J. Simon has pointed out to me that the Solovay and Strassen probabilistic primality test, construed as inference, also satisfies these criteria for being ampliative.
[9] According to Isaac Levi.

Levi, I. 1980. *Enterprise of Knowledge*. MIT Press.

Loui, R. 1987. Defeat among arguments. *Computational Intelligence* 3.

Loui, R. 1988. The curse of Frege. *Proc. Theoretical Aspects of Reasoning about Knowledge.* Morgan Kaufman.

Moore, R. 1985. Semantical considerations on nonmonotonic logic. *Artificial Intelligence* 25.

Pollock, J. 1987. Defeasible reasoning. *Cognitive Science* 11.

Poole, D. 1985. On the comparison of theories. *Proc. Intl. Joint Conf. AI.* Morgan Kaufman.

Sampson, J., and Weiner, E., preparers. 1989. *Oxford English Dictionary.* Clarendon Press.

Simari, G., and R. Loui. 1991. On the logic of defeasible reasoning. *Artificial Intelligence*, forthcoming.

# 8 Probabilistic Semantics for Nonmonotonic Reasoning

Judea Pearl

## 8.1  Why Probabilistic Semantics? Or, Conventions versus Norms

In nonmonotonic logics, defeasible sentences are usually interpreted as conversational conventions, as opposed to descriptions of empirical reality (McCarthy 1986, Reiter 1987). For example, the sentence "Birds fly" is taken to express a communication agreement such as: "You and I agree that whenever I want you to conclude that some bird does not fly, I will say so explicitly; otherwise you can presume it does fly." Here the purpose of the agreement is not to convey information about the world but merely to guarantee that in subsequent conversations, all conclusions drawn by the informed match those intended by the informer. Once the agreement is accepted by an agent, the meaning of the sentence acquires a dispositional character: "If $x$ is a bird and I have no reasons to presume the contrary, then I am disposed to believe that $x$ flies." Neither of these interpretations invokes any statistical information about the percentage of birds that fly nor any probabilistic information about how strongly the agent believes that a randomly chosen bird actually flies.

However, the probabilistic statement $P[(Fly(x)|Bird(x)] = High$ (to read: "If $x$ is a bird, then $x$ probably flies") offers such a clear interpretation of "Birds fly", that it is hard to refrain from viewing defeasible sentences as fragments of probabilistic information, albeit subjective in nature. With such declarative statements it is easier to define how the fragments of knowledge should be put together coherently, to characterize the set of conclusions that one wishes a body of knowledge to entail, and to identify the assumptions that give rise to undesirable conclusions, if any.

The reasons are several. First, semantics has traditionally been defined as a relation between the speaking agent and entities external to the agent. Probabilistic information is, by its very nature, a declarative summarization of constraints in a world external to the speaker. As such, it is empirically testable (at least in principle), it is often shared by many agents, and conclusions are less subject to dispute. Second, in many cases, it is the transference of probabilistic knowledge that is the ultimate aim of common conversations, not the speaker's pattern of dispositions (which are often arbitrary). In such cases, the empirical facts that caused the agent to commit to a given pattern of dispositions are more important than the dispositions themselves, because it is those empirical facts that the listening agent is about to confront in the future. Finally, being a centuries-old science, the study of probabilistic inference has accumulated a wealth of theoretical results that provide shortcuts between the semantics and the intended conclusions. This facilitates quick generation of meaningful examples and counterexamples, quick proofs of necessity or impossibility, and thus, effective communication among researchers.

But even taking the extreme position that the only purpose of default statements is to establish conversational conventions, probabilists nevertheless believe that, while we are in the process of uncovering and formulating those conventions, we cannot totally ignore their empirical origin. Doing so would resemble the hopeless task of formulating qualitative physics in total ignorance of the quantitative laws of physics, or, to use a different metaphor, designing speech-recognition systems oblivious to the laws of phonetics.

The quest for probabilistic semantics is motivated by the assumption that the conventions of discourse are not totally arbitrary, but rather, respect certain universal norms of coherence, norms that reflect the empirical origin of these conventions. Probabilistic semantics, by summarizing the reality that compelled the choice of certain conventions over others, should be capable of revealing these norms. Such norms should tell us, for example, when one convention is incompatible with another, or when one convention should be a natural consequence of another, examples of both will be illustrated in section 8.4.

The benefits of adopting probabilistic norms apply not only to syntactical approaches to nonmonotonic reasoning, but also to semantical approaches, such as those based on model preference (McCarthy 1980). Inferences based on model preference are much less disciplined than those based on probability, because the preferences induced by the various sentences in the knowledge base are not constrained a priori, and can, in general, be totally whimsical. Indeed, such a wide range of approaches to nonmonotonic reasoning can be formulated as variants of preference-based semantics (Shoham 1987), that highly sophisticated restrictions must be devised to bring the ensuing inferences in line with basic standards of rationality (Lehmann and Magidor 1988) (see section 8.6.2).

## 8.2 Nonmonotonic Reasoning Viewed as Qualitative Probabilistic Reasoning

To those trained in traditional logics, symbolic reasoning is the standard, and nonmonotonicity a novelty. To students of probability, on the other hand, it is symbolic reasoning that is novel, not nonmonotonicity. Dealing with new facts that cause probabilities to change abruptly from very high values to very low values is a commonplace phenomenon in almost every probability exercise and. naturally, has never attracted special attention among probabilists. The new challenge for probabilists is to find ways of abstracting out the numerical character of high and low probabilities, and cast them in linguistic terms that reflect the natural process of accepting and retracting beliefs. Thus. while nonmonotonic reasoning is commonly viewed as an extension to standard logic, it can also be viewed as an exercise in qualitative probability, much like physicists view current AI research in naive physics.

In research on qualitative physics, it is customary to discretize and abstract real quantities around a few "landmark" values (Kuipers 1986). For example, the value 0 defines the abstraction: positive, negative and zero. In probability, the obvious landmarks are $\{0, \frac{1}{2}, 1\}$, where 0 and 1 represent $FALSE$ and $TRUE$, respectively, and $\frac{1}{2}$ represents the neutral state of total ignorance. However, direct qualitative reasoning about $\{0, 1\}$ reduces to propositional logic, while reasoning with the intervals $[0, \frac{1}{2}]$ and $[\frac{1}{2}, 1]$ is extremely difficult—to process pieces of evidence properly and determine if a given probability should fall above $\frac{1}{2}$ requires almost the full power of numerical probability calculus (Bacchus 1988).

Following the tradition of qualitative reasoning in physics and mathematics, two avenues are still available for qualitative analysis:

1. "Perturbation" analysis, to determine the direction of CHANGE induced in the probability of one proposition as a result of learning the truth of another, and

2. An "order-of-magnitude" analysis of proximities to the landmark values.

The first approach has been pursued by Wellman (1987) and Neufeld and Poole (1988), and the second by Adams (1975), Spohn (1988), Pearl (1988), and Geffner (1988, 1989).

### 8.2.1 Perturbation Analyses

Both Wellman (1987) and Neufeld and Poole (1988) investigated the logic behind the qualitative relation of *influence* or *support*, namely, the condition under which the truth of one proposition would yield an increase in the probability of another. Wellman's analysis focuses on variables with ordered domains (e.g., "An increase in quantity $a$ is likely to cause an increase in quantity $b$") as a means of providing qualitative aids to decisions, planning, and diagnosis. Neufeld and Poole, focused on the relation of *confirmation* between propositions (e.g., *Quaker(Nixon)* adds confirmation to *Pacifist(Nixon)*), and viewed this relation as an important component of nonmonotonic reasoning.

Both approaches make heavy use of conditional independence and its graphical representation in the form of Bayesian networks (Pearl 1988). The reason is that, if we define the relation "$A$ supports $B$" (denoted $S(A, B)$) as

$$S(A, B) \quad \text{iff} \quad P(B \mid A) \geq P(B), \tag{1}$$

then this definition in itself is too weak to yield interesting inferences. For example, whereas we can easily show symmetry $S(A, B) \Leftrightarrow S(B, A)$ and contraposition $S(A, B) \Leftrightarrow S(\neg B, \neg A)$, we cannot conclude cumulativity (i.e. that $S(A \wedge B, C)$ follows from $S(A, B)$ and $S(A, C)$), nor transitivity (i.e., that $S(A, C)$ follows from $S(A, B)$ and $S(B, C)$). For the latter to hold, we must assume that $C$ is conditionally independent of $A$, given $B$,

$$P(C \mid A, B) = P(C \mid B),$$

namely, that knowledge of $A$ has no influence on the probability of $C$, once we know $B$.

Conditional independence is a 3-place nonmonotonic relationship that forms a *semi-graphoid* (Pearl and Verma 1987, Pearl 1988). Semi-graphoids are structures that share some properties of graphs (hence the name) but, in general, are difficult to encode completely, in a compact way. The assumption normally made in probabilistic reasoning (as well as in most nonmonotonic logics, though not explicitly) is that if we represent dependence relationships in the form of a directed (acyclic) graph, then any link missing from the graph indicates the absence of direct dependency between the corresponding variables. For example, if we are given two defeasible rules, $a \rightarrow b$ and $b \rightarrow c$, we presume that $a$ does not have any direct bearing on $c$, but rather, that $c$ is independent of $a$, given the value of $b$. An important result from the theory of graphoids states that there is indeed a sound and complete procedure (called $d$-separation) of inferring conditional independencies from such a graph. However, this requires that the graph be constructed in a disciplined, stratified way: Every variable $x$ should draw arrows from all those perceived to have *direct influence* on $x$, that is, those that must be known to render $x$ independent of all its predecessors in some total order (e.g., temporal). A graph (directed and acyclic) constructed in this fashion is called a *Bayesian network* (Pearl 1988). In practice, this presumes that the knowledge provider has taken pains to identify all direct influences of each variable in the system.

Neufeld and Poole have assumed that if we take isolated default statements and assemble them to form a directed graph, the resulting graph would display all the dependencies that a Bayesian network would. Unfortunately, this is not always the case, and may lead to unsound conclusions. For example, from the defaults $A \rightarrow B$, $C \rightarrow \neg B$, we will conclude (using the $d$-separation criterion) that $A$ is independent of $C$ (since there is no active path between $A$ and $C$). Often, however, two classes $A$ and $C$ whose members differ substantially in one typical property ($B$ vs $\neg B$) will be found dependent on one another. The language of graphs may also be insufficient for expressing some independencies that are found useful in natural discourse. For example, having been told that $A$ supports $C$ and $B$ supports $C$, we tend to presume that $A$ and $B$ also supports $C$. This presumption. however, is not directly expressible in the language of directed graphs, nor can it be derived from the semantics of "support" given in equation (1).

Wellman has circumvented these difficulties by starting from a well structured Bayesian network, and by defining "support" in a more restrictive way. Instead of equation (1), Wellman's definition reads:

$$S^+(a, b, G) \quad \text{iff} \quad P(B \mid A, x) \geq P(B \mid x)$$

where $S^+(a, b, G)$ stands for "$a$ positively influences $b$, in the context of graph $G$", and the inequality should hold for every valuation $x$ of the direct predecessors of $b$ (in $G$). This stronger definition of support defines, in fact, the conditions under which inferences based on graphically derived dependencies are probabilistically sound. Compared with the system of Neufeld and Poole, soundness is acquired at the price of a more elaborate form of knowledge specification, namely, the structure of a Bayesian network.

### 8.2.2 Infinitesimal Analysis

Spohn (1988) has introduced a system of belief revision (called OCF for Ordinal Conditional Functions) which requires only integer-value addition, and yet retains the notion of conditionalization, a facility that makes probability theory context dependent, hence nonmonotonic. Although Spohn has proclaimed OCF to be "nonprobabilistic," the easiest way to understand its power and limitations is to interpret OCF as an infinitesimal (i.e., nonstandard) analysis of conditional probabilities.

Imagine an ordinary probability function $P$ defined over a set $W$ of possible worlds (or states of the world), and let the probability $P(w)$ assigned to each world $w$ be a polynomial function of some small positive parameter $\varepsilon$, for example, $\alpha$, $\beta\varepsilon$, $\gamma\varepsilon^2$, and so on. Accordingly, the probabilities assigned to any subset $A$ of $W$, as well as all conditional probabilities $P(A|B)$, will be rational functions of $\varepsilon$. Now define the OCF function $\kappa(A|B)$ as

$$\kappa(A|B) = \text{lowest } n \text{ such that } \lim_{\varepsilon \to 0} P(A|B)/\varepsilon^n \text{ is non-zero.} \qquad (2)$$

In other words, $\kappa(A|B) = n$ iff $P(A|B)$ is of the same order as $\varepsilon^n$, or equivalently, $\kappa(A|B)$ is of the same order of magnitude as $[P(A|B)]^{-1}$.

If we think of $n$ for which $P(w) = \varepsilon^n$ as measuring the degree to which the world $w$ is disbelieved (or the degree of surprise were we to observe $w$), then $\kappa(A|B)$ can be thought of as the degree of disbelief (or surprise) in $A$, given that $B$ is true. It is easy to verify that $\kappa$ satisfies the following properties:

1. $\kappa(A) = \min\{\kappa(w) | w \in A\}$
2. $\kappa(A) = 0$ or $\kappa(\neg A) = 0$, or both
3. $\kappa(A \cup B) = \min\{\kappa(A), \kappa(B)\}$
4. $\kappa(A \cap B) = \kappa(A|B) + \kappa(B)$ \hfill (3)

These reflect the usual properties of probabilistic combinations (on a logarithmic scale) with *min* replacing addition, and addition replacing multiplication. The result is a probabilistically sound calculus, employing integer addition, for manipulating order of magnitudes of disbeliefs. For example. if we make the following correspondence between linguistic quantifiers and $\varepsilon^n$:

$$P(A) = \varepsilon^0 \quad A \text{ is believable} \qquad\qquad \kappa(A) = 0$$

$P(A) = \varepsilon^1$   $A$ is unlikely          $\kappa(A) = 1$

$P(A) = \varepsilon^2$   $A$ is very unlikely       $\kappa(A) = 2$

$P(A) = \varepsilon^3$   $A$ is extremely unlikely   $\kappa(A) = 3$

then Spohn's system can be regarded as a nonmonotonic logic to reason about likelihood (contrast with the modal logic of Halpern and Rabin 1987). It takes sentences in the form of quantified conditional sentences, for example, "Birds are likely to fly" (written $\kappa(\neg f|b) = 1$), "Penguins are most likely birds" (written $\kappa(\neg b \mid p) = 2$), "Penguins are extremely unlikely to fly," (written $\kappa(f|p) = 3$), and returns quantified conclusions in the form of "If $x$ is a penguin-bird then $x$ is extremely unlikely to fly" (written $\kappa(f|p \wedge b) = 3$).

The weakness of Spohn's system, shared by numerical probability, is that it requires the complete specification of a distribution function before reasoning can commence. In other words, we must specify the $\kappa$ associated with every world $w$. In practice, of course, such specification need not be enumerative, but can use the decomposition facilities provided by Bayesian networks. However, this too might require knowledge that is not readily available in common discourse. For example, we might be given the information that birds fly (written $\kappa(\neg f|b) = 1$) and no information at all about properties of non-birds, thus leaving $\kappa(f \wedge \neg b)$ unspecified. Hence, inferencial machinery is required for drawing conclusions from partially specified models, like those associating a $\kappa$ with isolated default statements. Such machinery is provided by the conditional logic of Adams (1975), to be discussed next.

Adams's logic can be regarded a bi-valued infinitesimal analysis, with input sentences specifying $\kappa$ values of only 0 and 1, corresponding to "likely" and "unlikely" rankings. However, instead of insisting on a complete specification of $\kappa(w)$, the logic admits fragmentary sets of conditional sentences, treats them as constraints over the distribution of $\kappa$, and infers only such statements that are compelled to acquire high likelihood in every distribution $\kappa(w)$ satisfying these constraints.

Because of its importance as a bridge between probabilistic and logical approaches, we will provide a more complete introduction to Adams's logic, using excerpts from chapter 10 of Pearl 1988. We will see that the semantics of infinitesimal probabilities (called $\varepsilon$-semantics in Pearl 1988) leads to a two-level architecture for nonmonotonic reasoning:

1. A conservative, consistency-preserving *core*, embodied in a semimonotonic logic, which derives only conclusions that are safe relative to the addition of new domain knowledge.

2. An adventurous *shell*, sanctioning a larger body of less grounded inferences. These inferences reflect probabilistic independencies that are not explicit in the input, yet, based on familiar patterns of discourse, are presumed to hold in the absence of explicit dependencies.

## 8.3   The Conservative Core

### 8.3.1   $\varepsilon$-Semantics

We consider a default theory $T = \langle F, \Delta \rangle$ in the form of a database containing two types of sentences: factual sentences $(F)$ and default statements $(\Delta)$. The factual sentences describe findings or observations specific to a given object or a situations; for example, $p(a)$ asserts that individual $a$ has the property $p$. The default statements are of the type "$p$'s are typically $q$'s", written $p(x) \to q(x)$ or simply $p \to q$, which is short for saying "any individual $x$ having property $p$ typically has property $q$". The properties $p, q, r \dots$ can be compound boolean formulas of some atomic predicates $p_1, p_2, \dots p_n$, with $x$ as their only free variable. However, no ground defaults (e.g., $p(a) \to q(a)$) are allowed in $F$ and no compound defaults (e.g., $p \to (q \to r)$) are allowed in $\Delta$. The default statement $S': p \to \neg q$ will be called the *denial* of $S: p \to q$.

Nondefeasible generic statements such as "all birds are animals" can be written $Birds(x) \land \neg Animal(x) \to FALSE$. This facilitates the desirable distinction between a generic law-like rule "all $p$'s are $q$'s" (to be encoded in $\Delta$ as $p \land \neg q \to FALSE$) and a factual observation $p(a) \supset q(a)$, which must enter $F$ as $\neg p \lor q$. Indeed, the theory $\langle \{p(a)\}, \{p \land \neg q \to FALSE\} \rangle$, will give rise to totally different conclusions (about $a$) than $\langle \{p(a), \neg p(a) \lor q(a)\}, \{ \ \} \rangle$, in conformity with common use of conditionals. A more natural treatment of nondefeasible conditionals is given in (Goldszmidt and Pearl 1989) where a new connective $\Rightarrow$ is used to retain the law-like character of these statements. However, to simplify our discussion we will henceforth assume that all statements are defeasible.

Let $L$ be the language of propositional formulas, and let a *truth-valuation* for $L$ be a function $t$ that maps the sentences in $L$ to the set $\{1, 0\}$, (1 for *TRUE* and 0 for *FALSE*) such that $t$ respects the usual Boolean connectives. To define a probability assignment over the sentences in $L$, we regard each truth valuation $t$ as a world $w$ and define $P(w)$ such that $\sum_w P(w) = 1$. This assigns a probability measure to each sentence $s$ of $L$ via $P(s) = \sum_w P(w) w(s)$.

We now interpret $\Delta$ as a set of restrictions on $P$, in the form of *extreme conditional probabilities*, infinitesimally removed from either 0 or 1. For example, the sentence $Bird(x) \to Fly(x)$ is interpreted as $P(Fly(x)|Bird(x)) \geq 1 - \varepsilon$, where $\varepsilon$ is understood to stand for an infinitesimal quantity that can be made arbitrarily small, short of actually being zero.

The conclusions we wish to draw from a theory $T = \langle F, \Delta \rangle$ are, likewise, formulas in $L$ that, given the input facts $F$ and the restrictions $\Delta$, are forced to acquire extreme high probabilities. In particular, a propositional formula $r$ would qualify as a *plausible conclusion* of $T$, written $F \hspace{0.1em}\vdash_\Delta r$, whenever the restrictions of $\Delta$ force $P$ to satisfy $\lim_{\varepsilon \to 0} P(r|F) = 1$.

It is convenient to characterize the set of conclusions sanctioned by this semantics in terms of the set of facts-conclusion pairs that are entailed by a given $\Delta$. We call this relation *$\varepsilon$-entailment*[1] formally defined as follows:

*Definition:* Let $\mathscr{P}_{\Delta,\varepsilon}$ stand for the set of distributions licensed by $\Delta$ for any given $\varepsilon$, i.e.,

$$P_{\Delta,\varepsilon} = \{P : P(v|u) \geq 1 - \varepsilon \text{ and } P(u) > 0 \text{ whenever } u \to v \in \Delta\} \tag{4}$$

A conditional statement $S: p \to q$ is said to be *$\varepsilon$-entailed* by $\Delta$, if every distribution $P \in \mathscr{P}_{\Delta,\varepsilon}$ satisfies $P(q|p) = 1 - O(\varepsilon)$, (i.e., for every $\delta > 0$ there exists a $\varepsilon > 0$ such that every $P \in \mathscr{P}_{\Delta,\varepsilon}$ would satisfy $P(q|p) \geq 1 - \delta$).

In essence, this definition guarantees that an $\varepsilon$-entailed statement $S$ is rendered highly probable whenever all the defaults in $\Delta$ are highly probable. The connection between $\varepsilon$-entailment and plausible conclusions, is simply:

$$F \hspace{0.1em}\vdash_\Delta r \text{ iff } (F \to r) \text{ is } \varepsilon\text{-entailed by } \Delta \tag{5}$$

### 8.3.2 Axiomatic Characterization

The conditional logic developed by Adams (1975) faithfully represents this semantics by qualitative inference rules, thus facilitating the derivation of new sound sentences by direct symbolic manipulations on $\Delta$. The essence of Adams's logic is summarized in the following theorem, restated for default theories in (Geffner and Pearl 1988).

---

[1] Adams (1975) named this $p$-entailment. However, $\varepsilon$-entailment better serves to distinguish this from weaker forms of probabilistic entailment, section 4.

THEOREM 1:    Let $T = \langle F, \Delta \rangle$ be a default theory where $F$ is a set of ground proposition formulas and $\Delta$ is a set of default rules. $r$ is a plausible conclusion of $F$ in the context of $\Delta$, written $F \mathrel{\vdash_\Delta} r$, iff $r$ is derivable from $F$ using the following rules of inference:

**Rule 1**   (Defaults) $(p \rightarrow q) \in \Delta \Rightarrow p \mathrel{\vdash_\Delta} q$

**Rule 2**   (Logic Theorems) $p \mathrel{\vdash} q \Rightarrow p \mathrel{\vdash_\Delta} q$

**Rule 3**   (Cumulativity) $p \mathrel{\vdash_\Delta} q, p \mathrel{\vdash_\Delta} r \Rightarrow (p \wedge q) \mathrel{\vdash_\Delta} r$

**Rule 4**   (Contraction) $p \mathrel{\vdash_\Delta} q, (p \wedge q) \mathrel{\vdash_\Delta} r \Rightarrow p \mathrel{\vdash_\Delta} r$

**Rule 5**   (Disjunction) $p \mathrel{\vdash_\Delta} r, q \mathrel{\vdash_\Delta} r \Rightarrow (p \vee q) \mathrel{\vdash_\Delta} r$

Rule 1 permits us to conclude the consequent of a default when its antecedent is all that has been learned and this permission is granted regardless of the content of $\Delta$. Rule 2 states that theorems that logically follow from a set of formulas can be concluded in any theory containing those formulas. Rule 3 (called *triangularity* in Pearl 1988 and *cautious monotony* in Lehmann and Magidor 1988) permits the attachment of any established conclusion ($q$) to the current set of facts ($p$), without affecting the status of any other derived conclusion ($r$). Rule 4 says that any conclusion ($r$) that follows from a fact set ($p$) augmented by a derived conclusion ($q$) also follows from the original fact set alone. Finally, rule 5 says that a conclusion that follows from two facts also follows from their disjunction.

**Some Meta-Theorems:**

**T-1**   (Logical Closure) $p \mathrel{\vdash_\Delta} q, p \wedge q \mathrel{\vdash} r \Rightarrow p \mathrel{\vdash_\Delta} r$

**T-2**   (Equivalent Contexts) $p \equiv q, p \mathrel{\vdash_\Delta} r \Rightarrow q \mathrel{\vdash_\Delta} r$

**T-3**   (Exceptions) $p \wedge q \mathrel{\vdash_\Delta} r, p \mathrel{\vdash_\Delta} \neg r \Rightarrow p \mathrel{\vdash_\Delta} \neg q$

**T-4**   (Right Conjunction) $p \mathrel{\vdash_\Delta} r, p \mathrel{\vdash_\Delta} q \Rightarrow p \mathrel{\vdash_\Delta} q \wedge r$

**Some Non-Theorems:**

(Transitivity) $p \supset q, q \mathrel{\vdash_\Delta} r \Rightarrow p \mathrel{\vdash_\Delta} r$

(Left Conjunction) $p \mathrel{\vdash_\Delta} r, q \mathrel{\vdash_\Delta} r \Rightarrow p \wedge q \mathrel{\vdash_\Delta} r$

(Contraposition) $p \mathrel{\vdash_\Delta} r \Rightarrow \neg r \mathrel{\vdash_\Delta} \neg p$

(Rational Monotony)

$$p \mathrel{\vdash_\Delta} r, \text{NOT}(p \mathrel{\vdash_\Delta} \neg q) \Rightarrow p \wedge q \mathrel{\vdash_\Delta} r \tag{6}$$

This last property (similar to CV of conditional logic) has one of its antecedents negated, hence, its consequences cannot be derived from $\Delta$ using the five rules above. It is, nevertheless, a desirable feature of a consequence relation, and was proposed by Makinson as a standard for nonmonotonic logics (Lehmann and Magidor 1988). Rational monotony can be restored within $\varepsilon$-semantics if we limit out attention to families of distributions $P_\varepsilon$ that are parameterized by $\varepsilon$ and are analytic in $\varepsilon$ (Goldszmidt et al 1990). Alternatively, rational monotony obtains if we interpret $\varepsilon$ as a nonstandard infinitesimal (in a non-standard analysis), which also amounts to interpreting $p \rightarrow q$ as an OCF constraint $\kappa(q|p) < \kappa(\neg q|p)$ (see section 8.4.1 and Pearl 1990).

The reason transitivity, positive conjunction, and contraposition are not sanctioned by the $\varepsilon$-semantics is clear: There are contexts in which they fail. For instance, transitivity fails in the penguin example—all penguins are birds, birds typically fly, yet penguins do not. Left conjunction fails when $p$ and $q$ create a new condition unshared by either $p$ or $q$. For example, if you marry Ann ($p$) you will be happy ($r$), if you marry Nancy ($q$) you will be happy as well ($r$), but if you marry both ($p \wedge q$), you will be miserable ($\neg r$). Contraposition fails in situations where $\neg p$ is incompatible with $\neg r$. For example, let $p \rightarrow r$ stand for *Birds* $\rightarrow$ *Fly*. Now imagine a world in which the only nonflying objects are a few sick birds. Clearly, *Bird* $\rightarrow$ *Fly* holds, yet if we observe a nonflying object we can safely conclude that it is a bird, hence $\neg r \rightarrow p$, defying contraposition.

THEOREM 2 ($\Delta$-monotonicity):   The inference system defined in theorem 1 is monotonic relative to the addition of default rules, that is,

$$\text{if } p \mathrel{\vert\!\sim}_\Delta r \text{ and } \Delta \subseteq \Delta', \text{ then } p \mathrel{\vert\!\sim}_{\Delta'} r \tag{7}$$

The proof follows directly from the fact that $\mathscr{P}_{\Delta',\varepsilon} \subseteq \mathscr{P}_{\Delta,\varepsilon}$ because each default statement imposes a new constraint on $\mathscr{P}_{\Delta,\varepsilon}$. Thus, the logic is nonmonotonic relative to the addition of new facts (in $F$) and monotonic relative to the addition of new defaults (in $\Delta$). Full nonmonotonicity will be exhibited in section 8.4, where we consider stronger forms of entailment.

### 8.3.3   Consistency and Ambiguity

An important feature of the system defined by rules 1–5 is its ability to distinguish theories portraying inconsistencies (e.g., $\langle p \rightarrow q, p \rightarrow \neg q \rangle$), from those conveying ambiguity (e.g., $\langle p \wedge q, p \rightarrow r, q \rightarrow \neg r \rangle$), and those conveying exceptions (e.g., $\langle p \rightarrow q, p \wedge r \rightarrow \neg q \rangle$).

*Definition:* $\Delta$ is said to be *$\varepsilon$-consistent* if $\mathscr{P}_{\Delta,\varepsilon}$ is non-empty for every $\varepsilon > 0$, else, $\Delta$ *is $\varepsilon$-inconsistent*. Similarly, a set of default statements $\{S_\alpha\}$ is said to be *$\varepsilon$-consistent with* $\Delta$ if $\Delta \cup \{S_\alpha\}$ is $\varepsilon$-consistent.

*Definition:* A default statement $S$ is said to be *ambiguous*, given $\Delta$, if both $S$ and its denial are consistent with $\Delta$.

THEOREM 3 (Adams 1975): If $\Delta$ is $\varepsilon$-consistent, then a statement $S$: $p \to q$ is $\varepsilon$-entailed by $\Delta$ iff its denial $S'$: $p \to \neg q$ is $\varepsilon$-inconsistent with $\Delta$.

In addition to rules 1–5 of theorem 1, the logic also possesses a systematic procedure for testing $\varepsilon$-consistency (hence, $\varepsilon$-entailment), involving a moderate number of propositional satisfiability tests.

*Definition:* Given a truth-valuation $t$, a default statement $p \to q$ is said to be *verified* under $t$ if $t$ assigns the value 1 to both $p$ and $q$. $p \to q$ is said to be *falsified* under $t$ if $p$ is assigned a 1 and $q$ is assigned a 0. A default statement $S$: $p \to q$ is said to be *tolerated* by a set $\Delta'$ of such statements if there is a $t$ that verifies $S$ and does not falsify any statement in $\Delta'$.

THEOREM 4 (Adams 1975): Let $\Delta$ be a finite set of default statements. $\Delta$ is $\varepsilon$-consistent iff in every non-empty subset $\Delta'$ of $\Delta$ there exists at least one statement that is tolerated by $\Delta'$.

COROLLARY 1 (Goldszmidt and Pearl 1989): Consistency (hence entailment) can be tested in $|\Delta|^2/2$ propositional satisfiability tests.

The procedure is simply to find every default statement that is tolerated by $\Delta$, remove those from $\Delta$, and repeat the process on the remaining set of statements, until there are no more default statements left. If this process leads to an empty set then $\Delta$ is $\varepsilon$-consistent, else it is inconsistent.

If the material counterpart of $p \supset q$ of each statement $p \to q$ in $\Delta$ is a Horn expression, then consistency can be tested in time quadratic with the number of literals in $\Delta$.

When $\Delta$ can be represented as a network of default rules, the criterion of theorem 4 translates into a simple graphical test for consistency, generalizing that of Touretzky (1986):

COROLLARY 2 (Pearl 1987a): Let $\Delta$ be a *default network*, that is, a set of default statements $p \to q$ where both $p$ and $q$ are atomic propositions (or negation thereof). $\Delta$ is consistent iff for every pair of conflicting arcs $p_1 \to q$ and $p_2 \to \neg q$

1. $p_1$ and $p_2$ are distinct, and
2. There is no cycle of positive arcs that embraces both $p_1$ and $p_2$.

Theorems 3, 4, and their corollaries are valid only when $\Delta$ consists of purely defeasible conditionals. For mixtures of defeasible and nondefeasible statements, consistency and entailment require a slightly modified procedure (Goldszmidt and Pearl 1989). This procedure attributes a special meaning to a strict conditional $a \Rightarrow b$, different than the material implication $a \supset b$. For example, conforming to common usage of conditionals, it proclaims $\{a \Rightarrow b, a \Rightarrow \neg b\}$ as inconsistent and will entail $a \Rightarrow b$ from $\neg b \Rightarrow \neg a$ but not from $\neg a$. Another extension of $\varepsilon$-semantics, permitting defaults to be given different strength, is treated in (Goldszmidt and Pearl 1991).

### 8.3.4  Illustrations

To illustrate the power of $\varepsilon$-semantics and, in particular, the syntactical and graphical derivations sanctioned by theorems 1, 3, and 4, consider the celebrated "Penguin triangle" of figure 8.1. $T$ comprises the sentences:

$$F = \{Penguin\ (Tweety), Bird(Tweety)\}, \tag{8}$$

$$\Delta = \{Penguin \rightarrow \neg fly, Bird \rightarrow Fly, Penguin \rightarrow Bird\}; \tag{9}$$

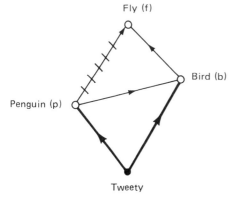

**Figure 8.1**
A network representing the knowledge base of equations (8) and (9). Heavy arcs represent evidence about individuals, thin arcs represent default statements, slashed arcs represent default denials. The arc between Penguin and Bird imposes specificity preference, yielding the conclusion "Tweety does not fly."

Although $\Delta$ does not specify explicitly whether penguin-birds fly, the desired conclusion is derived in three steps, using rules 1 and 3 of theorem 1:

1. *Penguin* (*Tweety*) $\vdash_\Delta \neg Fly$ (*Tweety*) (from Rule 1)
2. *Penguin* (*Tweety*) $\vdash_\Delta Bird$ (*Tweety*) (from Rule 1)
3. *Penguin* (*Tweety*), *Bird* (*Tweety*) $\vdash_\Delta \neg Fly$ (*Tweety*)
   (Applying rule 3 to lines 1, 2)

Note that preference toward subclass specificity is maintained despite the defeasible nature of the rule *Penguin* $\rightarrow$ *Bird*, which admits exceptional penguins in the form of non-birds.

We can also derive this result using theorems 3 and 4 by showing that the denial of the conclusion $p \wedge b \rightarrow \neg f$ is $\varepsilon$-inconsistent with

$$\Delta = \{p \rightarrow \neg f, b \rightarrow f, p \rightarrow b\}. \tag{10}$$

Indeed, no truth-valuation of $\{p, b, f\}$ can verify any sentence in

$$\Delta' = \{p \rightarrow \neg f, p \rightarrow b, p \wedge b \rightarrow f\} \tag{11}$$

without falsifying at least one other sentence.

Applying theorem T-3 to the network of figure 8.1 yields another plausible conclusion. *Bird* $\rightarrow \neg Penguin$, stating that when one talks about birds one does not have penguins in mind, that is, penguins are exceptional kind of birds. It is a valid conclusion of $\Delta$ because every $P$ in $\mathscr{P}_{\Delta, \varepsilon}$ must yield $P(p \mid b) = O(\varepsilon)$. Of course, if the statement *Bird* $\rightarrow$ *Penguin* is artificially added to $\Delta$, inconsistency results; as $\varepsilon$ diminishes below a certain level (1/3 in our case), $\mathscr{P}_{\Delta, \varepsilon}$ becomes empty. This can be predicted from purely topological considerations (corollary 2), since adding the arc *Bird* $\rightarrow$ *Penguin* would create a cycle of positive arcs embracing "bird" and "penguin," and these sprout two conflicting arcs toward "fly." Moreover, theorem 3 implies that if a network becomes inconsistent by the addition of $S$, then that network $\varepsilon$-entails its denial, $S'$. Hence, the network of Figure 8.1 $\varepsilon$-entails *Bird* $\rightarrow \neg Penguin$. By the same graphical method one can easily show that the network also $\varepsilon$-entails the natural conclusion, *Fly* $\rightarrow \neg Penguin$. This contraposition of *Penguin* $\rightarrow \neg Fly$ is sanctioned only because the existence of flying objects that are not penguins (i.e., normal birds) is guaranteed by the other rules in $\Delta$.

## 8.4    The Adventurous Shell

The preceding adaptation of Adams's logic of conditionals yields a system of defeasible inference with rather unique features:

1. The system provides a formal distinction between exceptions, ambiguities, and inconsistencies and offers systematic methods of testing and maintaining consistency.

2. Multiple extensions do not arise, and preferences among arguments (e.g., toward higher specificity) are respected by natural deduction.

3. There is no need to specify abnormality relations in advance (as in circumscription); such relations (e.g., that penguins are abnormal birds) are automatically inferred from the knowledge base.

However, default reasoning requires two facilities: one which forces conclusions to be retractable in the light of new refuting evidence; the second which protects conclusions from retraction in the light of new but irrelevant evidence. Rules 1–5 excel on the first requirement but fail on the second. For instance, in the example of figure 8.1, if we are told that Tweety is also a blue penguin, the system would retract all previous conclusions (as ambiguous), even though there is no rule which in any way connects color to flying. (The opposite is true in default logics—they excel on the second requirement but do not retract conclusions refuted by more specific information, unless all exceptions are enumerated in advance [Reiter 1987].)

The reason for this conservative behavior lies in our insistence that any issued conclusion attains high probability in *all* probability models licensed by Δ and one such model reflects a world in which blue penguins do fly. It is clear that if we want the system to respect the communication convention that, unless stated explicitly, properties are presumed to be *irrelevant* to each other, we need to restrict the family of probability models relative to which a given conclusion must be checked for soundness. In other words, we should consider only distributions which minimize dependencies relative to Δ, that is, they embody dependencies which are absolutely implied by Δ, and no others.

### 8.4.1    System Z

One way of suppressing irrelevant properties is to restrict our attention to the "most normal" or "least surprising" probability models that comply with the constraints in $\Delta$. This can be most conveniently done within the nonstandard analysis of Spohn (see section 8.2.2), where $\kappa(w)$ represents the degree of surprise associated with world $w$. To ratify a sentence $p \to q$ within this paradigm, we must first find the minimal $\kappa$ distribution permitted by the constraints in $\Delta$ and, then, test whether $\kappa(q|p) < \kappa(\neg q|p)$ holds in this distribution.

Translating the constraints of equation (4) to the language of nonstandard analysis, yields

$$\kappa(v \wedge u) < \kappa(\neg v \wedge u) \quad \text{if } u \to u \in \Delta \tag{12.a}$$

where $\kappa$ of a formula $f$ is given by

$$\kappa(f) = \min_w \{\kappa(w) : w \models f\} \tag{12.b}$$

Remarkably, these constraints admit a unique minimal $\kappa$ distribution whenever $\Delta$ is $\varepsilon$-consistent. Moreover, finding this minimal distribution, which was named $\mathbf{Z}$-ranking in Pearl 1990, requires no more computation than testing for $\varepsilon$-consistency according to corollary 1. We first identify all default statements in $\Delta$ that are tolerated by $\Delta$, assign to them a $\mathbf{Z}$-rank of 0, and remove them from $\Delta$. Next we assign a $\mathbf{Z}$-rank of 1 to every default statement that is tolerated by the remaining set, and so on. Continuing in this way, we form an ordered partition of $\Delta = (\Delta_0, \Delta_1, \Delta_2, \ldots, \Delta_K)$, where $\Delta_i$ consists of all statements tolerated by $\Delta - \Delta_0 - \Delta_1 - \ldots \Delta_{i-1}$. This partition uncovers a natural priority among the default rules in $\Delta$, and represents the relative "cost" associated with violating any of these defaults, with preference given to the more specific classes.

Once we establish the $\mathbf{Z}$-ranking on defaults, the minimal ranking on worlds is given as follows:

THEOREM 5 (Pearl 1990):    Out of all ranking functions $\kappa(w)$ satisfying the constraints in equation (12) the one that achieves the lowest $\kappa$ for each world $w$ is unique and is given by

$$\mathbf{Z}(w) = \min\{n : w \models (v \supset u), \mathbf{Z}(v \to u) \geq n\} \tag{13}$$

In other words, $\mathbf{Z}(w)$ is equal to 1 plus the rank of the highest-ranked default statement falsified in $w$.

Given $\mathbf{Z}(w)$, we can now define a useful extension of $\varepsilon$-entailment, which was called *1-entailment* in Pearl 1990.

*Definition* (1-entailment):    A formula $g$ is said to be *1-entailed* by $f$, in the context $\Delta$, (written $f \mathrel{|\!\sim}_1 g$), if $g$ holds in all minimal-$\mathbf{Z}$ worlds satisfying $f$. In other words,

$$f \mathrel{|\!\sim}_1 g \quad \text{iff} \quad \mathbf{Z}(f \wedge g) < \mathbf{Z}(f \wedge \neg g) \tag{14}$$

Note that $\varepsilon$-entailment is clearly a subset of 1-entailment.

Lehmann (1989) has extended $\varepsilon$-entailment in a different way, syntactically closing it under the *rational monotony* rule of equation 6, thus obtaining a new consequence relation which he called *rational closure*. Goldszmidt and Pearl (1990) have shown that 1-entailment and rational closure are identical whenever $\Delta$ is $\varepsilon$-consistent. Thus, the procedure of testing $\varepsilon$-consistency also provides a $|\Delta^2|/2$-time procedure for testing entailment in rational closure.

Figure 8.2 represents a knowledge base formed by adding three rules to that of figure 8.1:

1. "Penguins live in the antarctic"    $p \to a$

2. "Birds have wings"    $b \to w$

3. "Animals that fly are mobile"    $f \to m$

The numerical labels on the arcs stand for the $\mathbf{Z}$-ranking of the corresponding rules. The following are examples of plausible consequences that can be drawn from $\Delta$ by the various systems discussed in this section (ME will be discussed in section 8.4.2):

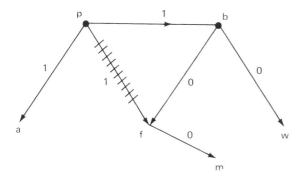

**Figure 8.2**
A knowledge base containing six defaults together with their $\mathbf{Z}$-labels.

| $\varepsilon$-entailed | 1-entailed | $ME$-entailed |
|---|---|---|
| $b \wedge p \mathrel{\vdash_\Delta} \neg f$ | $\neg b \mathrel{\vdash_1} \neg p$ | $p \mathrel{\vdash_{ME}} w$ |
| $f \mathrel{\vdash_\Delta} \neg p$ | $\neg f \mathrel{\vdash_1} \neg b$ | $p \wedge \neg a \mathrel{\vdash_{ME}} \neg f$ |
| $b \mathrel{\vdash_\Delta} \neg p$ | $\neg f \mathrel{\vdash_1} m$ | $p \wedge \neg a \mathrel{\vdash_{ME}} w$ |
| $p \wedge a \mathrel{\vdash_\Delta} b$ | $\neg m \mathrel{\vdash_1} \neg b$ | |
| | $p \wedge \neg w \mathrel{\vdash_1} b$ | |

1-entailment sanctions many plausible inference patterns that are not $\varepsilon$-entailed, among them chaining, contraposition and discounting irrelevant features. For example, from the knowledge base of figure 8.2 we can now conclude that birds are mobile, $b \mathrel{\vdash_1} m$, and that immobile objects are non-birds, $\neg m \mathrel{\vdash_1} \neg b$, and that green birds still fly. On the other hand, 1-entailment does not permit us to conclude that penguins who do not live in the antarctic still do not fly, $p \wedge \neg a \to \neg f$.

The main weakness of 1-entailment is its inability to sanction property inheritance from classes to exceptional sub-classes. For example, from $\Delta = \{a \to b, c \to d\}$ we cannot conclude $a \wedge \neg b \wedge c \to d$. Likewise, given the knowledge base of figure 8.2, 1-entailment will not sanction the conclusion that penguins have wings ($p \to w$) by virtue of being birds (albeit exceptional birds). The reason is that according to the Z-ranking procedure all statements conditioned on $p$ should obtain a rank of 1, and this amounts to proclaiming penguins an exceptional type of birds in *all* respects, barred from inheriting *any* bird-like properties (e.g., laying eggs, having beaks). To sanction property inheritance across exceptional classes, a more refined ordering is required which also takes into account the *number* of defaults falsified in a given world, not merely their rank orders. One such refinement is provided by the maximum-entropy approach (Goldszmidt, Morris, and Pearl 1990) where each world is ranked by the sum of weights on the defaults falsified by that world. Another refinement is provided by Geffner's conditional entailment (Geffner 1989), where the priority of defaults induces a *partial* order on worlds. These two refinements will be summarized next.

### 8.4.2 The Maximum Entropy Approach

The maximum-entropy (ME) approach (Pearl 1988) is motivated by the convention that, unless mentioned explicitly, properties are presumed to be independent of one another, such presumptions are normally embedded in probability distributions that attain the maximum entropy subject to a set of constraints. Given a set $\Delta$ of default rules and a family of probability distributions that are admissible relative the constraints conveyed by $\Delta$ (i.e., $P(\beta_r \rightarrow \alpha_r) \geq 1 - \varepsilon \, \forall r \in \Delta$), we single out a distinguished distribution $P^*_{\varepsilon,\Delta}$ having the greatest entropy $-\sum_w P(w) \log(w)$, and define entailment relative to this distribution by

$$f \mathrel{\vphantom{|}\rule[0.1ex]{0.6em}{0.08ex}\!\!\!\sim}_{\text{ME}} g \quad \text{iff} \quad P^*_{\varepsilon,\Delta}(g|f) \underset{\varepsilon \rightarrow 0}{\rightarrow} 1. \tag{15}$$

An infinitesimal analysis of the ME approach also yields a ranking function $\kappa$ on worlds, where $\kappa(w)$ corresponds to the lowest exponent of $\varepsilon$ in the expansion of $P^*_{\varepsilon,\Delta}(w)$ into a power series in $\varepsilon$. It can be shown that this ranking function can be encoded parsimoniously by assigning an integer weight $\kappa_r$ to each default rule $r \in \Delta$ and letting $\kappa(w)$ be the sum of the weights associated with the rules falsified by $w$. The weight $\kappa_r$, in turn, reflects the "cost" we must add to each world $w$ that falsifies rule $r$, so that the resulting ranking function would satisfy the constraints conveyed by $\Delta$, namely,

$$\min\{\kappa(w): w \models \alpha_r \wedge \beta_r\} < \min\{\kappa(w): w \models \alpha_r \wedge \neg\beta_r\}, \quad r: \alpha_r \rightarrow \beta_r \in \Delta. \tag{16}$$

These considerations lead to a set of $|\Delta|$ nonlinear equations for the weights $\kappa_r$, which, under certain conditions, can be solved by iterative methods. Once the rule weights are established, ME-entailment is determined by the criterion of equation (15), translated to

$$f \mathrel{\vphantom{|}\rule[0.1ex]{0.6em}{0.08ex}\!\!\!\sim}_{\text{ME}} g \quad \text{iff} \quad \min\{\kappa(w): w \models f \wedge g\} < \min\{\kappa(w): w \models f \wedge \neg g\} \tag{17}$$

where

$$\kappa(w) = \sum_{r: w \models \alpha_r \wedge \neg\beta_r} \kappa_r$$

We see that ME-entailment requires minimization over worlds, a task that is $NP$-hard even for Horn expressions (Ben-Eliyahu 1990). In practice, however, this minimization is accomplished quite effectively in network type databases, yielding a reasonable set of inference patterns. For example, in the database of figure 8.2, ME-entailment will sanction the desired consequences $p \mathrel{\vphantom{|}\rule[0.1ex]{0.6em}{0.08ex}\!\!\!\sim} w$, $p \wedge \neg a \mathrel{\vphantom{|}\rule[0.1ex]{0.6em}{0.08ex}\!\!\!\sim} \neg f$ and $p \wedge \neg a \mathrel{\vphantom{|}\rule[0.1ex]{0.6em}{0.08ex}\!\!\!\sim} w$ and, moreover, unlike 1-entailment it will conclude $c \wedge p \mathrel{\vphantom{|}\rule[0.1ex]{0.6em}{0.08ex}\!\!\!\sim}_1 \neg f$ from $\Delta \cup \{c \rightarrow f\}$, where $c$ is an irrelevant property.

An interesting feature of the ME approach is its sensitivity to the format in which the rules are expressed. This is illustrated in the following example. From $\Delta$ = {Swedes are blond, Swedes are well mannered}, ME will conclude that dark-haired Swedes are still well mannered, while no such conclusion will be drawn from $\Delta$ = {Swedes are blond and well mannered}. This sensitivity might sometimes be useful for distinguishing fine nuances in natural discourse, indicating, for example, that behavior and hair color are two independent qualities (as opposed, say, to hair color and eye color). However, it stands at variance with most approaches to default reasoning, where $a \rightarrow b \wedge c$ is treated as a shorthand notation of $a \rightarrow b$ and $a \rightarrow c$.

The failure to respond to causal information (see Pearl 1988: 463, 519 and Hunter 1989) prevents the ME approach from properly handling tasks such as the Yale shooting problem (Hanks and McDermott 1986), where rules of causal character should be given priority over other rules. This weakness may perhaps be overcome by introducing causal operators into the ME formulation, similar to the way causal operators are incorporated within other formalisms of nonmonotonic reasoning (e.g., Shoham 1986, Geffner 1989).

### 8.4.3   Conditional Entailment

Geffner (1989) has overcome the weaknesses of 1-entailment by introducing two new refinements. First, rather than letting rule priorities dictate a ranking function on worlds, a partial order on worlds is induced instead. To determine the preference between two worlds, $w$ and $w'$, we examine the highest priority default rules that distinguish between the two, that is, that are falsified by one and not by the other. If all such rules remain unfalsified in one of the two worlds, then this world is the preferred one. Formally, if $\Delta[w]$ and $\Delta[w']$ stand for the set of rules falsified by $w$ and $w'$, respectively, then $w$ is preferred to $w'$ (written $w < w'$) iff $\Delta[w'] \neq \Delta[w']$ and for every rule $r$ in $\Delta[w] - \Delta[w']$ there exists a rule $r'$ in $\Delta[w'] - \Delta[w]$ such that $r'$ has a higher priority than $r$ (written $r \prec r'$). Using this criterion, a world $w$ will always be preferred to $w'$ if it falsifies a proper subset of the rules falsified by $w'$. Lacking this feature in the Z-ordering has prevented 1-entailment from concluding $p \mathrel{\vert\kern-0.4em\sim} w$ in the example of figure 8.2.

The second refinement introduced by Geffner is allowing the rule-priority relation, $\prec$, to become a partial order as well. This partial order is determined by the following interpretation of the rule $\alpha \rightarrow \beta$; if $\alpha$ is all that we know, then, regardless of other rules that $\Delta$ may contain, we are authorized to assert $\beta$. This means that $r: \alpha \to \beta$ should get a higher priority than any argument (a chain of rules) leading from $\alpha$ to $\neg\beta$ and, more generally, if a set of rules $\Delta' \subset \Delta$ does not tolerate $r$, then at least one rule in $\Delta'$ ought to have a lower priority than $r$. In figure 8.2, for example, the rule $r_3: p \wedge \neg f$ is not tolerated by the set $\{r_1: p \to b, r_2: b \to f\}$, hence, we must have $r_1 \prec r_3$ or $r_2 \prec r_3$. Similarly, the rule $r_1: p \to b$ is not tolerated by $\{r_2, r_3\}$, hence, we also have $r_2 \prec r_1$ or $r_3 \prec r_1$. From the asymmetry and transitivity of $\prec$, these two conditions yield $r_2 \prec r_3$ and $r_2 \prec r_1$. It is clear, then, that this priority on rules will induce the preference $w < w'$ whenever $w$ validates $p \wedge b \wedge \neg f$ and $w'$ validates $p \wedge b \wedge f$; the former falsifies $r_2$, while the latter falsifies the higher priority rule $r_3$. In general, we say that a proposition $g$ is *conditionally entailed* by $f$ (in the context of $\Delta$) if $g$ holds in all the preferred worlds of $f$ induced by every priority ordering admissible with $\Delta$.

Conditional entailment bridges the conditional and dispositional approaches to default reasoning. It rectifies the shortcomings of 1-entailment and ME-entailment. However, having been based on model minimization as well as on enumeration of subsets of rules, its computational complexity might be overbearing. A proof theory for conditional entailment and its unification with causal theories can be found in Geffner 1989.

### 8.4.4 Dialectic Approaches

Dialectic approaches attempt to supplement the probabilistic interpretation of defaults with a set of assumptions about conditional independence drawn on the basis of the syntactic structure of $\Delta$. For a default $p \to q$, these approaches assume the probability of $q$ to be high not only when $p$ is all that is known, but also in the presence of an additional body of evidence which does not provide an *argument* against $q$ (Loui 1987, Pollock 1987). This interpretation is closer in spirit to the syntactic approaches to nonmonotonic reasoning proposed by Reiter (1980) and McDermott and Doyle (1980), which allow us to infer $q$ from $p$ in the absence of "proofs" for $\neg q$.

In the systems reported in Geffner and Pearl 1988 and Geffner 1988, these ideas take the form of an additional inference rule, similar to:

RULE 6:   Irrelevance

If $p \to r \in \Delta$ and $I_\Delta(q, \neg r \mid p)$, then $p \wedge q \vdash_\Delta r$,

where the predicate $I_\Delta(q, \neg r \mid p)$, which reads: "$q$ is irrelevant to $\neg r$ given $p$," expresses the conditional independence $P(r \mid p) \approx P(r \mid p, q)$.

The mechanism for evaluating the irrelevance predicate $I_\Delta(q, \neg r|p)$ appeals to the set $\psi'$ of wffs formed by converting each default $p \to q$ in $\Delta$ into a corresponding material implication $p \supset q$. In essence, $q$ is then said to be *relevant to* $\neg r$ given $p$, if there is a a set $\psi'$ of implications in $\psi$ which permit an *argument* for $\neg r$ to be constructed, i.e if $\psi'$, $p$, $q \vdash \neg r$, with the set of wffs $\psi' \cup p, q$ being logically consistent. The set $\psi'$ is called the *support* of the argument for $\neg r$. If $q$ is not relevant to $\neg r$ given $p$, then $q$ is assumed to be *irrelevant to* $\neg r$ in that context, and $I_\Delta(q, \neg r|p)$ thus holds.

This simple extension permits us to infer, for instance, that red birds are likely to fly given a default stating that birds fly, as "redness" does not induce any argument in support of not flying. Further refinements are installed to insure that arguments for $\neg r$ that are blocked by $p$ (or its consequences) do not bear on the predicate $I_\Delta$. With this refinement, most examples analyzed in the literature yield the expected results.

Dialectic approaches constitute an alternative way of extending the inferential power of the core set of probabilistic rules. An advantage of these approaches over those based on maximum entropy is intelligibility: derivations under this approach can usually be justified in a more natural fashion. On the other hand, these approaches lack the foundational basis of a principle like maximum entropy, making it difficult to justify and make precise the form these extensions should take.

## 8.5   Do People Reason with Extreme Probabilities (or Lotteries and other Paradoxes of Abstraction)

Neufeld and Poole (1988) have raised the following objection (so-called Dingo Paradox) in connection with the theorem of exceptions (T-3). We saw that the penguin triangle (fig. 8.1) sanctions the conclusion *Bird* → ¬*Penguin* by virtue of the fact that penguins are an exceptional class of birds (relative to flying). Similarly, if "sandpipers" are birds that build nests in sand, we would conclude *Bird* → ¬*Sandpiper*. Continuing in this manner through all types of birds, and assuming that every subclass of birds has a unique, distinguishing trait, we soon end up with the conclusion that birds do not exist—birds are not penguins, not sandpipers, not canaries, and so on—thus ruling out all types of birds.

This paradox is a variant of the celebrated Lottery Paradox (Kyburg 1961): Knowing that a lottery is about to have one winner is incompatible with common beliefs that each individual ticket is, by default, a loser. Indeed, the criterion provided by ε-semantics would proclaim the overall set of such statements ε-inconsistent, since the set of conditional probabilities

$$P(Loser(i) | Ticket(i)) \geq 1 - \varepsilon \qquad i = 1, 2, \ldots, N$$

cannot be satisfied simultaneously for $\varepsilon < 1/N$. Perlis (1987) has further shown that every default logic is bound to suffer from some version of the lottery paradox if we insist on maintaining deductive closure among beliefs.

Are these paradoxes detrimental to ε-semantics, or to nonmonotonic logics in general? I would like to argue that they are not. On the contrary, I view these paradoxes as healthy reminders that in all forms of reasoning we are dealing with simplified abstractions of real-world knowledge, that we may occasionally step beyond the boundaries of one abstraction and that, in such a case, a more refined abstraction should be substituted.

Predicate logic and probability theory are two such abstractions, and ε-semantics offers an abstraction that is somewhere between logic and probability. It requires less input than probability theory (e.g., we need not specify numerical probabilities), but more input than logic (e.g., we need to distinguish between defaults, $a \rightarrow b$, and observations, $\neg a \vee b$). It is more conservative than logic (e.g., it does not sanction transitivity), but more adventurous than probability theory (e.g., it admits conclusions even if their probabilities approach 1 very slowly, such as $= (1 - \varepsilon)^N$.

Each abstraction constitutes an expedient simplification of reality, tailored to serve a specialized set of tasks. Each simplification is supported by a different symbol processing machinery and by a set of norms, to verify whether the simplification and its supporting machinery are still applicable. The lottery paradox represents a situation where ε-semantics no longer offers a useful abstraction of reality. Fortunately, however, the consistency norms help us identify such situations in advance, and alert us (in case our decisions depend critically on making extensive use of the disjunction axiom) that a finer abstraction should be in order (perhaps full-fledged probability theory).

Probabilities that are infinitesimally close to 0 and 1 are very rare in the real world. Most default rules used in ordinary discourse maintain a non-vanishing percentage of exceptions, simply because the number of objects in every meaningful class is finite. Thus, a natural question to ask is, why study the properties of an abstraction that applies only to extreme probabilities? Why not develop a logic that characterizes moderately high probabilities, say probabilities higher than 0.5 or 0.9—or more ambitiously, higher than $\alpha$, where $\alpha$ is a parameter chosen to fit the domains of the predicates involved? Further, why not develop a logic that takes into account utility information, not merely probabilities, thus formalizing reasoning about actions, in addition to beliefs (Doyle 1988)?

The answer is that any such alternative logic would be too complicated; it would need to invoke many of the axioms of arithmetic, and would require more information than is usually available. Almost none of the patterns of reasoning found in common conversation will remain sound relative to such semantics. Take, for example, the logic of "majority," namely, interpreting the default rule $a \to b$ to mean "The majority of $a$s are $b$s," or $P(b|a) > 0.5$. Only the first two axioms of theorem 1 remain sound in this interpretation. Even the cumulativity axiom (rule 3, theorem 1), which is rarely disputed as a canon of default reasoning, is flatly violated by some proportions (e.g., $P(q|p) = 0.51$ and $P(r|p) = 0.51$ could yield $P(r|p \wedge q) = 0.02$, in case $P(\neg q \wedge \neg r) = 0$.)

How, then, do people reason qualitatively about properties and classes, proportions and preferences? It appears that, if the machinery invoked by people for such tasks stems from approximating numerical information by a set of expedient abstractions, then the semantics of extreme probabilities is one of the most popular among these abstractions. The axioms governing this semantics (i.e., rules 1–5, theorem 1) appears to have been thoroughly entrenched as inference rules in plausible reasoning. For example, from the sentences "Most students are males" and "Most students will get an A," the cumulativity axiom would infer "Most male students will get an A." This conclusion can be grossly incorrect, as shown in the paragraph above, yet it is a rather common inference made by people, given these two inputs. In conclusion, it appears that the machinery of plausible reasoning reflects a remarkable agreement with the rules of "almost all" logic.[2]

## 8.6   Relations to Other Nonmonotonic Systems

The logic closest in spirit to the probabilistic approaches presented in the preceding sections are those based on model preferences, where conclusions

---

[2] In an earlier version of this paper, as well as in Pearl 1988, I have speculated that this agreement indicates that plausible reasoning is more in line with the rules of "almost all" logic than with those of "support" or "majority" logics. I am now in the opinion that this agreement is more reflective of tacit assumptions of independence than of the type of logic chosen by people to reason about proportions. In our example, the conclusion "most students will receive an A" reflects the assumption that grades are independent of gender. The same holds for my analysis of the Simpson paradox (Pearl 1988).

are sanctioned relative to the minimal (or least abnormal) models of the theory. The reason for this closeness is that, if we regard probability weights as measures of "normality," then probability theory is essentially a theory of preferences among models. The main point of departure, however, is that in probability theory formulae are scored by the *sum of the weights* on models that validate the formulae while in model-preference logic a formula assumes the weight of its *maximal-weight* model. The practical implications of this difference is best illustrated by comparing qualitative and probabilistic approaches to abduction.

### 8.6.1  Probabilistic and Qualitative Abduction

In the probabilistic approach, abduction is considered the task of finding the "most probable explanation" of the evidence observed, namely, seeking an instantiation of a set of explanatory variables that attains the highest probability, conditioned on the evidence observed. Assume that we have a probability function $P$ defined on the set $W$ of possible worlds. One way of accounting for abductive beliefs is to posit that, at any state of knowledge, beliefs are fully committed to a world that has the highest probability. In other words, a proposition $A$ is *believed* if $A$ holds in some $w^* \in W^*$, where $W^* \subseteq W$ is the set of most probable worlds,

$$W^* = \{w^* \mid P(w^*) \geq P(w) \ \forall w \in W\}.$$

To maintain coherence, we also demand that any set of propositions that are simultaneously believed, must hold in the same $w^*$. Nonmonotonic behavior is obtained by conditionalization; given a body of evidence (facts) $e$, the probability function $P(w)$ shifts to $P(w|e)$ and this yields a new set of most probable worlds

$$W_e^* = \{w^* \mid P(w^*|e) \geq P(w|e) \ \forall w \in W\}.$$

which, in turn, results in a new set of beliefs.

This approach to abduction was explored in Pearl 1987b, where a world was defined as an assignment of values to a set of interdependent variables (e.g., assignment of *TRUE-FALSE* values to a set of diseases in medical diagnosis), and the worlds in $W^*$ were called *most probable explanations* (MPE). It was shown that the task of finding a most probable explanation of a body of evidence is no more complex than that of computing the probability of a single proposition. In singly connected networks (directed trees with unrestricted orientation) the task can be accomplished in linear time, using a parallel and distributed message-passing process. In multiply connected networks, the problem is NP-hard; however, clustering, conditioning and stochastic simulation techniques can offer practical solutions in reasonable time if the network is relatively sparse. Applications to circuit and medical diagnosis are described in Geffner and Pearl 1987, Pearl 1988, and Peng and Reggia 1987.

The MPE approach provides a bridge between probabilistic reasoning and nonmonotonic logic. Like the latter, the method provides systematic rules that lead from a set of factual sentences (the evidence) to a set of conclusion sentences (the accepted beliefs) in a way that need not be truth-preserving. However, whereas the input-output sentences are categorical, the medium through which inferences are produced is numerical, and the parameters needed for complete specification of $P(w)$ may not be readily available. In modeling man-made systems such as digital circuits this problem is not too severe, because all internal relationships are provided with the system's specifications. However, in medical diagnosis, as well as in reasoning about everyday affairs, the requirement of specifying a complete probabilistic model is too cumbersome and can be justified only in cases where critical decisions are at stake.

The qualitative approaches demand fewer judgments in constructing the knowledge base, but suffer from the lack of rating among competing explanations and, closely related to it, the lack of rating among pending information sources. To overcome this deficiency, the qualitative approaches make explicit appeal to explanatory scenarios, and seek scenarios that are both coherent and parsimonious.

A major challenge facing and the qualitative approaches is to enforce an appropriate separation between the *prospective* and *retrospective* modes of reasoning so as to capture the intuition that predictions should not trigger suggestions. To use my favorite example: "Sprinkler On" predicts "Wet Grass," "Wet Grass" suggests "Rain," but "Sprinkler On" should not suggest "Rain." In the probabilistic approach such separation is enforced via the patterns of independencies that are assumed to accompany causal relationships. In the qualitative approaches the separation is accomplished in two ways. One is to label sentences as either *causally established* (i.e., explained) or *evidentially established* (i.e., conjectured) and subject each type to a different set of inference rules (Pearl 1988a; Geffner 1989). The second method is to regard abduction as a specialized metaprocess that operates on a causal theory (Poole 1987; Reiter 1987).

In qualitative theories simplicity is enforced by explicitly encoding the preference of simple theories over complex ones, where simple and complex are given syntactical definitions, for example, smallest number of (cohesive) propositions (Thagard 1989) or minimal covering (Reiter 1987; Reggia et al. 1983). These syntactic ratings do not always coincide with the notion of plausibility, for example, two common diseases are often more plausible than a single rare disease in explaining a given set of symptoms (Reggia 1989). In probabilistic theories, coherence and simplicity are managed together by one basic principle—maximum posterior probability.

### 8.6.2   Relation to Model Preference Semantics

The model preference approach to nonmonotic reasoning (Shoham 1987) leaves room for widely different interpretations of defaults, ranging from the adventurous to the conservative. The adventurous approach takes the statement $A \rightarrow B$ to mean: Every world where $A \wedge B$ holds has a prima facie preference over the corresponding world where $A \wedge \neg B$ holds, everything else being equal (the terms "world" and "models" are used interchangeably in the literature). Conflicts are later resolved by extra logical procedures (Selman and Kautz 1988). The conservative school (Lehmann and Magidor 1988, DelGrande 1988) takes $A \rightarrow B$ to be a faint reflection of a preexisting preference relation, saying merely: $B$ holds in all the most preferred worlds compatible with $A$. Whether a collection of such faint clues is sufficient to reveal information (about the preference relation) that entails a new statement $x \rightarrow y$, depends on the type of restrictions the preference relation is presumed to satisfy.

Lehmann and Magidor (1988) have identified the class of preference relations, whose consequence relation satisfies a reasonable set of rationality requirements including, for example, cumulativity and rational monotony. In essence, the restriction is that states of worlds be *ranked* (e.g., by some numerical score $r$) such that a state of lower rank is preferred to a state of higher rank. Lehmann and Magidor proved that the consequence relation induced by this class of ranked worlds coincides exactly with Adams's $\varepsilon$-entailment relation defined in equation (4) and, of course, its properties coincide with rules 1–5 of theorem 1.

It is remarkable that two totally different interpretations of defaults yield identical sets of conclusions and identical sets of reasoning machinery. Note that, even if we equate rank with probability, the interpretation $P(B|A) > 1 - \varepsilon$ is different from the model preference interpretation, because, for any finite $\varepsilon$, the former permits the most probable world of $A$ to be incompatible with $B$. Fortunately, the two interpretations coincide in the language of non-standard analysis (see sections 8.2.2 and 8.4.1). Based on this coincidence, it is now possible to transport shortcuts and intuitions across semantical lines. For example, theorem 3 establishes a firm connection between preferential entailment and preferential consistency. Similarly, theorems 4 and 5 determine the complexity of proving entailment in model preference semantics.

Perhaps the deepest point of tension between probability and traditional nonmonotonic logics revolves around the issue of specificity-based arguments, that is, finding ways to ensure that inferences be based on the most specific classes for which information is available (e.g., the inference that a penguin cannot fly must override the inference that a bird can fly). In the case of Reiter's default logic (Reiter 1980), this requires semi-normal rules, which explicitly enumerate exceptions (e.g. birds fly, unless they are penguins or ostriches or ...). In the case of circumscription, we must supply priorities among abnormalities (McCarthy 1986). Touretzky (1986) has argued that the enumeration of exceptions places an impractical burden on the management of inheritance networks, and he showed how attention to "inferential distance" in the network can assure priority for more specific arguments without such explicit enumeration. In section 8.3, we saw that specificity-based priorities were obtained naturally from probability theory, even if numerical probabilities are not used, provided that we interpret defaults as statements of high conditional probability, infinitesimally close to one. Identical facility is provided by the conditional logics of Lehmann and Magidor (1988) and of DelGrande (1988).

What sets these systems apart from circumscription and Reiter's default logics is the distinction between *knowledge* and *facts* ($\Delta$ and $F$) a distinction that, for some reason has not been totally accepted throughout the nonmonotonic community. Intuitively, the knowledge component specifies the tendency of things to happen, that is, relations that hold true in all worlds, while the facts or "observations" describe that which actually happened, that is, one particular world. In other words, the knowledge base $\Delta$ contains information that is equivalent to meta inference rules, telling us how to process "observations" to get conclusions about a particular situation or a particular individual.

In section 8.3 we saw, for example, that it makes a profound difference whether the sentence "all penguins are birds" is treated as a rule $p \rightarrow b$ in the knowledge base $\Delta$, or as observational formula $\neg p \lor b$ in $F$. The latter would represent the English sentence "It has been observed that Tweety is either a non-penguin or a bird." The former is treated as constraint that shapes the set of admissible probability distributions (or $\kappa$ rankings) while the latter serves as evidence upon which the admissible distributions are to be conditioned. The former gives the intended results, properly treating penguins as subclass of birds. The latter does not, because the observation $\neg p \vee b$ can be totally subsumed by other observations, say $p \wedge b$, thus yielding identical conclusions regardless of whether penguins are a subclass of birds or birds are a subclass of penguins.[3]

## Acknowledgments

I am grateful to Ernest Adams, Hector Geffner, Moises Goldszmidt, Daniel Lehmann, David Makinson, Menachen Magidor, and Paul Morris for providing helpful comments on several topics of this paper. This work was supported in part by National Science Foundation Grant #IRI-8821444 and Naval Research Laboratory Grant #N00014-87-K-2029. An earlier version of this paper was presented at the First International Conference on Principles of Knowledge Representation and Reasoning (KR '89), Toronto, May 1989.

## References

Adams, E. 1975. *The logic of conditionals*. Dordrecht, Netherlands: D. Reidel.

Bacchus, F. 1988. Representing and reasoning with probabilistic knowledge. Ph.D. dissertation, Dept. of Computer Science, University of Alberta, Edmonton.

Ben-Eliyahu, R. 1990. Minimizing Horn-Clause violations is NP-hard UCLA Cognitive Systems Laboratory, Computer Science Dept., *Technical Report* R-158.

DelGrande, J. P. 1988. An approach to default reasoning based on first-order conditional logic; revised report. *Artificial Intelligence*, 36:63-90.

Doyle, J. 1988. On universal theories of defaults. *Technical Report* CMU-CS-88-11. Carnegie Mellon University.

Geffner, H., and J. Pearl. 1988. A framework for reasoning with defaults. UCLA Cognitive Systems Laboratory, *Technical Report* 870058 (R-94), March 1988. Also in Kyburg et al. (eds.) *Knowledge Representation and Defeasible Reasoning*, Kluwer, pp. 61-87 1990.

Geffner, H. 1988. On the logic of defaults. *Proceedings of the National Conference on AI (AAAI-88)*, St. Paul, 449-454.

---

[3] The story of the paper (Geffner and Pearl 1988) exemplifies the traditional resistance to distinguishing between knowledge and observations. This paper was rejected by the CSCSI-88 Conference Committee, because the referee would not allow conclusions to change as sentences move from $F$ to $\Delta$.

Geffner, H. 1989. Default reasoning: causal and conditional theories. Ph.D. dissertation, UCLA Computer Science Department, Cognitive Systems Laboratory *Technical Report* (R–137).

Goldszmidt, M., and J. Pearl. 1989. On the consistency of defeasible databases. *Proceedings of the 5th Workshop on Uncertainty in AI.* Windsor, Canada, 134–141. Also, *Uncertainty in AI–5.* North Holland, 1990, 87–97.

Goldszmidt, M., and J. Pearl. 1990. On the relation between rational closure and System-Z. *Proceedings, Third International Workshop on Nonmonotonic Reasoning.* S. Lake Tahoe, CA, May 1990, 130–140.

Goldszmidt, M., and J. Pearl. 1991. System $Z^+$: A formalism for reasoning with variable-strength defaults. *Proceedings of the National Conference on AI (AAA–91).* Anaheim, CA.

Goldszmidt, M., P. Morris, and J. Pearl. 1990. A maximum entropy approach to non-monotonic reasoning. *Proceedings of the National Conference on AI (AAAI–90).* Boston, MA, pp. 646–652.

Halpern, J. Y., and M. Rabin. 1987. A logic to reason about likelihood. *Artificial Intelligence* 32 (3):379–406.

Hanks, S., and D. V. McDermott. 1986. Default reasoning, nonmonotonic logics, and the frame problem. *Proceedings of the 5th National Conference on AI (AAAI–86).* Philadelphia, 328–333.

Hunter, D. 1989. Causality and maximum entropy updating. *International Journal of Approximate Reasoning* 3(1):87–114.

Jaynes, E. T. 1979. Where do we stand on maximum entropy? In *The maximum entropy formalism.* R. D. Levine and M. Tribus, eds. Cambridge: MIT Press.

Kuipers, B. 1986. Qualitative simulation. *Artificial Intelligence,* 29:289–338.

Kyburg, H. E. 1961. *Probability and the logic of rational belief.* Middleton, Conn.: Wesleyan University Press.

Lehmann, D., and Magidor, M. 1988. Rational logics and their models: a study in cumulative logics. Department of Computer Science, Hebrew University, Jerusalem, Israel, *Technical Report* TR–88–16.

Lehmann, D. 1989. What does a conditional knowledge base entail? *Proceedings of the First International Conference on Principles of Knowledge, Representation, and Reasoning,* 212–222. San Mateo: Morgan Kaufmann.

Loui, R. 1987. Defeat among arguments: A system of defeasible inference. *Computational Intelligence.*

McCarthy, J. 1980. Circumscription—A form of non-monotonic reasoning. *Artificial Intelligence* 13(1), 27–70.

McCarthy, J. 1986. Applications of circumscription to formalizing common-sense knowledge. *Artificial Intelligence* 28(1):89–116.

McDermott, D. V., and J. Doyle. 1980. Non-monotonic logic 1. *Artificial Intelligence* 13(1,2): 41–72.

Neufeld, E., and D. Poole. 1988. Probabilistic semantics and defaults. *Proceedings of the 4th AAAI Workshop on Uncertainty in AI.* Minneapolis. 275–281.

Pearl, J. 1987. Deciding consistency in Inheritance Networks. UCLA Cognitive Systems Laboratory, *Technical Report* 870053 (R–96).

Pearl, J. 1987. Distributed revision of composite beliefs. *Artificial Intelligence* 33(2):173–215.

Pearl, J. 1988. *Probabilistic reasoning in intelligent systems: networks of plausible inference.* San Mateo: Morgan Kaufmann.

Pearl, J., and T. S. Verma. 1987. The logic of representing dependencies by directed graphs. *Proceedings of the 6th National Conference on AI ( AAAI–87 )*, Seattle, 374–379.

Pearl, J. 1990. System Z: A natural ordering of defaults with tractable applications to nonmonotonic reasoning. In R. Parikh (ed.), *Theoretical Aspects of Reasoning about Knowledge* (TARK–III). San Mateo: Morgan Kaufmann, pp. 121–135.

Peng, Y., and J. A. Reggia. 1987. Plausibility of diagnostic hypotheses. *Proceedings of the 5th National Conference on AI ( AAAI–86 )*, Philadelphia, 140–145.

Perlis, D. 1987. On the consistency of common sense reasoning. *Computational Intelligence,* 2:180–190.

Poole, D. L. 1987. Defaults and conjectures: Hypothetical reasoning for explanation and prediction. *Research Report* CS–87–54, University of Waterloo.

Pollock, J. 1987. Defeasible Reasoning, *Cognitive Science,* 11:481–518.

Reggia, J. A. 1989. Measuring the plausibility of explanatory hypotheses. *Behavioral and Brain Sciences.* 12(3):486–487.

Reggia, J. A., D. S. Nau, and Y. Wang. 1983. Diagnostic expert systems based on a set-covering model. *International Journal of Man-Machine Studies* 19:437–460.

Reiter, R. 1980. A logic for default reasoning. *Artificial Intelligence* 13:81–132.

Reiter, R. 1987. A theory of diagnosis from first principles. *Artificial Intelligence* 32(1):57–95.

Reiter, R. 1987. Nonmonotonic reasoning. In *Annual review of computer science* 2, 147–186. Palo Alto, Calif.: Annual Reviews.

Selman, B. and H. Kautz. 1988. The complexity of model-preference default theories. *Proc. CSCSI–88,* Seventh Canadian Conference on Artificial Intelligence, Edmonton, Alberta, 102–109.

Shoham, Y. 1986. Chronological ignorance: Time, nonmonotonicity, necessity, and causal theories. *Proceedings of the 5th National Conference on AI ( AAAI–86 )*, Philadelphia, 389–393.

Shoham, Y. 1987. Nonmonotonic logics: meaning and utility. *Proceedings of International Joint Conference on AI ( IJCAI–87 )*, Milan, 388–393.

Spohn, W. 1988. A general non-probabilistic theory of inductive reasoning, *Proceedings of the 4th Workshop on Uncertainty in AI,* Minneapolis, 315–322. Also, in W. L. Harper and B. Skyrms, eds. *Causation in Decision, Belief Change, and Statistics,* Vol. 2. Reidel, Dordrecht, Netherlands, 1988, 105–134.

Thagard, P. 1989. Explanatory coherence. *Behavioral and Brain Sciences* 12(3):435–468.

Touretzky, D. 1986. *The mathematics of inheritance systems.* Los Altos, Calif.: Morgan Kaufmann.

Wellman, M. 1987. Probabilistic semantics for qualitative influences. *Proceedings of the National Conference on AI ( AAAI–87 )*, Seattle, 660–664.

# 9 OSCAR: A General Theory of Rationality

John L. Pollock

## 9.1 Philosophy and AI

My ultimate objective is the construction of a general theory of rationality, and its implementation on a computer. The enterprise is a blend of philosophy and artificial intelligence. OSCAR is the system of automated reasoning that will result. The present work describes the first stages in the construction of the theory and the automated reasoning system.[1]

Implementing a theory of reasoning on a computer can be regarded either as an exercise in computer modeling, or as an attempt to build a machine that thinks. This is the difference between weak and strong AI. I favor the latter construal of the enterprise, but that will not make any difference for present purposes. Philosophers may wonder whether there is any philosophical point to actually carrying out the computer modeling. To them, it may seem that all that is important is the *possibility* of building an automated reasoner that models the theory of reasoning. Their view would be that actually building the system is the business of AI, not philosophy. However, the refining and the modeling of theories of reasoning go hand in hand in a way that philosophers have generally overlooked. I recommend this as *the* proper way to pursue philosophical investigations of reasoning. It is probably the only way to get theories of reasoning wholly right. One does not have to spend long constructing computer models of theories of reasoning to discover that they almost never do precisely what we expect them to do, and sorting out why leads to the discovery of subtle errors in the theories. From the comfort of his armchair, a philosopher will be able to discover some of the more obvious counterexamples to a flawed theory, but there are often subtle difficulties that do not emerge in simple cases and will generally be overlooked by mere reflection. However, when a computer model is applied to complicated cases, the difficulties become apparent. The computer thus becomes a mechanical aid in the discovery of counterexamples. I cannot emphasize too strongly how important this is. Computer modeling has led me to make profound changes in my own theories. Philosophers may not fully appreciate what a powerful

---

[1] My *How to Build a Person* constitutes a philosophical prolegomenon to the present work. The main thesis of that book is that we can literally build a person by constructing a system that adequately mimics human rationality. The present work begins the construction of that system.

technique this is until they try it, but once they try it they will never be content to do without it. I predict that this will become an indispensable tool for philosophy over the next twenty years.

## 9.2   Intellection

I turn now to an initial sketch of some important features of rationality. Rationality can be divided into *theoretical rationality* and *practical rationality*. Theoretical rationality is concerned exclusively with the rationality of beliefs, and it comprises the subject matter of epistemology. Assessing the rationality of a belief amounts to determining whether it ought to be held in the present epistemological circumstances. So the issue is really one of belief updating. Belief updating is accomplished by reasoning, broadly construed. The kind of reasoning involved in belief updating is called *theoretical reasoning*.

Practical rationality encompasses all aspects of rationality other than theoretical rationality. This includes most centrally the rationality of actions, but it also includes the rationality of nondoxastic mental states like desires, intentions, emotions (for instance, a fear can be rational or irrational), and so on. The point of ascribing rationality or irrationality to nondoxastic states has to do with their role in reasoning about actions. Such reasoning is called *practical reasoning*.

I will identify the theory of rationality with the theory of correct reasoning. The theory of epistemic rationality is thus the theory of theoretical reasoning, and the theory of practical rationality is the theory of practical reasoning. I will refer to the processes of theoretical and practical reasoning jointly as *intellection*. Rationality is thus identified with the operation of intellection. It must be recognized, however, that this involves a narrow construal of rationality, and there is no implication that the beliefs and actions of rational agents should always be the result of reasoning. The difficulty is that reasoning is slow. Many aspects of reasoning would seem to be essentially serial. Human beings gain speed by employing their inherently slow hardware for parallel processing. Much of reasoning cannot be done in parallel, so human processing includes many "nonintellectual" processes (processes that are not part of intellection) that also issue in beliefs and actions. For instance, a human being does not have to pull out a pocket calculator and compute trajectories in order to catch a baseball or get out of the way of a bus.

I used to refer to these nonintellectual processes as "quick and dirty," but the psychologist Lynn Cooper has impressed upon me that they need not be at all dirty. For example, our built-in procedures for computing trajectories are incredibly accurate. Their shortcoming is not inaccuracy but inflexibility. They achieve their speed by building in assumptions about the environment, and when those assumptions fail then the processes may yield wildly inaccurate answers. For instance, if we see that a baseball is going to bounce off a telephone pole, we had best wait until it ricochets before predicting its trajectory. Our built-in "trajectory module" cannot handle this situation accurately, so we use intellection to temporarily override it until the situation becomes one that can be handled accurately by the trajectory module. I will refer to modules like the trajectory module as *Q&I modules* ("quick and inflexible").

It must not be supposed that human Q&I modules are primarily concerned with motor skills. Psychological evidence strongly suggests that most everyday inductive and probabilistic inference is carried out by Q&I modules.[2] In this case, the modules really are dirty. Accurate probabilistic reasoning is in many cases computationally unfeasible, and so humans appear to rely upon processes like Tversky's "representativeness heuristic", which often yield results incompatible with the probability calculus. This is not to say, however, that it is unreasonable to rely upon such approximation methods. The alternative of explicit reasoning is too slow for many practical purposes.

I would urge that much ordinary inductive inference is also the result of Q&I modules. Inductive inference *can* be carried out intellectually—by explicit reasoning from explicitly stated data—and scientists try to do that. But this requires the storage and processing of huge databases, which is exhaustive of system resources and computationally expensive. Only in science do we tend to accumulate an explicit body of data, peruse it, and then engage in explicit inductive reasoning about it. Instead, we normally employ procedures that allow us to use the data as we acquire it and then forget it, forming provisional generalizations that we modify as we go along. This is much more efficient, but it is subject to pitfalls having to do with the possibility of non-independent data which cannot be judged non-independent because it is no longer recalled.

We do not want to require rational agents, human or otherwise, to make inductive inferences only by explicit inductive reasoning. That is too slow

---

[2] Tversky and Kahneman [1974].

and computationally too difficult for many practical purposes. In this connection it is interesting to reflect upon much of the machine learning literature. Although I will not try to substantiate this here, I would suggest that many of the systems developed there are best viewed as Q&I systems. They are conclusion-drawers, but not reasoners. Reasoning is a step-by-step sequential process, but many machine learning systems do nothing like that.[3] This does not make them any the less interesting. A general-purpose automated cognizer with humanlike cognitive powers will have to be provided with potent Q&I modules to supplement explicit reasoning.

The advantage of Q&I modules is speed. The advantage of intellection, on the other hand, is extreme flexibility. It seems that it can in principle deal with any kind of situation, but it is slow. In complicated situations we may have no applicable Q&I modules, in which case we have no choice but to underake explicit reasoning about the situation. In other cases, human beings accept the output of the Q&I modules *unless* they have some explicit reason for not doing so. Intellection is used to monitor the output and override it when necessary. In sum, the rolc of intellection should be (1) to deal with cases to which built-in Q&I modules do not apply, and (2) to monitor and override the output of Q&I modules as necessary.

### 9.3 Interactions between Theoretical Reasoning and Practical Reasoning

Within philosophy, it tends to be the case that either theoretical reasoning is discussed in isolation from practical reasoning, or the attempt is made to reduce theoretical reasoning to practical reasoning by identifying it with practical reasoning about what to believe.[4] But neither strategy can be completely successful. The two kinds of reasoning cannot be entirely separated, because there are important interactions between them. First, practical reasoning must be based upon knowledge of the agent's current situation. For instance, it may require a prior estimate of the likelihood of actions having different outcomes. Such knowledge must be the result of theoretical reasoning. Thus any practical reasoning must presuppose prior theoretical reasoning. This has the immediate consequence that theoretical reasoning cannot be viewed as just a special kind of practical reasoning.

---

[3] For instance, think of Holland et al. [1986].
[4] The latter has also been urged in AI by Jon Doyle [1988] and [1988a].

By and large, epistemologists have tried to ignore practical reasoning in their investigations of theoretical reasoning, but that cannot be entirely satisfactory either. The difficulty is that theoretical reasoning is often guided by practical reasoning about how best to reason. For instance, a mathematician addressing an unsolved problem may spend more time considering how to approach the problem than he does in actually constructing trial proofs. Similarly, an experimental scientist may spend more time considering what experiments to perform or what hypotheses to test than he does in evaluating the data that results from the experiments. In each case the rational agent is conducting practical reasoning about what theoretical reasoning he should perform.

In precisely what ways can practical reasoning affect the course of theoretical reasoning? At the very least, it can affect the strategies we employ in attempting to answer questions. We can learn that certain natural (default) strategies are unlikely to be effective in specific circumstances, and we can discover new strategies that are effective. The latter are often obtained by analogy from previous problem solving.

On the other hand, it is commonly asserted that practical reasoning cannot affect belief directly because belief is not under voluntary control. Theoretical reasoning is "directly causally efficacious" in belief formation in a sense in which practical reasoning is not. Notice that practical reasoning appears to be directly causally efficacious in the formation of intentions and desires in precisely the same way theoretical reasoning is directly causally efficacious in belief formation. Intentions and desires are not under voluntary control either. It is only actions that are under voluntary control.

Even in the case of actions the situation is a bit murky. *Turning off the light* is an action, but it is not something that we can do infallibly. If we try to turn off the light, circumstances may intervene to prevent it. Perhaps we should say that, in a strict sense, *turning off the light* is not under voluntary control. Action theorists distinguish between *basic actions*, which need not be performed *by* performing other actions, and *nonbasic actions*, which can only be performed by doing something else. *Turning off the light* is a nonbasic action. Raising your arm is supposed to be a basic action. The observation that beliefs are not under the direct control of practical reasoning seems to amount to no more than that beliefs are not basic actions. Beliefs *are*, to some extent, under the control of practical reasoning. If one desires not to have a certain belief, one can take steps that affect one's beliefs indirectly. For instance, one can avoid thinking about the evidence supporting the belief. The only difference between beliefs and nonbasic actions seems to be that beliefs are somewhat more difficult to control—even indirectly.

It must be possible for the rational agent to use practical reasoning to direct the course of theoretical reasoning (and also to direct the course of practical reasoning itself). On the other hand, because practical reasoning presupposes theoretical reasoning, some theoretical reasoning must be possible without practical reasoning. To avoid an infinite regress, a rational agent must have built-in default reasoning strategies for both theoretical reasoning and practical reasoning. The agent must be able to employ these default strategies without engaging in practical reasoning about how to reason. The general architecture of rational thought can thus be diagrammed as in figure 9.1.

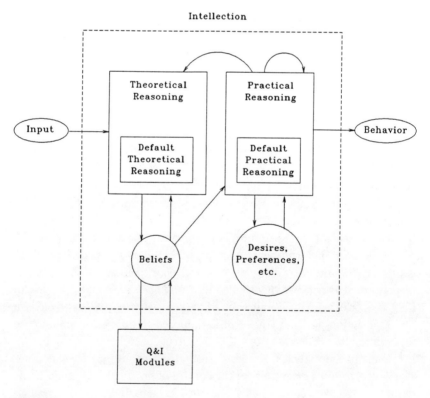

**Figure 9.1**
The architecture of rational thought

## 9.4   Introspective Reasoners

In order to perform practical reasoning about how to reason, an agent must be able to think about its own reasoning. I will refer to a reasoner with such capabilities as an *introspective reasoner*. The construction of an introspective reasoner is a tricky process. It involves the ability to reason, and then "move up a level" to form beliefs about what reasoning has occurred. We want the reasoner to direct future reasoning by relying upon generalizations it has formed about the efficacy of certain kinds of reasoning in the past. This requires not only the ability to reason inductively, but also the ability to evaluate the truth values of beliefs in the light of subsequent information. The latter is not just a matter of revising the earlier beliefs, but of forming beliefs *about* whether the earlier beliefs are true. Only in that way can the reasoner inductively generalize about what kinds of reasoning are apt to be reliable or unreliable in yielding true conclusions under particular circumstances.

Reasoning requires a system of mental representation—what in the philosophical literature is called a *language of thought*.[5] Reasoning consists of manipulating sentences in the language of thought. An introspective reasoner must be able to think about the sentences in its own language of thought and observe their manipulation. For this to be possible, the reasoner's system of mental representation must incorporate something analogous to quotation names of those sentences. If $p$ is a sentence in the language of thought, let «$p$» be its quotation name.

The construction of an introspective reasoner will begin with a *planar reasoner* that lacks the ability to move up a level and observe itself. A planar reasoner can still reason about reasoning, in the same way it reasons about anything else, but it will have no special mechanisms for use in reasoning specifically about reasoning. I assume that the planar reasoner has the ability to perform inductive reasoning. To this planar reasoner we must then add an *introspective module* and a *truth-evaluation module*. The default theoretical reasoning module can be viewed as consisting of a planar reasoning module, the introspective monitoring module, and the truth-evaluation module, combined as in figure 9.2. Note that this is all part of default theoretical reasoning, because the system must perform this much reasoning *before* it can apply practical reasoning to the question of how to

[5] The term is from Fodor [1975].

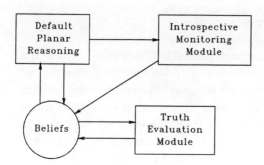

**Figure 9.2**
Default theoretical reasoning

reason. The introspective module enables the reasoner to acquire beliefs about its own reasoning. It will accomplish this by adding procedures to the reasoner that, under appropriate circumstances, lead the reasoner to adopt beliefs of the form

I believe «$p$»;

I believe «$p$» on the basis of «$q_1$», ..., «$q_n$»;

when it does in fact hold that belief on that basis.[6]

The addition of such an introspective module to a planar reasoner creates no obvious difficulties, but there are grave difficulties associated with the addition of a truth-evaluation module. The obvious proposal is to adopt an analogue of Tarski's T-schema[7]:

From p, infer $\lceil \ll p \gg$ is true$\rceil$.

From $\lceil \ll p \gg$ is true$\rceil$, infer $p$.[8]

The problem is that incorporating these rules into a reasoner will lead immediately to the liar paradox. The resulting inconsistency will be catastrophic in any reasoner that is able to draw all possible deductive consequences from its beliefs. There is a massive literature in philosophical logic regarding how to avoid the liar paradox, and that all becomes relevant

---

[6] These procedures must be interest-driven, in the sense of section six. The reasoner should adopt these beliefs only if it is previously interested in them.
[7] Tarski [1956].
[8] These must also be interest-driven. In the sense of section six, the first would be a backwards reason and the second a forwards reason.

here.[9] Thus the liar paradox, which initially appears to be a purely logical puzzle, becomes resurrected as an obstacle to AI. I think that this will not be unusual. A great many familiar philosophical problems arise in a new guise when we start modeling actual reasoning.

Within the context of describing an introspective reasoner, I am tempted by a radical solution to the liar paradox. I am inclined to think that, despite the inconsistency, the T-schema is an accurate description of our rules for reasoning about truth. Any attempt to avoid the liar paradox by restricting the T-schema seems ad hoc and unmotivated. My suggestion is that the solution to building an introspective reasoner that that does not collapse in the face of the liar paradox lies in damage control rather than damage avoidance. When an introspective reasoner gets into trouble, it is able to apply practical reasoning to the situation and back out gracefully without necessarily solving the problem that led to the difficulty. This is a general phenomenon of considerable importance. It is illustrated by a number of situations. For instance, mathematicians tend to be very cautious about accepting the results of complicated proofs. But the proof, if correct, is simply an exercise in deductive reasoning. How is such caution possible? Why doesn't their rational architecture force them to just automatically accept the conclusion? The answer seems to be that they have learned from experience that complicated deductive reasoning is error-prone. Practical reasoning about theoretical reasoning has the power to intervene and prevent acceptance of the conclusion until the proof is adequately checked. That practical reasoning has this power is just a brute fact about our rational architecture.

The gambler's fallacy provides another illustration of this phenomenon. Contrary to popular opinion, reasoning in accordance with the gambler's fallacy is not automatically irrational. Such reasoning proceeds in terms of a perfectly good defeasible reason of the form ⌜Most $A$'s are $B$'s, and this is an $A$, so (defeasibly) this is a $B$⌝. In the case of the gambler's fallacy, there is a defeater for this prima facie reason, but it is surprisingly difficult to say precisely what the defeater is.[10] Most people who consciously refrain from reasoning in accordance with the gambler's fallacy do so not because they understand precisely what is wrong with it, but because they know from

---

[9] For a sampling of the literature on the liar paradox, see Martin [1970] and [1984].
[10] For a detailed discussion of the reasoning involved in the gambler's fallacy and the defeater responsible for making the reasoning ultimately incorrect, see chapter nine of my *Nomic Probability and the Foundations of Induction.*

experience that they get into trouble when they reason that way. Again, it is practical reasoning that intervenes to prevent the theoretical reasoning.

A related phenomenon is common in any intellectual discipline. An investigator formulating a theory will frequently encounter difficulties that he cannot answer in the early stages of the investigation, but this does not automatically move him to give up his investigation. He may suspect that there is a way for the theory to handle the difficulty even if he cannot initially see what it is. This can be a perfectly reasonable attitude based upon the observation that the theory has been successful in avoiding many other difficulties whose solutions were not intially obvious. If the investigator were constrained to blindly follow the canons of theoretical reasoning, he would have to give up the theory *until* he is able to resolve the difficulty, but because he anticipates that he will eventually be able to resolve it, he instead retains the theory and continues to look for a solution to the problem while developing the theory in other ways. This example is particularly interesting because the investigator may literally have inconsistent beliefs but postpone giving up any of them. Instead of rejecting the beliefs, he retains them but does not draw any conclusions from the resulting contradiction. Practical reasoning imposes a kind of damage control that encapsulates the problem until a solution is found.

My suggestion is that precisely the same phenomenon is involved in the liar paradox. Reasoning about the liar sentence gets us into cognitive difficulties. We do not immediately see our way out of them, but we do not simply go crazy as a result. Instead, practical reasoning intervenes to encapsulate the problem until we find a solution. The difference between this case and the previous case is that there may be no solution to the liar paradox. If the T-schema is an accurate description of part of our rational architecture, then our rational architecture is logically inconsistent, and there is nothing we can do about it. However, for an introspective reasoner, that need not be catastrophic.

All of these examples illustrate that in an introspective reasoner, practical reasoning can intervene to prevent theoretical reasoning that would otherwise occur. Such intervention does not result from the mere fact that we would prefer not to adopt certain conclusions which are repugnant to us for one reason or another. The intervention results from the threat of *purely cognitive* difficulties. At this stage it is not clear how to give a precise formulation of the rules of practical reasoning that are involved.

## 9.5   Defeasibility

Theoretical reasoning can lead not only to the adoption of new beliefs, but also to the retraction of old beliefs. Similarly, practical reasoning can lead to the formation of intentions, but also to the retraction of intentions. In philosophy, reasoning is said to be *defeasible* in the sense that correct reasoning can lead first to the adoption of a conclusion, and subsequently to its retraction. Both practical reasoning and theoretical reasoning are defeasible. This aspect of reasoning has been called "nonmonotonic" in AI work.[11]

In AI there is the common impression that defeasible reasoning consists of jumping to conclusions or making "tentative guesses."[12] It is supposed that defeasible reasoning is less secure than normal reasoning, and should only be countenanced for the sake of computational efficiency. What is overlooked is that defeasible reasoning *is* normal reasoning. Its use is not just a matter of computational efficiency. It is logically impossible to reason successfully about the world around us using only deductive reasoning. *All* interesting reasoning outside of mathematics involves defeasible steps. For instance, our basic information about the world comes from sense perception. Things appear certain ways to us, and we take that to be a reason for believing that they are that way. Clearly, this reason is defeasible, but our reasoning in this way is no mere matter of convenience. As years of work in epistemology has made clear, there is in principle no way to logically deduce the state of the world from the way it appears.[13] Moving on up the epistemic ladder, we use induction to form general beliefs summarizing observed regularities. If a regularity has been observed to hold in every case, that gives us a reason for thinking that it holds in general. If it has only been observed to hold in most cases, that gives us a reason for thinking it will continue to hold in most cases. Such inductive reasoning is defeasible, and it cannot be replaced by deductive reasoning. There is no

---

[11] The work on defeasible reasoning in philosophy stems mainly from the publications of Roderick Chisholm and myself. See Chisholm [1957], [1966], [1977], and Pollock [1967], [1970], [1974], [1986], [1987]. See also Kyburg [1974] and [1983]. For a sampling of the work in AI, see Delgrande [1988], Etherington [1987], Etherington and Reiter [1983], Loui [1987], McCarthy [1980] and [1984], McDermott and Doyle [1980], Moore [1985], Nute [1988], Pearl [1988], Pollock [1987], Poole [1985] and [1988], Reiter [1980], and Reiter and Criscuolo [1981].

[12] Doyle [1979].

[13] For further discussion of this point, see my *Contemporary Theories of Knowledge*, 39ff.

way to deduce general conclusions from finitely many observations. Given that a generalization holds most of the time, we can use that to infer that it will hold in further unobserved cases. This inference is also defeasible. It takes ⌜Most $A$'s are $B$'s, and this is an $A$⌝ to be a defeasible reason for ⌜This is a $B$⌝. The upshot of all this is that defeasible reasoning is not just common—it is thoroughly pervasive and absolutely essential. Almost everything we believe is believed at least indirectly on the basis of defeasible reasoning, and things could not have been any other way.[14]

Reasoning proceeds in terms of reasons. Within theoretical reasoning, some reasons are *conclusive reasons*, in the sense that they logically entail their conclusions. Others support their conclusions only defeasibly. The latter are *prima facie reasons*, and the considerations that can lead to the retraction of conclusions based upon prima facie reasons are *defeaters*. Notice that prima facie reasons and defeaters make theoretical reasoning defeasible already at the level of default planar reasoning. We do not require an introspective reasoner for defeasibility (although introspection is required for the acquisition of some important kinds of defeaters).[15]

## 9.6 Interest-Driven Reasoning

We can think of human reasoning as consisting of three processes: (1) constructing arguments supporting conclusions in which we are interested, and the subsequent adoption of beliefs on the basis of the arguments we find; (2) retracting arguments and beliefs in the face of defeaters; (3) the reinstatement of arguments and the readoption of beliefs when defeaters are themselves defeated or retracted. The first process is familiar from the AI literature on automated deduction, but the other two processes are unique to defeasible reasoning.

In searching for arguments, an introspective reasoner can bring to bear the full power of its practical reasoning, as informed by all of its prior experience. This would seem to be the only reason that an experienced

---

[14] In chapter one of Pollock [*How to Build a Person*], I argue that there is a purely computational reason why a sophisticated cognizer will function better with an appearance/reality distinction and a merely defeasible connection between appearance and reality. This provides a deeper reason for the necessity of defeasible reasoning.

[15] I have in mind reliability defeaters, which defeat a prima facie reason by noting that it is an unreliable indicator of the truth of the conclusion under circumstances of the sort in which the system presently finds itself.

mathematician is better at finding proofs than an equally intelligent math student. However, as we have seen, an introspective reasoner must be built on top of a non-introspective reasoner, and the searches of the latter are guided exclusively by the built-in procedures that constitute the default strategies for the introspective reasoner. The default reasoner may be quite good at constructing proofs that are not too difficult, but it is unlikely to provide any real competition for a human mathematician. On the other hand, a full-blown introspective reasoner might turn out to be capable of anything that a human mathematician can do.

It is of interest to reflect upon how work on automated theorem proving fits into the present scheme. Automated theorem provers have been able to prove some very difficult theorems, but it is noteworthy that they do so by employing domain specific heuristics, and generally by tailoring the proof procedures to the problem in ways that are chosen by a human operator rather than by the program itself.[16] I would suggest that this is best viewed as an approximation to part of an introspective reasoner, with the human operator providing the introspection and practical deliberation that alters the default reasoning strategies of the automated reasoner. Accordingly, such results show little about the unaided powers of a default non-introspective reasoner.

The first step in constructing OSCAR has been concerned with the default strategies the system employs in searching for arguments—the default monotonic reasoner. Although there is a massive literature on searching for arguments, I have not found it very helpful in the present context. This is for three reasons. First, most of the literature on automated deduction is concerned with resolution-based systems, about which I will say more below. Although resolution refutation is complete for first order logic, it is not at all obvious how to extend it to encompass defeasible reasoning. Second, most automated deduction systems embrace a very limited range of argument structures. For instance, most (not all) such systems eschew any kind of suppositional reasoning (for instance, con-ditionalization, or reasoning by cases). Such a narrow view of arguments is provably unproblematic for deductive reasoning in the predicate calculus, because the resulting system is still complete, but at this time we have no reason to expect it to be equally unproblematic for reasoning in general. Third, as I have indicated, the more impressive results in automated rea-

---

[16] For an overview, see Wos [1988].

soning have been achieved by systems working under the direction of human operators, and as such they do not model default non-introspective reasoning.

The operation of the monotonic reasoner seems to be generally the same whether the arguments are deductive or defeasible. Accordingly, it has proven expedient to begin the construction of OSCAR by building a purely deductive reasoner. The deductive reasoner carries out the first of the three processes (searching for arguments) that comprise default theoretical reasoning. I will briefly sketch the structure of the deductive reasoner, and then make some remarks about how it is modified to incorporate defeat and reinstatement, thus creating a general purpose default reasoner that does both deductive and defeasible reasoning.

It is a familiar point that we could build a reasoning system that systematically generates all possible arguments, and it would be complete for, say, the predicate calculus. Using this system, if we want to establish a certain conclusion we have to just wait until the system gets to it. This is the so-called British Museum algorithm. But such a system would be hopelessly inefficient. The behavior of any reasonable theorem prover must be guided by what it is trying to prove rather than just reasoning randomly until it happens upon its desired conclusion. All actual theorem provers are guided in some way or other. I will propose a general account of how this works in human default reasoning. The basic idea is that reasoning proceeds both forwards and backwards (it uses forwards chaining and backwards chaining). We reason forwards from our existing beliefs, and backwards from what we are interesting in proving, and try to bring the two chains of reasoning together. Reasoning backwards can be regarded as deriving interests from interests. A reasoning system that combines such forward and backward reasoning will said to be *interest-driven*.

It is natural to suppose that backward reasoning is just forward reasoning done in reverse, and that in any given instance we *could* just reason in one direction or the other without combining the two. I was astonished to stumble upon considerations that show that this view of reasoning is fundamentally mistaken. There are profound differences between random forward reasoning and backward reasoning, and neither is replaceable by the other. They are both absolutely essential for reasoning, and there is a definite logic governing when to use one and when to use the other. The choice is not just a matter of convenience. We literally could not arrive at our conclusions in any but the simplest cases without using both kinds of reasoning. This point becomes obvious when we look at concrete examples of reasons. For instance, if we are investigating deductive reasoning in the propositional calculus, we might propose that the following are among the reasons we employ:

*Backwards reasons*:

| | |
|---|---|
| adjunction: | $\{p, q\}$ is a reason for $(p \,\&\, q)$ |
| addition: | $p$ is a reason for $(p \lor q)$ |
| | $q$ is a reason for $(p \lor q)$ |
| $\sim\sim$ introduction: | $p$ is reason for $\sim\sim p$ |

*Forwards reasons*:

| | |
|---|---|
| simplification: | $(p \,\&\, q)$ is a reason for $p$ |
| | $(p \,\&\, q)$ is a reason for $q$ |
| $\sim\sim$ elimination: | $\sim\sim p$ is a reason for $p$ |
| modus ponens: | $\{(\sim p \lor q), p\}$ is a reason for $q$ |

It takes only a moment's reflection to realize that the reasons listed under "backwards reasons" are *only* of use in backwards reasoning, and those listed under "forwards reasons" are only of use in random forward reasoning. For instance, consider addition. Suppose we could use addition in random forward reasoning. Then if we adopted $p$, we would be led to adopt every disjunction containing $p$ as one disjunct. But there are infinitely many such disjunctions, and most are useless in any given problem. In point of fact, we only use addition when we have some reason to be interested in the resulting disjunction. Much the same point can be made about adjunction. Suppose we could use it in random forward reasoning, and we adopted $p$ and $q$. Then we would be led to adopt $(p \,\&\, q)$. That does not seem so bad, but it would not stop there. We would go on to adopt $[(p \,\&\, q) \,\&\, p]$, $(q \,\&\, p)$, $[(q \,\&\, p) \,\&\, (p \,\&\, q)]$, $[(q \,\&\, p) \,\&\, [(p \,\&\, q) \,\&\, p]]$, $(p \,\&\, [(q \,\&\, p) \,\&\, [(p \,\&\, q) \,\&\, p]])$, and so on without limit. Obviously, we do not do that, and a reasoning system that performed in this way would be crippled. This largely useless reasoning would continually get in its way, taking up its resources and preventing it from making more useful inferences.

The use of simplification in backward reasoning would be even more catastrophic. Suppose we are interested in $q$. Backwards reasoning with simplification would lead us to adopt interest in $(p \,\&\, q)$, for *every* $p$, and then backwards reasoning with adjunction (which is presumably acceptable) would lead us to adopt interest in $p$. Thus interest in anything would automatically lead to interest in everything, which would completely vitiate the interest restrictions in interest driven reasoning. Similar reflection on the other reasons indicates that in each case, they can only function in the category in which they are listed.

The somewhat surprising conclusion to be drawn from this is that some reasons are of use in backward reasoning, and others are of use in random forward reasoning, and individual reasons may not play both roles. In fact, I have yet to find *any* reason that can play both roles (although I would stop short of affirming that as a general principle). Reasons can be classified as *forwards reasons*, which can be used in a forward direction for deriving beliefs from beliefs, and *backwards reasons*, which can be used in a backwards direction for deriving interests from interests. Given the distinction between these two kinds of reasons, we can describe much reasoning as proceeding in terms of the following rules:

*R-DEDUCE:*
If $X$ is a forwards reason for $q$, and you adopt some member of $X$ and already believe the others, then adopt $q$.

*INTEREST-ADOPTION:*
If you are interested in $q$, and $X$ is a backwards reason for $q$, then become interested in the members of $X$. If you already believe all the members of $X$ then adopt $q$.

*DISCHARGE-INTEREST:*
If you are interested the members of $X$ as a way of getting $q$, and you adopt some member of $X$ and already believe the others, then adopt $q$.

These rules form the basis for a simple automated reasoning system.

## 9.7   Suppositional Reasoning

A point that has often been overlooked by epistemologists, and to a large extent by AI theorists as well, but not by logicians, is that reasoning is *suppositional*. Epistemologists have tended to adopt a linear model of reasoning according to which all arguments are constructed by repeatedly drawing conclusions from previous beliefs that constitute reasons for the conclusions. This is what I call "linear reasoning." The simplest way to see that this cannot be a completely general account of reasoning is to note that deductive reasoning can lead to a priori knowledge of "truths of reason." For instance, we can obtain conclusions like $[(p \& q) \supset q]$ or $(p \lor \sim p)$ that do not depend upon any premises. Linear reasoning can only draw conclusions from previously adopted beliefs, so such a priori knowledge cannot be obtained by linear reasoning. Instead, we employ several kinds of rules enabling us to embed "subsidiary arguments" within the main argument and draw conclusions within the main argument that are related to conclusions drawn in the subsidiary arguments. Familiar examples are rules governing conditionalization, reductio ad absurdum, reasoning by cases (dilemma), and some form of universal generalization.

The use of subsidiary arguments constitutes *suppositional reasoning*, wherein we suppose something "for the sake of argument", reason using the supposition in the same way we reason about beliefs and interests nonsuppositionally, and then on the basis of conclusions drawn using the supposition we draw further conclusions that do not depend upon the supposition. For instance, in conditionalization, in order to establish a conditional $(p \supset q)$, we "suppose" the antecedent, try to derive the consequent from that supposition, and then "discharge" the supposition to infer the conditional. Similarly, in reductio ad absurdum, if we are trying to establish $p$, we may suppose $\sim p$, show that that leads to a contradiction, and then discharge the supposition to infer $p$. In both of these kinds of reasoning, what is crucial is the use of suppositions to get conclusions related to our desired conclusions, and their subsequent discharge. Within the supposition, we reason as if the supposed propositions were believed, using all the rules for adoption and interest adoption that are used in connection with linear reasoning.

It is fairly straightforward to build an automated reasoning system for the predicate calculus that does interest driven suppositional reasoning of the sort I have been describing.[17] This is accomplished by the subsystem of OSCAR that does exclusively deductive reasoning. It is extremely interesting to compare this part of OSCAR with more conventional work on automated reasoning in AI. OSCAR bears little similarity to other automated reasoning systems.[18] Most of those systems are based upon what is

---

[17] This system is described in my "Interest driven supposition reasoning" and *OSCAR: A General Theory of Reasoning.*

[18] The only major exception is Pelletier's THINKER [1985]. It is probably significant that Pelletier is a philosopher. OSCAR stands in stark contrast with, for instance, the systems of Lusk et al. [1984], [1985], Stickel [1985], [1986], Wos and Winker [1983], and others too numerous to mention. Systems to which OSCAR bears a distant resemblance are HARP

called "resolution refutation." Philosophers will recognize that as proof by reductio ad absurdum as applied to conjunctive normal forms. I think it is clear to everyone that resolution refutation is not descriptive of human reasoning. That was never the intent of the AI systems based upon it. Instead, they were designed with the idea that computers are better at certain kinds of "symbol crunching" than human beings, and automated reasoning systems can take advantage of that. This always struck me as reasonable, and so my expectation was that OSCAR would be slow compared to other automated reasoning systems. The purpose of the construction of this system was not to provide a competitor to more familiar systems of automated deduction, but rather to build a system modeling certain aspects of human reasoning and extendable to defeasible reasoning. To my surprise, however, the resulting automated theorem prover for the predicate calculus has turned out to be remarkably efficient, beating most standard systems on some hard problems. There are no established standards for comparing reasoning systems, but there are a few problems that have been run on a wide variety of reasoning systems and provide at least rough comparisons. The best known is the *Schubert steamroller problem.* That is the following problem in the predicate calculus:

$(\forall x)(Wx \supset Ax)$        $(\forall x)(\forall y)[(Cx \mathbin{\&} By) \supset Mxy]$

$(\forall x)(Fx \supset Ax)$        $(\forall x)(\forall y)[(Sx \mathbin{\&} By) \supset Mxy]$

$(\forall x)(Bx \supset Ax)$        $(\forall x)(\forall y)[(Bx \mathbin{\&} Fy) \supset Mxy]$

$(\forall x)(Cx \supset Ax)$        $(\forall x)(\forall y)[(Fx \mathbin{\&} Wy) \supset Mxy]$

$(\forall x)(Sx \supset Ax)$        $(\forall x)(\forall y)[(Wx \mathbin{\&} Fy) \supset {\sim}Exy]$

$(\exists w)Ww$        $(\forall x)(\forall y)[Wx \mathbin{\&} Gy) \supset {\sim}Exy]$

$(\exists f)Ff$        $(\forall x)(\forall y)[(Bx \mathbin{\&} Cy) \supset Exy]$

$(\exists b)Bb$        $(\forall x)(\forall y)[(Bx \mathbin{\&} Sy) \supset {\sim}Exy]$

$(\exists c)Cc$        $(\forall x)[Cx \supset (\exists y)(Py \mathbin{\&} Exy)]$

$(\exists s)Ss$        $(\forall x)[Sx \supset (\exists y)(Py \mathbin{\&} Exy)]$

(Oppacher and Suen [1985], [1988]), TPS (Andrews et al. [1983], [1985]), and the UT Natural Deduction Prover (Bledsoe [1977] and [1983], Bledsoe and Tyson [1975]), and the systems of Murray [1982] and Nevins [1974].

$(\exists g)Gg$                    $(\forall x)(Gx \supset Px)$

$(\forall x)[Ax \supset [(\forall w)(Pw \supset Exw) \vee (\forall y)((Ay \ \& \ (Myx \ \& \ (\exists z)(Pz \ \& \ Eyz))) \supset Exy)]]$

---

$(\exists x)(\exists y)[(Ax \ \& \ Ay) \ \& \ (\exists z)[Exy \ \& \ (Gz \ \& \ Eyz)]]$

This is a slightly whimsical symbolization of the following:

Wolves, foxes, birds, caterpillars, and snails are animals, and there are some of each of them. Also, there are some grains, and grains are plants. Every animal either likes to eat all plants or all animals much smaller than itself that like to eat some plants. Caterpillars and snails are much smaller than birds, which are much smaller than foxes, which in turn are much smaller than wolves. Wolves do not like to eat foxes or grains, while birds like to eat caterpillars but not snails. Caterpillars and snails like to eat some plants. Therefore, there is an animal that likes to eat a grain-eating animal.[19]

Many respected automated reasoning systems that are considered fast take a long time to do this problem. A system invented by Mark Stickel (not his latest) was reported to do this problem in 2 hours 53 minutes on a Symbolics 3600 computer, and the well-known ITP theorem prover, operating on a much faster computer and written in PASCAL (faster than LISP), was reported to do the problem in eleven minutes.[20] The fastest published time is attributed to a current system of Stickel, which does the problem in six seconds on a Symbolics 3600.[21] It is noteworthy that this time was obtained by using the system interactively in a way that allowed the human operator to tailor the reasoning strategies to this particular problem. Stickel notes that a more natural initial choice of strategy resulted in the system taking 1 hour 35 minutes. By way of contrast, OSCAR does this problem in thirteen seconds on a Symbolics 3600, and does this while operating in a completely automatic way. OSCAR seems equally fast on other problems.

OSCAR was not constructed with speed in mind, and is not even written very efficiently. A sustained effort at optimization should accelerate the system appreciably. OSCAR's speed does not result from fancy programming, but from the general architecture of the system. This suggests that that architecture may have an inherent advantage over resolution theorem provers. As this at least purports to be the architecture of human reasoning, this would seem to show something very interesting about human beings.

[19] Pelletier [1986], 203.
[20] These times are reported in Cohn [1985].
[21] Stickel [1986].

Granted that OSCAR is fast, *why* is it fast? The explanation appears to be that the interest driven architecture allows the system to find proofs while performing many fewer unnecessary inferences. For instance, on the steamroller problem, only 11 percent of the inferences performed by OSCAR are unnecessary to the final 42-line proof. By contrast, even on Stickel's fastest time his theorem prover performed 479 inferences, and when his theorem prover was not given special directions tailored to the problem, it performed 245,820 inferences. The other theorem provers for which he provides data performed between 1,106 and 26,190 inference steps. This means that between 91 percent and 99.98 percent of the inferences performed by these theorem provers were unnecessary. OSCAR is equally efficient on a broad range of problems. There is a set of test problems due to Pelletier (1986). In solving Pelletier's propositional calculus problems (numbers 1–17), OSCAR's average percentage of unnecessary inferences is only 8 percent, and on the pure predicate calculus problems (numbers 18–47), the redundancy figure only goes up to 26 percent. It appears that OSCAR's interest constraints are extremely effective in eliminating unnecessary inferences. This would seem to be the key to OSCAR's surprising speed, and it is directly attributable to the interest-driven architecture.

## 9.8    The Structure of Defeasible Reasoning

Recall that my present purpose is to describe a default non-introspective reasoner, which will eventually be incorporated into a general purpose reasoner. Thus far I have described how the system works as a monotonic reasoner. The next step is to extend it to defeasible reasoning.

What makes reasoning defeasible is that prima facie reasons can be defeated. Considerations that defeat prima facie reasons are *defeaters*. There are two importantly different kinds of defeaters. Where *P* is a prima facie reason for *Q*, *R* is a *rebutting defeater* if and only if *R* is a reason for denying *Q*. All work on nonmonotonic logic and defeasible reasoning has recognized the existence of rebutting defeaters, but it has often been overlooked that there are other defeaters too. For instance, suppose *x* looks red to me, but I know that *x* is illuminated by red lights and red lights can make things look red when they are not. This defeats the prima facie reason, but it is not a reason for thinking that *x* is *not* red. After all, red objects look red in red light too. This is an *undercutting defeater*. Undercutting defeaters attack the connection between the reason and the conclusion rather than attacking the conclusion directly. Where $P$ is a prima facie reason for $Q$, $R$ is an undercutting defeater if and only if $R$ is a reason for denying that $P$ would not be true unless $Q$ were true.

Theories of reasoning are basically procedural theories. They are concerned with what a reasoner should do next when it finds itself in any particular epistemological situation. Correct reasoning can involve numerous false starts, wherein a belief is adopted, retracted, reinstated, retracted again, and so forth. At each stage of reasoning, if the reasoning is correct then a belief held on the basis of that reasoning is justified, even if subsequent reasoning will mandate its retraction. *Epistemic justification*, in this sense, is a procedural notion consisting of the correct rules for belief updating having been followed by the system up to the present time in connection with the belief being evaluated. Justified belief is a dynamic notion having to do with the present state of the reasoning system. The justification of a belief can vary not just as a result of further perceptual input but also as one's reasoning progresses without further input. For instance, a person can be perfectly justified in holding beliefs that are logically inconsistent with one another, provided he has good reasons for believing them and his reasoning has not exposed the inconsistency. If he later discovers the inconsistency, then he becomes unjustified in continuing to hold both beliefs, and this change occurs without any new perceptual input.

Extending the interest driven deductive reasoner to accommodate defeasible reasoning requires keeping track of the bases upon which beliefs are held, retracting both beliefs and interests when defeaters are adopted, and keeping track of defeat so that beliefs and interests can be reinstated if defeaters are themselves defeated or retracted. The details of this are too complicated to pursue at the present time, but I do have a version of OSCAR that purports to do sophisticated defeasible reasoning.

In epistemology the concept of a prima facie reason has served primarily as a tool for the analysis of different kinds of epistemological problems. It has rarely been the subject of logical investigation in its own right. This contrasts sharply with AI, where nonmonotonic reasoning has been the subject of intensive logical investigation. Unfortunately, the AI work has been done without sufficient attention to actual epistemological examples of defeasible reasoning, and the resulting theories turn out to be inadequate for the description of human reasoning. To illustrate this with a simple example, none of the familiar AI theories of nonmonotonic reasoning can accommodate the use of prima facie reasons in conditional reasoning. For instance, knowing that $x$ is a bird and most birds can fly gives us a prima facie reason for thinking that $x$ can fly. This is a standard example from AI. Given this prima facie reason, if we know that there is a small animal in the next room and we are trying to identify it by the sounds it makes, we may among other things reason that if it is a bird then it can fly. No AI system of nonmonotonic reasoning can accommodate this inference. Our actual reasoning is very simple. We *suppose* that the animal is a bird, infer defeasibly that it can fly, and then discharge the supposition to conclude that if it is a bird then it can fly.[22]

The first success of the OSCAR project was the construction of an automated reasoning module that does reasonably sophisticated defeasible reasoning.[23] It was not a *total* success, however, because it was based upon some simplifying assumptions. It had three main shortcomings. First, it was not interest-driven. It drew every conclusion it could draw given its input. Second, it did not do suppositional reasoning, and correspondingly could not accommodate much purely deductive reasoning. Third, it ignored variations in strength between reasons, taking all reasons to be equally good. I now have an implementation of defeasible reasoning that avoids all of these shortcomings. It is constructed by extending the deductive reasoner described above. It is not yet adequately tested, but initial results are promising.

## 9.9 Conclusions

The objective of the OSCAR project is to design and build a general-purpose automated cognizer. This will be an introspective reasoner, built on top of non-introspective default theoretical and practical reasoners. The current stage of the project is concerned with the construction of the default theoretical reasoner. I have what purports to be a general purpose deductive and defeasible interest-driven reasoner. The next step will be to extend it (and test it further) by using it as the inference engine for systems that perform specific kinds of reasoning. My immediate target is the imple-

---

[22] For a more sustained critique of nonmonotonic reasoning systems, see chapter nine of my *Nomic Probability*.
[23] This is described in Pollock [1987].

mentation of at least parts of the theory of probabilistic and inductive reasoning described in my book on that topic.[24]

## Acknowledgments

This paper is reprinted, with minor revisions, from *The Journal of Theoretical and Experimental Artificial Intelligence.*

## References

Andrews, P. B., F. Pfenning, S. Issar, C. P. Klapper. 1985. The TPS Theorem Proving System. *8th International Conference on Automated Deduction.* J. H. Siekman, ed. Springer-Verlag.

Andrews, P. B., D. A. Miller, E. L. Cohen, and F. Pfenning. 1983. Automating higher order logic. *Automated Theorem Proving: After 25 Years.* W. W. Bledsoe and D. W. Loveland, eds. American Mathematical Society.

Bledsoe, W. 1977. Non-reduction theorem proving. *Artificial Intelligence* 9, 1–35.

Bledsoe, W. 1983. Some automatic proofs in analysis. *Automated Theorem Proving: After 25 Years.* W. W. Bledsoe and D. W. Loveland, eds. American Mathematical Society.

Bledsoe, W., and Tyson, M. 1975. The UT interactive theorem prover. University of Texas at Austin Math Department Memo ATP–17.

Boyer, R., and J. Moore. 1979. *A Computational Logic.* Academic Press.

Chisholm, Roderick. 1957. *Perceiving.* Cornell University Press.

Chisholm, Roderick. 1966. *Theory of Knowledge.* First edition. Prentice Hall.

Chisholm, Roderick. 1977. *Theory of Knowledge.* Second edition. Prentice Hall.

Cohn, A. 1985. On the solution of Schubert's steamroller in many sorted logic. *IJCAI85.*

Delgrande, J. P. 1988. An approach to default reasoning based on a first-order conditional logic: revised report. *Artificial Intelligence* 36, 63–90.

Doyle, J. 1979. A truth maintenance system. *Artificial Intelligence* 12, 231–272.

Doyle, J. 1988. On universal theories of default. Carnegie Mellon Computer Science Department, Technical Report CMU–CS–88–111.

Doyle, J. 1988a. Artificial intelligence and rational self-government. Carnegie Mellon Computer Science Department, Technical Report CMU–CS–88–124.

Etherington, D. 1987. Formalizing non-monotonic reasoning systems. *Artificial Intelligence* 31, 41–86.

Etherington, D., and Reiter, R. 1983. On inheritance hierarchies with exceptions. *Proceedings of AAAI–83.*

Fodor, J. 1975. *The Language of Thought.* Thomas Y. Crowell.

Hanks, S., and McDermott, D. 1987. Nonmonotonic logic and temporal projection. *Artificial Intelligence* 33, 379–412.

---

[24] Pollock [1990a].

Holland, J., K. Holyoak, R. Nisbett, and P. Thagard. 1986. *Induction*. Bradford/MIT Press.

Horty, J., Thomason, R., and Touretzky, D. 1987. A skeptical theory of inheritance in non-monotonic semantic nets. *Proceedings of AAAI-87*.

Kyburg, H., Jr. 1974. *The Logical Foundations of Statistical Inference*. Reidel.

Kyburg, H., Jr. 1983. The reference class. *Philosophy of Science 50*, 374–397.

Kyburg, H., Jr. 1979. Attitudes de dicto and de se. *Philosophical Review 87*, 513–543.

Loui, R. 1987. Defeat among arguments: a system of defeasible inference. *Computational Intelligence 3*.

Lusk, E., and R. Overbeek 1984. The automated reasoning system ITP. ANL–84–27, Argonne National Laboratory.

Lusk, E., W. McCune, R. Overbeek 1985. ITP at Argonne National Laboratory. *8th International Conference on Automated Deduction*. J. H. Siekman, ed. Springer-Verlag.

Martin, R. L. 1970. *The Paradox of the Liar*. Yale University Press.

Martin, R. L. 1984. *Recent Essays on Truth and the Liar Paradox*. Oxford University Press.

McCarthy, J. 1980. Circumscription—a form of non-monotonic reasoning. *Artificial Intelligence 13*, 27–39.

McCarthy, J. 1984. Applications of circumscription to formalizing common sense knowledge. *Proceedings of the Workshop on Nonmonotonic Reasoning*, 1984.

McDermott, D., and Doyle, J. 1980. Non-monotonic logic I. *Artificial Intelligence 13*, 41–71.

Moore, R. 1985. Semantic considerations on nonmonotonic logic. *Artificial Intelligence 25*, 75–94.

Murray, N. V. 1982. Completely non-clausal theorem proving. *Artificial Intelligence 18*, 67–85.

Nevins, A. 1974. A human oriented logic for automatic theorem proving. *Jour. Assoc. for Comput. Mach. 21*, 603–621.

Nute, D. 1988. Defeasible reasoning: a philosophical analysis in PROLOG. *Aspects of AI*. J. Fetzer, ed. Reidel.

Oppacher, F., and E. Suen. 1985. Controlling Deduction with Proof Condensation and Heuristics. *8th International Conference on Automated Deduction*. J. H. Siekman, ed. Springer-Verlag.

Oppacher, F., and E. Suen. 1988. HARP: A tableau-based theorem prover. *Journal of Automated Reasoning 4*, 69–100.

Pearl, J. 1988. *Probabilistic Reasoning in Intelligent Systems: Networks of Plausible Inference*. Morgan Kaufmann.

Pelletier, F. J. 1985. THINKER. *8th International Conference on Automated Deduction*. J. H. Siekman, ed. Springer-Verlag.

Pelletier, F. J. 1986. Seventy-five problems for testing automatic theorem provers. *Journal of Automated Reasoning 2*, 191–216.

Pollock, J. 1967. Criteria and our knowledge of the material world. *Philosophical Review 76*, 28–62.

Pollock, J. 1970. The structure of epistemic justification. *American Philosophical Quarterly*, monograph series 4, 62–78.

Pollock, J. 1974. *Knowledge and Justification*. Princeton University Press.

Pollock, J. 1986. *Contemporary Theories of Knowledge*. Rowan and Littlefield.

Pollock, J. 1987. Defeasible reasoning. *Cognitive Science 11*, 481–518.

Pollock, J. 1989. *How to Build a Person*. Bradford/MIT Press.

Pollock, J. 1989a. *OSCAR: a General Theory of Reasoning*. In preparation.

Pollock, J. 1990. Interest driven suppositional reasoning. *Journal of Automated Reasoning 6*, 419–462.

Pollock, J. 1990a. *Nomic Probability and the Foundations of Induction*. Oxford University Press.

Poole, D. 1985. On the comparison of theories: preferring the most specific explanation. *Proceedings of IJCAI–85*.

Poole, D. 1988. A logical framework for default reasoning. *Artificial Intelligence 36*, 27–48.

Reiter, R. 1980. On reasoning by default. *Artificial Intelligence 13*, 81–132.

Reiter, R., and Criscuolo, G. 1981. On interacting defaults. *Proceedings IJCAI–81*, 270–276.

Stickel, M. E. 1985. The KLAUS Automated Theorem Proving System. *8th International Conference on Automated Deduction*. J. H. Siekman, ed. Springer-Verlag.

Stickel, M. E. 1986. Schubert's steamroller problem: formulations and solutions. *Journal of Automated Reasoning 2*, 89–101.

Tarski, A. 1956. The concept of truth in formalized languages. *Logic, Semantics, and Metamathematics*. London.

Tversky, A., and D. Kahneman. 1974. Judgment under uncertainty: heuristics and biases. *Science 185*, 1124–1131.

Wos, L. 1988. *Automated Reasoning: 33 Basic Research Problems*. Prentice-Hall.

Wos, L., and S. Winker. 1983. Open questions solved with the assistance of AURA. *Automated Theorem Proving: After 25 Years*. W. W. Bledsoe and D. W. Loveland, eds. American Mathematical Society.

# 10  Models and Minds: Knowledge Representation for Natural-Language Competence

Stuart C. Shapiro and William J. Rapaport

## 10.1  Introduction

Knowledge representation is concerned, among other things, with the representation of information in artificial-intelligence (AI) computer systems. Few, if any, researchers claim at the outset to be working on an AI system whose abilities are co-extensive with human intellectual abilities, so most AI systems are designed to work on a narrower (if still broad) domain, such as vision, problem solving, robotics, or natural-language processing. It may be argued that in order to reach human-level abilities in any one of these areas, it is necessary to have human-level abilities in all the others. If that is true, then choosing an area of AI to work on is just a research strategy for working on general AI. In any case, the choice determines what one thinks are the problems to be worked on (initially) and the information that needs to be represented.

In this paper, we shall consider the information that needs to be represented by an AI system whose domain is general natural-language processing. By "natural-language processing," we mean the use of natural human languages (e.g., English) for the kind of communication with agents (human or computer) that humans engage in when they communicate with each other in those languages. In particular, we exclude the kinds of text processing that treat natural-language texts as uninterpreted strings of characters (such as producing a concordance), and we include both natural-language *generation* and natural-language *understanding*, for which we suggest the term *natural-language competence* (NLC). The quintessential NLC task is interactive dialogue, although other tasks (such as reading and summarizing a narrative or translating a text from one natural language to another) have been recognized by AI researchers as requiring the same abilities.

In order to focus on the information that an NLC system needs, it is useful to consider briefly, by way of contrast, the information needed by some other intelligent systems (remembering, however, that, as an NLC system is extended into a general intelligent system, it, too, will need such information). Robot systems (both for locomotion and for manipulation) and vision systems must operate in the here and now of the real world. The way the world really is (the subject of physics) is important to them, because they must operate in it. They must recognize multiple interactions with the same physical object as *being* interactions with the same physical object. This is the essence of the stereo vision problem: a mobile robot can go between two objects but must go around one; a manipulator needs at least two points of contact to grasp an object. On the other hand, although face-to-face dialogue often includes references to objects in the current environment, the essence of natural language is the ability to discuss the not-here and the not-now.

Distinguishing "knowledge representation" from "data storage" is not easy, but Brian Cantwell Smith's Knowledge-Representation Hypothesis is fairly well accepted:

Any mechanically embodied intelligent process will be comprised of structural ingredients that a) we as external observers naturally take to represent a propositional account of the knowledge that the overall process exhibits, and b) independent of such external semantical attribution, play a formal but causal and essential role in engendering the behaviour that manifests that knowledge. (Smith 1982:33)

As is often the case in AI, this takes key terms (such as "knowledge") on their pre-theoretic meaning, to be attributed (or not) to AI systems by the same criteria by which they are attributed to humans.

The declarative/procedural controversy (Winograd 1975) has fairly well died out, and it would seem that the "structural ingredients" in Smith's Knowledge-Representation Hypothesis, which are to be taken as the represented knowledge, could be either declarative or procedural. It is clear that the declarative knowledge of a system could be considered procedural to the extent that it plays a "causal and essential role in engendering ... behaviour". However, the distinction is still useful if worded in a slightly different way than it has been in the past. Let us consider as *procedural knowledge* that knowledge that *only* plays such a causal role, and let us consider as *declarative knowledge* that knowledge that the system can discuss with another. So, for example, humans act as though they know the grammar of their native language (competence), but most cannot describe that grammar at all, and no one has yet been able to describe it completely. So we would say that people have procedural knowledge of the grammar of their native language, but not declarative knowledge of it. In this paper, we shall concentrate on discussing the declarative knowledge needed by a system for human-level NLC abilities, rather than the procedural knowledge needed for NLC. (For a discussion of the latter, see Weischedel 1986.)

## 10.2   Intensional Knowledge Representation

Insofar as an AI/NLC system is considered a model of a cognitive agent, the information represented in its "mind" consists of the beliefs, knowledge, and other intentional (i.e., psychological) attitudes of the agent, together with the objects, properties, and relations that those attitudes are directed to. (On the information represented, cf. Brachman and Smith 1980; on the notion of "mind," cf. Rapaport 1988a.)

Thus, cognitive agents, whether human or computer, that engage in natural-language discourse and that have beliefs about the beliefs of other cognitive agents must be able to represent objects the way they believe them to be and the way they believe others believe them to be. They must be able to represent other cognitive agents both as objects of beliefs and as agents of beliefs. They must be able to represent their own beliefs, and they must be able to represent beliefs as objects of beliefs.

A fair number of AI researchers have described systems, both theoretical and implemented, that address these issues. One remaining controversy is the number of levels of representation required to solve the problem. Consider a cognitive agent, C, with beliefs about another cognitive agent, O. Let "A" be the term C uses in its belief structure to refer to O. That is, if C believes that some property holds of O, then the term "A" actually occurs in the structure representing that belief. Here are some questions to consider:

• Does "A" refer to O extensionally, as an object-in-the-world, or only intensionally, as C's conceptualization of O?

• Are two terms, "A" and "A*", needed to represent the above two cases?

• Now suppose that "P" is the structure representing one of C's beliefs, Q, and that C believes that O also holds Q. Does it make sense for "P" and "A" to occur in C's structure representing the belief that O holds Q, without being quoted, primed, or otherwise modified?

• Suppose that C has another belief about the belief Q; how is "P" used to represent that belief?

In a series of earlier papers, we have argued that such a system must represent and reason about *intensional*, as opposed to *extensional*, entities (Maida and Shapiro 1982; Rapaport and Shapiro 1984; Rapaport 1985, 1986a; Wiebe and Rapaport 1986; Shapiro and Rapaport 1987a). Briefly, this means that, instead of storing information about *objects in the world*, as vision and robot systems must, NLC systems store information about *mental objects* that may or may not even exist. Our theory of intensional knowledge representation answers the above questions as follows:

- "A" refers to O intensionally, as C's conceptualization of O.

- No additional term is needed to refer to O as an object-in-the-world.

- It does make sense for "P" and "A" to occur in the structure C uses to represent its belief that O holds Q, without modification.

- Similarly, "P" may be used without modification in the representation of other of C's beliefs about Q.

In Shapiro and Rapaport 1987a, we discuss the use of the SNePS propositional semantic network processing system (Shapiro 1979) to build an NLC system according to our theory of intensional knowledge representation. This system, referred to as CASSIE (the *C*ognitive *A*gent of the *S*NePS *S*ystem—an *I*ntelligent *E*ntity) is a particular application of SNePS, with a particular set of arc labels and case frames, together with a generalized ATN parsing/generating grammar (Shapiro 1982) for a fragment of English. We refer to SNePS with these arcs, case frames, and grammar as SNePS/CASSIE.

In a series of papers, John Barnden has critiqued this theory. In Barnden 1986a, he claims that, under it, there is no consistent way of dealing with sentence sequences such as:

**(1)**   That John is taller than Mary is Kevin's favorite proposition.

**(2)**   Bill believes Kevin's favorite proposition.

Here, Bill is O, that John is taller than Mary is Q, (2) expresses the belief that O believes Q, and (1) expresses another belief about Q. He has also objected that a knowledge-representation system such as ours "imputes" "arcane" theories to cognitive agents, cannot quantify over intensions, and cannot represent the differences between an entity and an idea of that entity (Barnden 1986b, 1989).

In this essay, we extend, deepen, and, we hope, clarify, our theory of intensional knowledge representation implemented in CASSIE, and we discuss how CASSIE handles Barnden's challenges. We hope thereby to shed light on general issues of the modeling of cognitive agents sophisticated enough to have beliefs about the beliefs of other cognitive agents.

## 10.3   Knowledge Representation Formalisms

### 10.3.1   Syntax and Semantics

A knowledge-representation formalism, like any language, has a syntax and a semantics. The syntax specifies those parts of the language (such as "terms" and "sentences") that can be given meanings (interpretations) by the semantics. Larger syntactic parts (such as sentences) are formed from smaller syntactic parts by putting the smaller parts together in various structured ways with the use of punctuation. We presume that the reader is already familiar with this (a typical example for a first-order language is discussed in Rapaport 1987).

Several different knowledge representation formalisms have been suggested for NLC systems. In the following sections, we survey a few of the major varieties, discussing their syntactic constructs and their intended domains of interpretation. (Other recent reviews of knowledge representation are Barr and Davidson 1981, Mylopoulos and Levesque 1984, Levesque 1986, and Kramer and Mylopoulos 1987. Recent collections of papers on knowledge representation relevant to NLC include Brachman and Levesque 1985, King and Rosner 1986, and Cercone and McCalla 1987.)

**10.3.1.1   Conceptual Dependency Theory.**   Conceptual Dependency theory (Schank and Rieger 1974, Schank 1975, Schank and Riesbeck 1981; cf. Hardt 1987) uses a knowledge-representation formalism consisting of sentences, called "conceptualizations", which assert the occurrence of events or states, and six types of terms: PPs—"real-world objects"; ACTs—"real-world actions"; PAs—"attributes of objects"; AAs—"attributes of actions"; Ts—"times"; and LOCs—"locations." (The glosses of these types of terms are quoted from Schank and Rieger 1974: 378–379.) The set of ACTs is closed and consists of the well-known primitive ACTs PTRANS (transfer of physical location), ATRANS (transfer of an abstract relationship), etc.

The syntax of an event conceptualization is a structure with six slots (or arguments), some of which are optional: actor, action, object, source, destination, and instrument. A stative conceptualization is a structure with an object, a state, and a value. Only certain types of terms can fill certain slots. For example, only a PP can be an actor, and only an ACT can be an action. Interestingly, conceptualizations themselves can be terms, although they are not one of the six official terms. For example, only a conceptualization can fill the instrument slot, and a conceptualization can fill the object slot if MLOC (mental location) fills the act slot. A "causation" is another kind of conceptualization, consisting only of two slots, one containing a causing conceptualization and the other containing a caused conceptualization.[1] Although, from the glosses of PP and ACT, it would seem that the intended domain of interpretation is the real world, the domain also must contain theoretically postulated objects such as: the "conscious processor" of people, in which conceptualizations are located; conditional events; and even negated events, which haven't happened.

**10.3.1.2 The KL-ONE Family.** KL-ONE (Brachman and Schmolze 1985) and its descendents, KL-TWO (Vilain 1985), KRYPTON (Brachman, Fikes, and Levesque 1983), and Loom (MacGregor and Bates 1987) separate their formalisms into two sub-languages—the definitional (or terminological) component, called the "TBox," and the assertional component, called the "ABox" (KL-ONE's separation is more rudimentary than that of the later systems). The ABox consists of sentences in a restricted first-order logic (e.g., KL-TWO doesn't allow any quantifiers) and are taken to assert truths in the domain of interest. Terms in the Abox have existential import. That is, constants represent individuals that exist in the domain, and an existentially quantified sentence of the form $\exists x P(x)$ asserts that an individual satisfying $P$ exists in the domain. Unary predicate symbols, relational predicate symbols, and function symbols in ABox sentences are themselves terms in the TBox. There are two types of terms in the TBox— concepts and relations (or roles). TBox sentences make assertions like, "A **family** is: a kind of **social-structure** with exactly 1 *male-parent* and this *male-parent* is a **man**; and a kind of **social-structure** with exactly 1 *female-parent* and this *female-parent* is a **woman**; and a kind of **social-structure** all

---

[1] Schank's notion of "causation," it should be noted, is such that two conceptualizations can "cause" *each other*. E.g., buying and selling events (both of which are ATRANSes) cause each other (cf. Schank and Riesbeck 1981:17).

of whose *child*ren are **persons**." Here, **family, social-structure, man, woman,** and **person** are concept terms; *male-parent, female-parent,* and *child* are relation terms; all other parts of the sentence are punctuation; and the sentence itself is taken as the definition of **family**. This last is most important—the sentence cannot be either true or false; it is simply a definition. If you think that this definition is incorrect, you cannot say, "No, you're wrong; a family isn't like that." You can only say, "Well, your concept of **family** is different from mine." Also, defining **family** in the TBox doesn't say that there are any in the domain of interest. That can only be said in the ABox by an existential statement such as $\exists x$**family**$(x)$ or by an ABox assertion such as **family** (Shapiro). TBox sentences about relations are also definitional. For example, we could use the relation *child* to define *son* as a *child* that is a **man**. NIKL (Moser 1983) is another descendent of KL-ONE and consists only of a TBox (in fact, it is the TBox of KL-TWO), so all sentences in NIKL are definitional.

**10.3.1.3  SNePS.**  The knowledge-representation formalism we are concerned with in this paper is SNePS/CASSIE. In this section, we give an introductory description of SNePS/CASSIE at the same level of detail we used for Conceptual Dependency and the KL-ONE family in the previous two sections.

The SNePS formalism consists of two parts, nodes and labeled, directed arcs. Nodes constitute the terms of the language; labeled, directed arcs are punctuation. Nodes are partitioned into atomic nodes, which have no arcs emanating from them, and molecular nodes, which do have arcs emanating from them. Every node represents some entity in the domain of discourse, and no two nodes represent the same entity. (We have called this the Uniqueness Principle.) The entity represented by a node is determined in one of two ways: it is determined *assertionally* by the subnetwork connected to the node via arcs pointing into it; it is determined *structurally* by the subnetwork connected to the node via arcs pointing out of it. (There are no cycles of arcs.) Once a node is created, it can get new arcs pointing into it, but the set of arcs pointing out of it can never change, so the structurally determined nature of a node is more characteristic of it than its assertionally determined nature. Notice that the semantics is not compositional, since the interpretation of an atomic node is not fixed independently of the nodes that get their structural interpretation by dominating it (having arcs that point out of them into it). In a sense, the semantics is circular—two nodes connected to each other each partially determine the other's meaning. A major escape from this circularity is the set of *sensory* nodes (cf. Rapaport 1988a), which are atomic nodes representing lexical entries of the language that CASSIE uses to communicate with other cognitive agents (e.g., people). The entity represented by a molecular node is structurally determined semicompositionally by the set of nodes it dominates[2] and by the labels of the arcs that connect it to them. For example, a node with a LEX arc to a sensory node represents the entity referred to by the lexeme that the sensory node represents, and a node with an OBJECT arc to a node $i$ and a PROPERTY arc to a node $j$ represents the proposition that the entity represented by $i$ has the property represented by $j$. This is the sense in which the arcs are punctuation.

Notice that some nodes (both molecular and atomic) represent propositions (we will call these *propositional nodes*), but all nodes are terms of the SNePS language. Thus, molecular nodes, whether they represent propositions or what are usually considered to be individuals, correspond more to functional terms in other languages than to sentences. Furthermore, every propositional node has an *assertion tag* that can be on or off. If propositional node $p$ represents proposition $[\![p]\!]$, then $p$'s assertion tag's being on represents the assertion, for CASSIE, that "I believe $[\![p]\!]$". The assertion tag's being off represents the absence of such belief. Finally, some propositional nodes can be interpreted by the SNePS Inference Package (SNIP) as *rule nodes*. Rule nodes represent deduction rules and are used for node-based deductive inference (Shapiro 1978; Shapiro and McKay 1980; McKay and Shapiro 1981; Shapiro, Martins, and McKay 1982).

The ideas outlined in this section will be expanded upon in the rest of this paper.

## 10.4  Semantics

### 10.4.1  Nodes, Mental Tokens, Concepts, and Actual Objects

Above, we said that instead of storing information about objects in the world, as vision and robot systems must, NLC systems store information about mental objects that may or may not even exist. CASSIE, as a cog-

---

[2] Only *semi*compositionally, because it partially assertionally determines the meaning of them.

nitive agent implemented in SNePS, is an "interpreted automatic formal system," to use Haugeland's (1985: 106) phrase. SNePS nodes are the tokens of CASSIE's mental language (cf. Fodor 1975, Stich 1983). As symbols of mental syntax, what do they denote? Our answer is that they denote elements of the domain that has been called "Aussersein": the domain of the objects of thought—the things we can think about, have beliefs about, and so forth, whether or not they exist or are true (Meinong 1904; Rapaport 1978, 1985; Shapiro and Rapaport 1987a). These elements can be called "mental objects" or "intensions." They are what we refer to as "concepts." So when we say that a node of SNePS/CASSIE represents a concept, we mean it in this way. Moreover, all representations of concepts are in CASSIE's mind. Thus, when CASSIE represents the beliefs of someone else, what is in her mind is CASSIE's representation of the beliefs of the other person, not the other person's actual beliefs. (We return to this in section 10.5.2.)

What is the relation between a concept (an intensional object in Aussersein) and objects in the world? Some concepts have objects in the world that *correspond to* them (Rapaport 1978 refers to the objects as the "Seincorrelates" of the concepts); some have one; some have more than one. Some have none: for instance, concepts of unicorns and square circles have no objects corresponding to them in the real world. The concept of the coffee cup that I[3] habitually use in and around my office has one object that corresponds to it. The concept of the straight-backed teak chair with black seat that I[4] have in my house has eight objects that correspond to it.

I[5] believe that I can recognize my coffee cup, but it may be that there is one exactly like it. If, some night, someone were to replace my coffee cup with one that looked exactly like it, I might not notice the difference (cf. The Ballad of Shakey's Pizza Parlor in Dennett 1982: 53–60). In that case, I would take the new cup to be my cup, the object that corresponds to the concept denoted by the mental token I have been using for that concept for years, and I would not create a new mental token for it. On the

[3] When "I" is used, the reader is invited to use a new mental token for a concept that is co-extensional with one of the two authors, but the reader does not know which.
[4] The reader may identify the referent of this "I" with the previous one, or may create a new mental token, again co-extensional with one of the two authors. In the latter case, the two "I's" might or might not refer to the same author, but in the former case, the reader is deciding that they refer to the same one, but still has not committed to which one.
[5] This now, surely, refers to the same author as one of the two previous "I's", and the reader should have no trouble deciding which.

other hand, I know I cannot distinguish my eight chairs at home, and have no beliefs about any individual one.

What do I mean by "my concept of X", and how does that relate to "your concept of X"? If my beliefs about X coincide exactly with your beliefs about X (no matter how long we discuss X, we find no disagreement), then our concepts of X are the same intensional objects (although there would be two nodes representing them, one in my mind, one in yours). However, if we disagree in the slightest about X, then our concepts of X are different intensional objects in Aussersein, even if one and the same object in the real world corresponds to them. This also applies to "CASSIE's concept of X" and "OSCAR's concept of X", where CASSIE and OSCAR (the Other SNePS Cognitive Agent Representation) are two different SNePS cognitive agents.[6]

### 10.4.2   Epistemological Ontology

What sorts of things are there in Aussersein? Since this is a question of what there is among mental objects, it is a question of epistemological ontology (cf. Rapaport 1985/1986). It can be answered by considering the naive ontology of things talked about in natural language—what the world would be like if it fit our language (Rapaport 1981; cf. Hobbs 1985).

One sort of mental object is people. I have beliefs about George Bush; so I have a concept of George Bush. My concept of George Bush includes beliefs that he is currently president of the United States, was vice-president of the United States, before that was director of the CIA, and so on. There is an object in the real world (at least, I believe so) that corresponds to the concept of a person named George Bush having these three properties. Depending on the rest of my beliefs about George Bush, there may or may not be an object in the real world corresponding to it (cf. Rapaport 1978).

Another sort of mental object is mental acts, such as acts of believing. Our concept of believing is being discussed in this essay, and there is a vast literature discussing other people's concepts of believing. Whether one believes that there is an object in the real world corresponding to believing depends on one's ontology (i.e., one's *non*-epistemological ontology), and the two authors of this paper sometimes disagree on that.

Another sort of mental object is propositions. Propositions are sometimes called "beliefs," "facts," or "truths," depending on what other beliefs

[6] Our OSCAR is, perhaps, a distant cousin of John Pollock's (1988) Oscar; cf. Rapaport, Shapiro, and Wiebe 1986.

the speaker has about the proposition being discussed. The ontological status of objects corresponding to propositions is as controversial as that of objects corresponding to believings.

There are other sorts of mental objects. Some are: properties, sentences, numbers, numerals, and truth values. These are all different sorts in the sense that we have different kinds of beliefs about them and believe that different kinds of properties are relevant to them.

When we discuss people, we refer to them by using a proper name, a definite noun phrase, or, sometimes, an indefinite noun phrase. We can refer to Ronald Reagan as "Ronald Reagan" or "Nancy Reagan's favorite actor." A particular understander at a particular time will take these referring expressions to refer to his or her own concept of Ronald Reagan, and may react accordingly.

When we discuss propositions, we often use the phraseology, "that ⟨clause⟩". For example, in the U.S. Declaration of Independence, we find, "We hold these truths to be self-evident, that all men are created equal, that they are endowed by their Creator with certain unalienable Rights, that among these are Life, Liberty and the pursuit of Happiness," and in Lincoln's Gettysburg Address we find, "a new nation conceived in liberty and dedicated to the proposition that all men are created equal." We could also refer to a proposition using a definite noun phrase, for example, "the first self-evident truth mentioned in the Declaration of Independence" or "Lincoln's favorite proposition." Whether the referent of "the first self-evident truth mentioned in the Declaration of Independence" *is the same as* the referent of "Lincoln's favorite proposition" depends on the particular beliefs of a particular understander.

People, believings, and propositions (those people, believings, and propositions that we have beliefs about) are denizens of the same universe—Aussersein. If CASSIE believes that Lincoln believed that all men are created equal, part of CASSIE's Lincoln concept is that he participates in a believing act (her concept of believing) directed to the proposition that all men are created equal (her concept of that proposition).

## 10.5 Topics in Knowledge Representation for Natural-Language Competence

In this section, we present short discussions of a series of topics we believe to be important for knowledge representation for NLC. We discuss these topics in terms of SNePS/CASSIE, not because we believe that they are only relevant to her, but because we feel that we can express ourselves most clearly using her as a model.

## 10.5.1   Knowledge and Belief

CASSIE needs to be able to represent her own beliefs. She should be able to represent them both *explicitly* (or consciously)—she must be able to *say* "I believe that $P$"[7]—and *implicitly* (or subconsciously)—she must be able to say "$P$" (and it must be the case that *we* can say, truthfully, that she believes that $P$). The latter is handled by *asserting* that $P$ (cf. section 10.3.1.3). The former is handled by having a node that represents CASSIE's self-concept (it has an "I"-pointer, similar to the "now"-pointer that marks (CASSIE's concept of) the current time (Rapaport, Shapiro, and Wiebe 1986; on the "now"-pointer, cf. Almeida and Shapiro 1983, Almeida 1987).

She must also be able to represent the beliefs of others: (a) *de re* belief reports ("John believes of Lucy that she is sweet", where 'Lucy' is the name that *CASSIE* uses to refer to the individual whom John believes to be sweet, whether or not that is how John would refer to her), (b) *de dicto* belief reports ("John believes that the girl next door is sweet", where 'the girl next door' is how CASSIE understands *John* to characterize her), and (c) quasi-indexical *de se* belief reports ("John believes that he* is rich", where the use of 'he' by CASSIE expresses what John would express with 'I'; cf. Castañeda 1966, Rapaport 1986a).[8] These are handled as shown in figures 10.1–10.3. In a linear, predicate language, these are, roughly,

(*de re*)   Name(b1, 'John') & Name(b2, 'Lucy') & Believes(b1, Sweet(b2))

(*de dicto*)   Name(b1, 'John') & Believes(b1, The-girl-next-door(b2)) & Believes(b1, Sweet(b2))

(*de se*)   Name(b1, 'John') & Believes(b1, Rich(b1))

Note that a sentence expressing a belief report can be *interpreted* as *de re* or *de dicto*, and the interpretation determines how the report will be

---

[7] She ought to be able to say this even if, in fact, she *doesn't* believe that $P$—perhaps she only *thinks* (mistakenly) that she believes that $P$.
[8] The '*' marks a quasi-indexical, or "logophoric" pronoun; cf. Sells 1987, Zubin in Rapaport, Segal, et al. 1989.

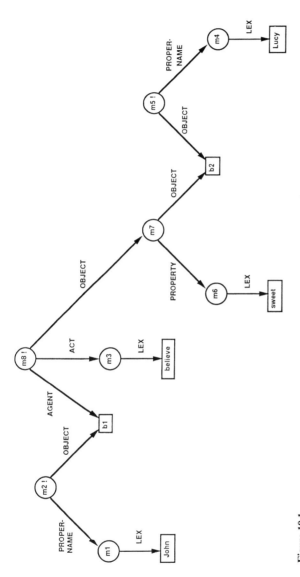

**Figure 10.1**
SNePS/CASSIE representation of the *de re* belief report, 'John believes of Lucy that she is sweet'.

m2 = b1 is named 'John'
m5 = b2 is named 'Lucy'
m8 = b1 believes that m7
m7 = b2 is sweet

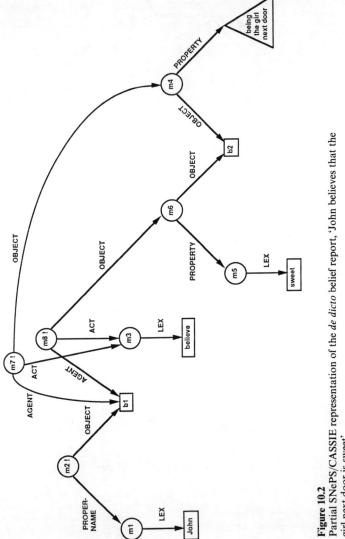

**Figure 10.2**
Partial SNePS/CASSIE representation of the *de dicto* belief report, 'John believes that the
girl next door is sweet'.
m2 = b1 is named 'John'                    m7 = b1 believes that m4
m8 = b1 believes that m6                   m4 = b2 is the girl next door
m6 = b2 is sweet                                   [partial representation]

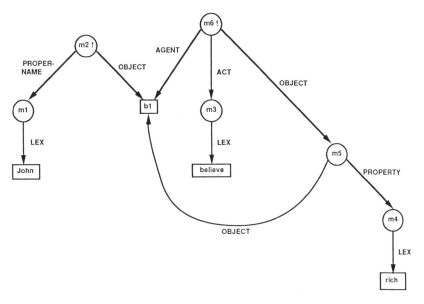

**Figure 10.3**
SNePS/CASSIE representation of the quasi-indexical, *de se* belief report, 'John believes that
he* is rich'.
m2 = b1 is named 'John'
m6 = b1 believes that m5
m5 = b1 is rich

represented. Once represented, the terms '*de re*' and '*de dicto*' no longer
apply (cf. Wiebe and Rapaport 1986). (The representation of a belief report
interpreted *de dicto* consists of two, linked representations of *de re* belief
reports. For a critique of this, see Wyatt 1990. The representation of *de se*
belief reports given here differs from that given in Rapaport and Shapiro
1984 and Rapaport 1986a. The reasons for the change are detailed in
Rapaport, Shapiro, and Wiebe 1986, and are related to our representation
for knowledge reports and the veridicality principle, described next.)

Arguably, there are also *de re, de dicto,* and *de se* knowledge reports;
these are represented similarly, replacing the sensory-node labeled with the
lexeme 'believe' by a sensory-node labeled 'know'. A rule of veridicality
(that what one knows is true) allows CASSIE to infer that if she believes
that John knows that *P*, then she believes that *P*. That rule is shown in
figure 10.4, roughly, it is:

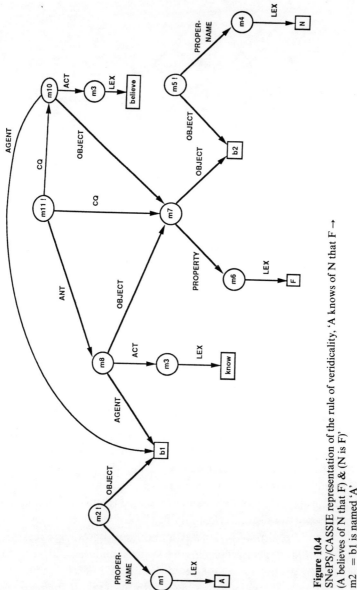

**Figure 10.4**
SNePS/CASSIE representation of the rule of veridicality, 'A knows of N that F →
(A believes of N that F) & (N is F)'
m2  = b1 is named 'A'
m5  = b2 is named 'N'
m11 = m8 → m10 & m7    [N.B.: The universal quantifers are not shown, for legibility.]
m8  = b1 knows that m7
m10 = b1 believes that m7
m7  = b2 is F

(Veridicality)

(CASSIE believes that $A$ knows of $N$ that F) $\rightarrow$

(CASSIE believes that $A$ believes of $N$ that F) & (CASSIE believes that $N$ is F)

(For a detailed justification of this rule, see Rapaport, Shapiro, and Wiebe 1986.)

### 10.5.2 Fully Intensional Knowledge Representation in SNePS

In order to distinguish the sort of intensional knowledge representation that we advocate, it will be useful to compare our theory with those of Hector-Neri Castañeda (1972, 1975ab, 1977) and Gottlob Frege (1892). We choose these, since, like ours, they are "fully intensional" in the sense that they do not use any notion of possible worlds. (There are, of course, possible-worlds analyses of Fregean theories, but Frege himself did not use them.)

One standard way to see how a semantic theory works is to test it on various "puzzles" (cf. Russell 1905). We shall give CASSIE the following puzzle (from Castañeda 1989; cf. Castañeda 1984):

Castañeda's Puzzle

The following seven statements, according to standard principles of logic, imply a contradiction:

**(1)**    At the time of the pestilence, Oedipus believed that: Oedipus's father was the same as his own father but the previous King of Thebes was not the same as his own father.

**(2)**    Oedipus's father was the same as the previous King of Thebes.

**(3)**    It was not the case that at the time of the pestilence Oedipus believed that: the previous King of Thebes was the same as his own father but the previous King of Thebes was not the same as his own father.

**(T1)**    For any individuals $x$ and $y$: if $x$ is (genuinely or strictly) identical with $y$, then whatever is true of $x$ is true of $y$, and vice versa.

**(T2)**    The sentential matrix occurring in (1) and (3), namely: 'at the time of the pestilence, Oedipus believed that: __ was the same as his own father but the previous King of Thebes was not the same as his own father', expresses something true of (a property of) the individual denoted by the singular term that by filling the blank in the matrix produces a sentence expressing a truth.

**(T3)**    The expression 'was the same as' in (2) expresses genuine or strict identity.

**(T4)**   The singular terms 'the previous King of Thebes' and 'Oedipus's father' have
exactly the same meaning and denotation in both direct and indirect speech.[9]

Frege's theory can resolve the contradiction by accepting (T1)–(T3) and
rejecting (T4). The rejection of (T4) is accomplished by his introduction of
the sense–reference distinction: On his theory, the singular terms mentioned in (T4) differ in sense and reference in direct and indirect speech.

Castañeda's theory resolves the contradiction by accepting (T1), (T2),
and (T4), but rejecting (T3). The meaning of a term is always a "guise" (a
kind of intensional entity that is "located" in the actual world); thus (T4) is
maintained. But 'is the same as' is taken as ambiguous among several
different kinds of "sameness" relations, chief of which are "consubstantiation" (*very* roughly, co-extensionality) and "consociation" (*very* roughly,
co-extensionality within an intensional context). In particular, (2) is taken
as expressing the consubstantiation of two guises. (For details, see Castañeda 1972, 1975b, 1977, and, especially, 1975a; cf. Rapaport 1978, 1985.)

On our SNePS/CASSIE theory, however, all of (T1)–(T4) can be accepted without contradiction. CASSIE interacts with other cognitive
agents in (fragments of) natural language, interpreting each sentence in
light of her previous beliefs (cf. Shapiro and Rapaport 1987a, Rapaport
1988a). In this regard, our theory is similar to Hans Kamp's Discourse Representation Theory (Kamp 1984 and forthcoming; Asher 1986, 1987). Imagine CASSIE being told sentences (1)–(3), in that order. There are several ways she can interpret the descriptions in these sentences depending
on her previous beliefs. Figure 10.5 shows one version of a SNePS semantic
network of concepts and propositions representing CASSIE's beliefs after
hearing (3).

After understanding (3), CASSIE believes the propositions represented
by the following molecular nodes:

• m2 (that someone—namely, the individual represented by atomic node
b1—is named 'Oedipus')

• m5 (that Oedipus believes that someone—namely, the individual represented by node b2—is named 'Oedipus')

---

[9] (T4) is ambiguous. The intended reading is that 'the previous King of Thebes' has exactly
the same meaning and denotation in both direct and indirect speech, and so does 'Oedipus's
father', not that the two descriptions have the same meaning and denotation as each other.

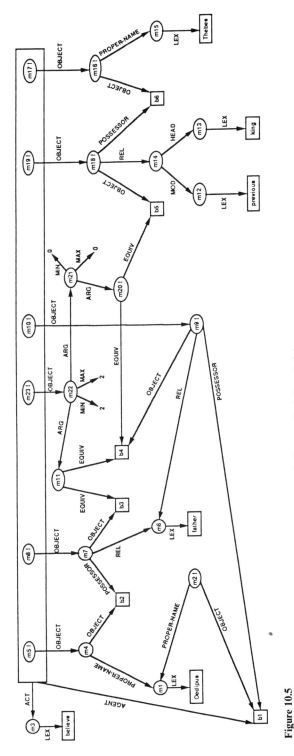

**Figure 10.5**
CASSIE's mind representing the information in sentences (1), (2), and (3) of Castañeda's Puzzle. Each node in the rectangle has an AGENT arc to node b1 and an ACT arc to node m3, so the nodes with OBJECT arcs pointing to them from the nodes in the rectangle represent propositions that CASSIE believes that Oedipus (represented by b1) believes.

- m8 (that Oedipus believes that someone—namely, the individual represented by node b3—is the father of the individual he believes to be Oedipus, that is, of the individual represented by b2)
- m9 (that the individual represented by node b4 is Oedipus's father)
- m10 (that Oedipus believes that the individual represented by b4 is his father)—that is, CASSIE believes that Oedipus believes that Oedipus's father is the same as his own father
- m16 (that something—namely, the individual represented by node b6— is named 'Thebes')
- m17 (that Oedipus believes that b6 is named 'Thebes')
- m18 (that something, b5, is Thebes's previous king)
- m19 (that Oedipus believes that b5 is Thebes's previous king)
- m20 (that b4 = b5, i.e., that Oedipus's father is Thebes's previous king)
- m23 (that Oedipus believes that m22, that is, that Oedipus believes *both* that m11 [i.e., that b3 = b4, i.e., that Oedipus's father is his own father] *and* that m21 [i.e., that it is not the case that m20, i.e., that b4 ≠ b5, i.e., that his own father ≠ Thebes's previous king]—i.e., CASSIE believes that Oedipus believes that Thebes's previous king is not the same as his own father)

(We are ignoring temporal information for simplicity, but without loss of generality; the representation of temporal information in SNePS is discussed in Almeida and Shapiro 1983, Almeida 1987.)

Note that there is no contradiction in this figure. To see why, consider each of (T1)–(T4):

**(T1)**  In SNePS, there are two ways to represent "sameness": (a) by following the Uniqueness Principle (cf. section 10.3.1.3) and using a single node, or (b) by using two nodes and asserting an "EQUIV"-proposition about them (such as propositional nodes m11 and m20 of figure 10.5; cf. Maida and Shapiro 1982, Rapaport 1986a). Only the former is genuine or strict identity; the latter is co-extensionality within a belief space (corresponding, roughly, to Castañeda's "consociation"). In SNePS, A is "true of" B if A is asserted of B. But if $x$ and $y$ are genuinely or strictly identical (i.e., are the same node), then surely whatever is true of one is true of the other. So SNePS/CASSIE accepts (T1).

**(T2)**   The hidden agenda behind (T2) concerns referential opacity and transparency. Thesis (T2) asserts that the blank in the quoted context is in a referentially transparent position. Now, SNePS/CASSIE distinguishes between *de re* and *de dicto* belief reports (cf. section 10.5.1). So there are really two versions of (T2) for us to consider. On the *de re* version, the issue concerns the network fragment that consists of (a) the representation of a *de re* report of the appropriate form minus (b) the node representing whatever fills the blank: Is this fragment asserted of whatever is represented by that node? In SNePS/CASSIE, it is; so SNePS/CASSIE accepts the *de re* version of (T2). On the *de dicto* version, the issue concerns the network fragment that consists of (a) the representation of a *de dicto* report of the appropriate form minus (b) the node representing whatever fills the blank: Is this fragment asserted of that blank filler? But recall that we represent *de dicto* belief reports using two representations of *de re* belief reports (cf. section 10.5.1). So, the answer here is the same as before: SNePS/CASSIE accepts the *de dicto* version of (T2), also. Figure 10.5 shows the *de dicto* interpretation of (1) with respect to "Oedipus's father," so the node representing the individual denoted by the term filling the blank is b3.

**(T3)**   Since CASSIE hears (2) *after* hearing (1), *she already has separate concepts of Oedipus's father* (represented by node b4 of Figure 5) *and the previous King of Thebes* (represented by node b5). So her representation of (2) has to be a proposition asserting that those nodes are "EQUIV"alent (represented by node m20). Hence, in this case, SNePS/CASSIE rejects (T3). However, if CASSIE had heard (2) *before* (1), her interpretation of (2) *could* be (and there is psychological evidence that it *should* be: see Anderson 1977, 1978; cf. Maida and Shapiro 1982) *two* propositions asserting of a *single* entity both that *it* was Oedipus's father and that *it* was the previous King of Thebes. In that case, SNePS/CASSIE would accept (T3).

**(T4)**   We now come to the heart of the matter (cf. section 10.4.1): All nodes in the semantic network representing CASSIE's mind represent concepts in CASSIE's mind only. They never represent concepts in any other cognitive agent's mind. Concepts that are represented as being in another cognitive agent's belief space are just CASSIE's concepts about which she has beliefs that the other cognitive agent has beliefs about them.

(We have made this methodologically solipsistic point in Wiebe and Rapaport 1986. Wilks (1986: 267) makes a similar point, calling this "recursive cognitive solipsism".) Thus, (T4) is too simplistically stated to be either accepted or rejected. If the understander takes the believer to have the same concept of the referent of the singular term as the understander herself, she will use exactly the same node for this occurrence in indirect speech as she uses for occurrences in direct speech. (Figure 10.5 shows CASSIE making this interpretation for both "Thebes" and "the previous King of Thebes.") However, if the understander chooses to allow for the believer's having a different concept of the referent of the singular term, then she will use a different node, and this occurrence in indirect speech will not have exactly the same meaning as an occurrence of the term in direct speech. (Figure 10.5 shows CASSIE making this interpretation for the second occurrence of "Oedipus" and for the occurrence of "Oedipus's father" in (1).)

Thus, we do not, and do not need to, reject any of (T1)–(T4), though we do reinterpret some of them.

### 10.5.3   Belief Spaces

We define a believer's *belief space* to be the set of nodes (and, by extension, the concepts represented by them) dominated by propositional nodes representing propositions believed by the believer. All the nodes in figure 10.5 are in CASSIE's belief space. All the nodes in figure 10.5 dominated by (and including) nodes m4, m7, m9, m16, m18, and m22 are in the belief space of CASSIE's concept of Oedipus, referred to as (Oedipus CASSIE) in the notation of Rapaport and Shapiro 1984, Rapaport 1986a, and Wiebe and Rapaport 1986. We say "CASSIE's concept of Oedipus" rather than just "Oedipus", because Oedipus's belief space is in his own mind, while all nodes in figure 10.5 are in CASSIE's mind. (Oedipus CASSIE)'s belief space contains the nodes representing concepts that CASSIE believes to be in Oedipus's belief space. That is the sense in which (Oedipus CASSIE)'s belief space is CASSIE's model of Oedipus's belief space.

*All* nodes in (Oedipus CASSIE)'s belief space are also in CASSIE's belief space. *Some* of the nodes in (Oedipus CASSIE)'s belief space are such that CASSIE and (Oedipus CASSIE) have nearly the same beliefs about them. That is the case when CASSIE believes that Oedipus has a mental token representing an intensional object in Aussersein that closely resembles the intensional object that the node represents for CASSIE. For example, both CASSIE and (Oedipus CASSIE) believe the proposition represented by node m16 in figure 10.5. Thus, CASSIE believes that Oedipus has nearly the same concept of Thebes (node b6) as she does. Similarly, CASSIE believes that she and Oedipus closely agree on the concept of the previous King of Thebes (node b5), as well as the concept of the being-the-father-of relation (node m6), etc. The reason that this is close agreement rather than exact sharing of concepts is that, for example, CASSIE's concept of Thebes includes certain beliefs about its previous king that are not shared by (Oedipus CASSIE).

When CASSIE allows for the possibility that Oedipus and she might have very different concepts of an individual satisfying some description, she uses two nodes, one just in her belief space and one in (Oedipus CASSIE)'s belief space. For example, in figure 10.5, node b1 represents Oedipus for CASSIE, whereas b2 represents Oedipus for (Oedipus CASSIE). Only in this way can the sentence "Oedipus believed that Oedipus's father was the same as his own father" say anything non-tautologous. "His own father" refers to (Oedipus CASSIE)'s father, represented by b4, whereas this occurrence of "Oedipus's father" refers to (Oedipus Oedipus CASSIE)'s father, represented by b3. (Oedipus CASSIE)'s belief that they are the same is represented by node m11.

It might be noticed that figure 10.5 does not show m11 as being believed by (Oedipus CASSIE). Instead, (Oedipus CASSIE) believes m22, which is the conjunction of m11 and m21. Reasoning within a belief space may be carried out by the SNePS Belief Revision system (SNeBR; Martins and Shapiro 1983, 1988), assuming that all believers accept SNeBR's rules of inference. A SNeBR belief space, consisting of a set of hypotheses and all propositions derived from them, may be initialized with all propositions believed by (Oedipus CASSIE) and all propositions believed by CASSIE to be "common knowledge." SNeBR's conclusions, which in this case would include m11, could then be installed into (Oedipus CASSIE)'s belief space by making them the objects of believings by (Oedipus CASSIE). This is another way in which CASSIE can use (Oedipus CASSIE)'s belief space as a model of Oedipus's belief space.

As another example, consider figure 10.6, which shows CASSIE's belief space after she has processed the two sentences of Barnden's challenge (cf. section 10.2). As before, nodes with assertion tags (exclamation marks) represent beliefs held by CASSIE. All the nodes in figure 10.6 are in CASSIE's belief space. The nodes in figure 10.6 dominated by (and including) node m6 are in the belief space of CASSIE's concept of Bill, i.e.,

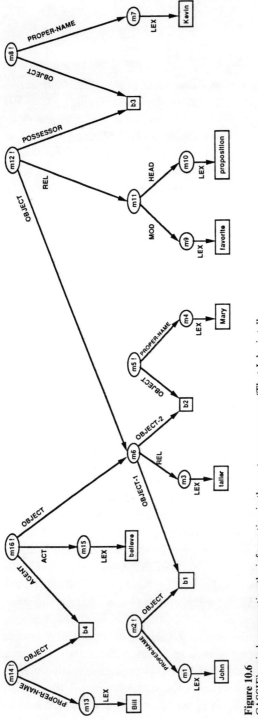

**Figure 10.6**
CASSIE's mind representing the information in the sentence sequence, 'That John is taller than Mary is Kevin's favorite proposition. Bill believes Kevin's favorite proposition.'

m2 = b1 is named 'John'      m16 = b4 believes that m6
m5 = b2 is named 'Mary'      m6 = b1 is taller than b2
m8 = b3 is named 'Kevin'     m12 = m6 is the m11 of b3
m14 = b4 is named 'Bill'     m11 = being the favorite proposition of

(Bill CASSIE). We say "CASSIE's concept of Bill" rather than just "Bill", because Bill's belief space is in his own mind and all nodes in figure 10.6 are in CASSIE's mind. (Bill CASSIE)'s belief space contains the nodes representing concepts that CASSIE believes to be in Bill's belief space. That is the sense in which (Bill CASSIE)'s belief space is CASSIE's model of Bill's belief space.

*All* nodes in (Bill CASSIE)'s belief space are also in CASSIE's belief space. However, CASSIE and (Bill CASSIE) may hold different beliefs about them. For example, since CASSIE gave a *de re* reading to "John is taller than Mary," she used nodes b1 and b2 to represent John and Mary, respectively. Node b1 represents the individual CASSIE believes to be named "John" and whom she believes that Bill believes to be taller than the individual represented by b2. CASSIE has no beliefs concerning the name that Bill uses when referring to the person represented by b1. Similarly, node m6 represents the proposition that CASSIE would express as "John is taller than Mary," and that she believes that Bill believes, although she, herself, doesn't believe it.

### 10.5.4   Concepts of Concepts: CASSIE as Cognitive Scientist

Now that we have explicated our understanding of the relationships among mental tokens, nodes, concepts, actual objects, concepts of different cognitive agents, and concepts in different belief spaces, we will briefly discuss concepts of concepts.

The first thing to note is that we have, in fact, not yet discussed concepts of concepts. We have, however, discussed concepts. That is, this paper is intended to explicate our concept of concepts. CASSIE has heretofore had beliefs about people, properties, believings, propositions, and the like, but she has not had any beliefs about concepts. If we started discussing cognitive science with CASSIE, we could give her such beliefs. She would then develop a concept of concepts, and might have a theory (a coherent set of beliefs) of how concepts relate to people. In this way, concepts are just another sort of mental object on the same level as intensional people, believings, and propositions. Whether concepts in Aussersein have objects in the real world corresponding to them is another controversy, which we do not want to pursue.

It is an intriguing idea that we could give CASSIE a theory of concepts different from the one we employed in implementing her. There would be no way for her to tell that her theory was not in accord with the facts, unless she made a prediction about her own behavior that was not confirmed, because she does not have access to the data structures used to implement SNePS.

If CASSIE thought about the issues raised in this paper, she might have nodes representing her concept of Oedipus, her concept of her concept of Oedipus, her concept of OSCAR, her concept of Oedipus as she believes OSCAR thinks of him, and her concept of OSCAR's concept of Oedipus. These would be different nodes, since they represent different intensional objects. (We return to this issue in our reply to Barnden in section 10.6.)

### 10.5.5   Plans

Plans are mental objects that need to be represented in NLC systems. Plans can be discussed, reasoned about, formulated, and followed.

It may be thought that any AI system that can represent and use rules, and that can evaluate a predicate by computation rather than by inference, can just use rules to represent plans. For example, Prolog is such a system, and one can view the Prolog rule,

$$p :- q, r, s.$$

either as the rule, "$p$ is true if $q$, $r$, and $s$ are true", or as the plan, "If you want to do $p$, first do $q$, then do $r$, and then do $s$." SNePS is also such a system, but in SNePS it is quite clear that rules can only be used as plans for reasoning, not as plans for acting.

To understand the problem, consider the Prolog rule,

$$p :- q, r, q.$$

This is bizarre as a rule—once $q$ is determined as true, why bother to do so again? However, as a plan for acting, it is reasonable—there are many plans that require performing the same act more than once (for an appropriate meaning of "the same" applied to acts). The strict left-right depth-first control structure of most implementations of Prolog guarantees that the subgoal $q$ is activated twice regardless of whether the rule is supposed to be a reasoning rule or a plan for acting.

We can see that the use of rules as acting plans in Prolog depends on a pun: ',' is simultaneously interpreted as the logical operator *AND* and as the programming-language *sequence* operator.

SNePS does not make this pun. The corresponding SNePS rule is:

$$q \vmapsto [r \vmapsto [q \vmapsto p]]].$$

(where '$\vee\!\!\rightarrow$' is "or-entailment"; cf. Shapiro 1979, Shapiro and Rapaport 1987a). Although this specifies the same order of subgoal triggering as the Prolog version, SNIP would not attempt to work on $q$ the second time. It would just reuse the results of the first effort. Therefore, SNePS rules cannot be used as plans for acting.

Is this a deficit in SNePS? No, for two reasons. First, this refusal to work on the same subgoal more than once is not only efficient, it is one of the mechanisms that allow SNIP to work with unrestricted recursive rules (Shapiro and McKay 1980, McKay and Shapiro 1981), a facility Prolog does not have. Second, the Prolog pun amounts to a semantic confusion between the logical notion of truth (or belief) and the practical notion of action.

People can explain plans to each other using natural language. For example, a student might be told, "To sum some numbers, choose an accumulator variable, set it to zero, and then successively add the numbers to it." This sentence expresses a plan, using certain grammatical structures to express the structure of the plan. The student's understanding of the plan can then be tested by asking questions about it. For example, one might ask, "What should the accumulator variable be initialized to when summing a sequence of numbers?"

Recently, we have designed, implemented, and experimented with an initial version of SNACTor, a version of SNePS/CASSIE that can be given plans and other instructions about how to act in a fragment of English, that can discuss these plans and instructions, and that can carry them out (Kumar, Ali, and Shapiro 1988; Kumar 1990). This version acts in the blocks-world domain, using graphics as a simulation of the world. Of course, for an NLC system, the major action carried out is the generation of language, so one might expect an NLC system to be able to understand plans about how to express itself in natural language, reason about such plans, discuss them, and use them. The AI literature on planning is vast (see Vere 1987), but we know of no current NLC system that does all this. We have made a start in this direction via an initial test of SNACTor as multi-media interface to a geographic information system, but more work is needed.

### 10.5.6   Truth

We have persistently avoided providing a standard Tarskian denotational semantics for our networks (although nothing prevents us from doing so, in the manner, e.g., that Kamp 1984 does for his theory). For one reason, this is because the entire network is definitional (like a NIKL network; cf. section 10.3.1.2). For another, we are more interested in *CASSIE's representation* of the external world than in either the external world itself or the *correctness* of her representation of it. (This is another manifestation of our methodological solipsism.)

Consider figure 10.5 again. Node m16, by its syntactic position in the network, represents a proposition that there is something named "Thebes". This something has the properties represented by the rest of the network connected to it, and subtly changes as the network grows (cf. the "pegs" of Landman 1986). One property is that the individual represented by b5 was its previous king. Again, this may be true, false, or just confused. It may be that the previous king was in some ways alike, and in some ways different from, CASSIE's concept of him. Would that make m18 false? Would it make m16 false?

The only construct in SNePS/CASSIE of any assertional import is the device that declares certain propositions (such as the one represented by m16) to be believed by CASSIE, and *these assertions are true by virtue of being made*—CASSIE is just built that way.

If CASSIE utters a sentence generated from a proposition she believes, we might agree or disagree with that sentence. Just as with a person, we might say the sentence is true or false, or we might say that CASSIE is confused: "Your concept of Thebes is somehow different from mine. Let's discuss it."

## 10.6   Replies to Barnden's Objections

John Barnden (1986ab, 1989) has made several points that he presents as clarifications or objections to our intensional knowledge-representation theory as expressed in Maida and Shapiro 1982 and Rapaport and Shapiro 1984 (however, the reader should consult Rapaport 1986a and Shapiro and Rapaport 1987a for more recent formulations). We feel that some of Barnden's points are valid complaints about lack of clarity (or timidity) in our earlier papers, some stem from his confusion about our theory, and some stem from actual differences in our theories. In this section, we summarize Barnden's points and reply to them.

Barnden wonders whether we want our nodes to "ambassadorially represent" intensions or objects in the world, or denote one or the other

(1986a: 412). We are not sure we understand what Barnden means by "ambassadorially represents," but suspect that we would accept the idea that we intend nodes to ambassadorially represent intensions. We would not, however, accept Barnden's conclusion that, therefore, they *denote* objects in the world. Our ideas here were spelled out in section 10.4.1.

Barnden wonders whether we want our network to model a cognitive agent, to be used by a cognitive agent, or to be a theoretical tool (1986a: 412). The answer to this is: all three. It is a theoretical tool for understanding cognition; it uses the methodology of AI, in which one of the best theoretical tools is a computer model; and, in that sense, it is also a model of the mind of a cognitive agent. However, sometimes, a model of X *is* an X, and we believe that this is one of those cases (see section 10.7). Thus, the network also is used by a cognitive agent—CASSIE.

Barnden says that belief is a relation between an extensional person and an intensional proposition (1986a: 412–413) and that, therefore, "in determining what a proposition denoted by a node states, we sometimes 'dereference' the concepts denoted by argument nodes and sometimes we do not" (Barnden 1986a: 413). Instead, we believe that belief is an intentional stance ascribed to people (see Dennett 1978) and therefore is a relation between an intensional person and an intensional proposition (see section 10.5.3).

Barnden goes on to suppose that we would have practical problems building "a system that translates network fragments into natural-language statements. ... [W]e do not want the language generator coming out with a statement to the effect that a *concept of* Bill believes something, or to the effect that Bill believes some *truth-value*" (Barnden 1986a: 413; italics in original). That our system has no such problems may be seen from the CASSIE conversations below and in Shapiro and Rapaport 1987a and Shapiro 1989. See also the discussion of natural-language expressions that refer to intensional people and propositions in section 10.5.3, and the discussion of concepts of concepts in section 10.5.4.

As noted in section 10.2, Barnden suggests that we have no consistent way of dealing with sentence sequences such as

(1)  That John is taller than Mary is Kevin's favorite proposition.

(2)  Bill believes Kevin's favorite proposition.

because the node representing the proposition would have to be dereferenced in one context and not in the other (1986a: 413–414).

However, we have given these sentences to CASSIE, and the conversation went as follows:

: That John is taller than Mary is Kevin's favorite proposition.

I understand that that John is taller than Mary is Kevin's favorite proposition

: Bill believes Kevin's favorite proposition.

I understand that Bill believes of John that he is taller than Mary.

Input sentences are on the lines beginning with the ":" prompt. The other lines are CASSIE's responses. CASSIE's response to a statement is the phrase "I understand that" prefixed to a sentence that she generates from the belief structure formed while analyzing the input statement. CASSIE's belief space after hearing these two sentences is shown in figure 10.6. Node m6 is built when CASSIE understands the subject clause of sentence (1). Then it is given the property of being Kevin's favorite proposition. When CASSIE reads "Kevin's favorite proposition" in sentence (2), she takes it referentially to refer to the proposition represented by m6, and attaches it as the object of Bill's believing. Although CASSIE believes that the proposition represented by m6 is Kevin's favorite proposition, she does not express it that way, because she prefers to express propositions by giving their propositional content. The sentence comes out "... believes of John that he is taller than Mary" rather than "... believes that John is taller than Mary", because that is CASSIE's way of explicitly showing that a *de re* reading of "John" is appropriate.

A more general problem that Barnden sets for knowledge-representation systems is what he calls the "imputation problem" (1986b). Consider the following:

**(S)** Mike believes that the water is boiling.

**(S')** Mike believes that the water is forcibly expelling some water vapor.

and suppose that boiling = forcibly expelling some water vapor. Clearly, one of (S), (S') might be true while the other is false. Now suppose that X is an NLC program that represents 'The water is boiling' in its knowledge-representation language as:

**(F)** $\exists v [forcibly\text{-}expel(w, v) \land is\text{-}water\text{-}vapor(v)]$

According to Barnden, if X then represents (S) as:

**(G)**   $B(mike, \exists v [\,forcibly\text{-}expel(w, v) \wedge is\text{-}water\text{-}vapor(v)\,])$

then X *imputes* its own theory of boiling to Mike. (One might say that (G) is a *de dicto* belief report; cf. section 10.5.1.) Barnden sees this as a problem insofar as such an imputation is "harmful" (not all are), and he proposes a

> strategy for ameliorating the imputation problem in the case of representation schemes intended for ... [cognitive modeling]:
> STRATEGY 1. Make sure that all explications that the representation scheme induces are cognitively reasonable for human beings. In particular, do not explicate propositional attitudes in terms of arcane theoretical constructs.
> (Barnden 1986b: 341)

According to Barnden (1986b: 345f), this is the strategy pursued by SNePS even though an imputation problem remains: Consider

**(S15)**   Mike believes [*de re*] that Jim's mother is clever

(which we prefer to express as 'Mike believes of Jim's mother that she is clever'), and suppose

**(\*)**   George believes that Mike believes of Jim's mother that she is clever.

Now, how should these be represented by SNePS/CASSIE? The representation of (S15) might be as shown in figure 10.7a or 10.7b. That is, roughly,

**(S15a)**   Believes(Mike, Clever(b3)) & Mother-of(Jim, b3)

i.e., Mike believes of Jim's mother (b3) that she (b3) is clever, or

**(S15b)**   Believes(Mike, Clever(b4)) & Mother-of(Jim, b3) & Equiv(b4, b3)

i.e., Mike believes of someone (b4) who is equivalent to Jim's mother (b3) that she (b4) is clever. Accordingly, CASSIE's representation of (\*) might be as shown in figure 10.8a or 10.8b. That is, roughly,

**(\*a)**   Believes(George, Believes(Mike, Clever(b3))) & Believes(George, Mother-of(Jim, b3))

or

**(\*b)**   Believes(George, Believes(Mike, Clever(b4))) & Believes(George, Mother-of(Jim, b3)) & Believes(George, Equiv(b4, b3)).

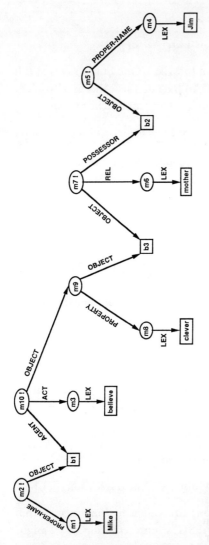

**Figure 10.7a**
One possible SNePS/CASSIE representation of (S15a), the *de re* belief report, 'Mike believes of Jim's mother that she is clever.'

m2 = b1 named 'Mike'        m10 = b1 believes that m9

m5 = b2 is named 'Jim'        m9   = b3 is clever

m7 = b3 is the mother of b2

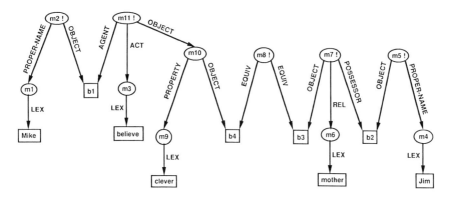

**Figure 10.7b**
Another possible SNePS/CASSIE representation of (S15b), the *de re* belief report, 'Mike believes of Jim's mother that she is clever.'

m2 = b1 is named 'Mike'          m8 = b4 is the same as b3
m5 = b2 is named 'Jim'           m11 = b1 believes that m10
m7 = b3 is the mother of b2      m10 = b4 is clever

Barnden says of CASSIE that she must represent (*) as in (*b),[10] which imputes a belief about Equiv to George, in violation of STRATEGY 1.

Our reply is quite simple: CASSIE would not represent (*) as in (*b) but as in (*a), which does not make the "harmful" imputation. But suppose that CASSIE's representations of (S15) and (*) were (S15b) and (*b): Is this "cognitively reasonable"? On the (b)-representations, CASSIE believes that George believes that there are two concepts: there is George's concept of Mike's concept of a clever person, and there is George's concept of Jim's mother; and CASSIE believes that George believes that these two concepts are equivalent. But this equivalence is not an arcane imputation to George; it is (merely) *CASSIE's* belief.[11]

Barnden also raises two further objections (1986b: 346; 1989, section 4): CASSIE has no way to quantify over intensions and no way to make statements about intensions themselves. For example, how would she represent the following?

[10] Actually, he says, *de dicto*, that Maida and Shapiro (1982) must represent (*) thus; cf. Barnden 1986b:345f.
[11] Arguably, (a) is less plausible than (b): On (a), CASSIE believes that George believes that there is a single concept: George's concept of Mike's concept of someone who *is*, on George's belief, Jim's mother. But surely it is plausible (and perhaps more so) for George to distinguish between his own concept of Jim's mother and Mike's concept of the clever person.

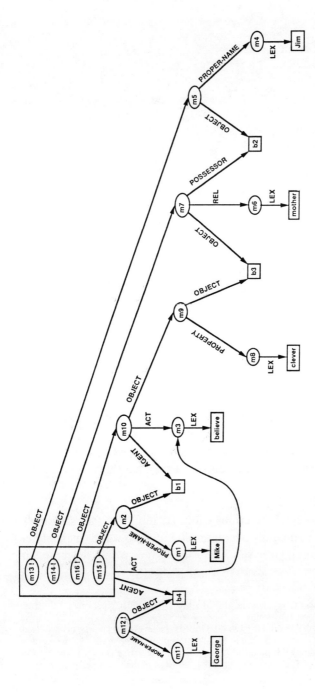

**Figure 10.8a**
One possible SNePS/CASSIE representation of (*a), 'George believes that Mike believes of
Jim's mother that she is clever.'

m12 = b4 is named 'George'                m14 = b4 believes that m7
m16 = b4 believes that m10               m13 = b4 believes that m5
m15 = b4 believes that m2

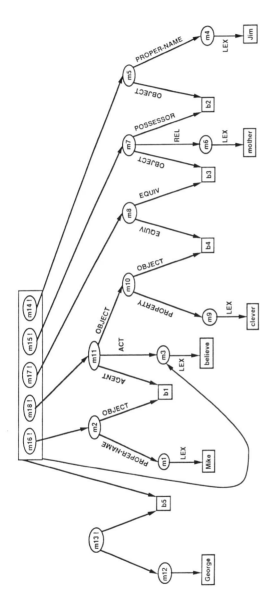

**Figure 10.8b**
Another SNePS/CASSIE representation of (*b), 'George believes that Mike believes of
Jim's mother that she is clever.'

m13 = b5 is named 'George'          m15 = b5 believes that m7
m18 = b5 believes that m11          m14 = b5 believes that m5
m16 = b5 believes that m2           m17 = b5 believes that m8

**(3)**    Mike believes everything Bill believes.

**(4a)**   Mike believes that some house he has a hazy idea of is red.

**(4b)**   Mike believes that someone is a spy, but he has only a hazy idea of whom it might be.

The representation of (3) is simple; see figure 10.9. Roughly, it is:

$\forall v1$ [Bill believes v1 $\rightarrow$ Mike believes v1]

The representations of (4a) and (4b) are a bit trickier. We must distinguish the concept of the house (or the spy) from the concept of the *idea of* the house (or the *idea of* the spy). (Cf. our earlier discussion of the difference between a concept and a concept of a concept.) We propose, tentatively, to represent this as in figure 10.10. Then (4a) and (4b) would be represented as in figures 10.11 and 10.12.[12]

## 10.7   Conclusions: Building Minds

We have discussed knowledge representation—more accurately, we feel, the representation of beliefs—in the context of AI systems having what we call natural-language competence. Knowledge representation for natural-language competence is different from knowledge representation for robot or vision systems, because the goal of an NLC system is not to make its way in the real world, but to converse with humans about all the topics that humans discuss—real, imaginary, theoretical, and impossible.

We have also attempted to clarify, extend, and deepen our theory of intensional knowledge representation. The main points were that there is no need for multiple terms in the belief-representation language of a cognitive agent for representing other cognitive agents in their roles as objects of belief and in their roles as agents of beliefs. Neither is there a need for multiple terms to represent propositions in their roles of propositions held by the cognitive agent, objects of normal beliefs, and objects of beliefs about believing them.

---

[12] The representation of (4b) is a bit more tentative than that of (4a), since it requires a theory of how to represent "knowing who": 'Mike has a (hazy) idea who the spy is' should probably be represented similarly to 'Mike knows who the spy is.'

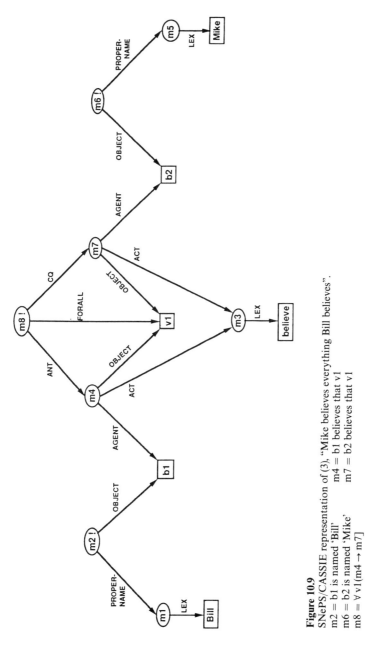

**Figure 10.9**
SNePS/CASSIE representation of (3), "Mike believes everything Bill believes".
m2 = b1 is named 'Bill'      m4 = b1 believes that v1
m6 = b2 is named 'Mike'      m7 = b2 believes that v1
m8 = ∀ v1(m4 → m7)

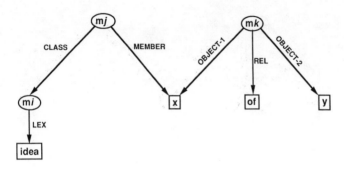

**Figure 10.10**
SN3PS/CASSIE case frame for 'x is an idea of y':
m$j$ = x is a (member of class) m$i$
m$k$ = x is (an idea) of y

We are now comfortable in adopting what Searle 1980 refers to as the strong AI position: an Artificial Intelligence *is* a cognitive agent and *has* a mind. Perhaps a computer simulation of a hurricane is not a hurricane (cf. Rapaport 1988b), and certainly a model of a horse is not a horse. But a wind-tunnel simulation of air flow *is* air flow, a wind-tunnel model of an airfoil *is* an airfoil, a wave-tank model of a wave *is* a wave, a model of a statue of a horse *is* a statue of a horse, and a computer model of a mind (if successful) *is* a mind (cf. Rapaport 1986b). As John Haugeland (1985: 255) says,

Perhaps Artificial Intelligence should be called 'Synthetic Intelligence' to accord better with commercial parlance. Thus artificial diamonds are fake imitations, whereas synthetic diamonds are genuine diamonds, only manufactured instead of dug up.... Despite the name, AI clearly aims at genuine intelligence, not a fake imitation.

Thus, SNePS/CASSIE is both a model of a mind (some arbitrary, individual mind) and a mind itself (CASSIE's mind), and a node of SNePS/CASSIE is both a model of a concept as well as being (in Barnden's phrase) "something that is *used by* [CASSIE] as a basis for its normal cognitive processing" (Barnden 1986a: 411).

The task facing researchers in knowledge representation for NLC is to design a mind with the ability to handle the range and complexity of thoughts that humans have.

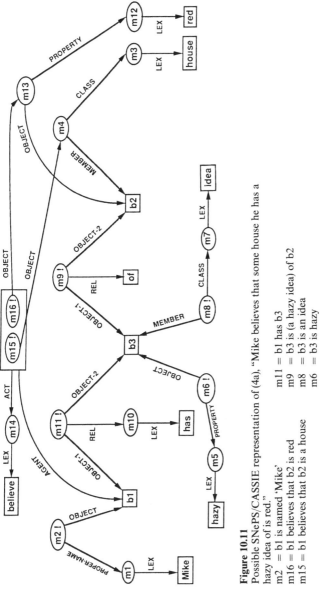

**Figure 10.11**
Possible SNePS/CASSIE representation of (4a), "Mike believes that some house he has a hazy idea of is red."

m2 = b1 is named 'Mike'
m16 = b1 believes that b2 is red
m15 = b1 believes that b2 is a house

m11 = b1 has b3
m9 = b3 is (a hazy idea) of b2
m8 = b3 is an idea
m6 = b3 is hazy

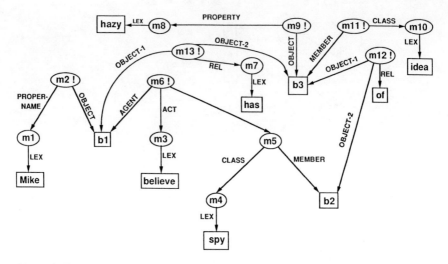

**Figure 10.12**
Possible SNePS/CASSIE representation of (4b), 'Mike believes that someone is a spy, but
he has only a hazy idea of whom it might be.'

m2 = b1 is named 'Mike'            m13 = b1 has b3
m6 = b1 believes that m5           m12 = b3 is (an idea) of b2
m5 = b2 is a spy                   m11 = b3 is an idea
                                   m9  = b3 is hazy

## Acknowledgments

This work was supported in part by the National Science Foundation
under Grant IRI–8610517 (Rapaport and Shapiro), and in part by the
Air Force Systems Command, Rome Air Development Center, Griffis
Air Force Base, New York 13441–5700, and the Air Force Office of
Scientific Research, Bolling AFB DC 20332 under Contract No. F30602–
85–C–0008, which supported the Northeast Artificial Intelligence Consortium (NAIC) (Shapiro).

The first author is grateful to Norman Sondheimer and the USC/Infor-
mation Sciences Institute for their support and hospitality during his
sabbatical year.

Both authors are grateful to Soon Ae Chun for her work on CASSIE's
grammar, and to the members of SNeRG (the SNePS Research Group),
for their contributions and discussion.

Earlier versions of portions of this essay appeared in Shapiro and Rapaport 1987b and Shapiro and Rapaport 1988.

# References

Almeida, M. J. 1987. Reasoning about the Temporal Structure of Narratives. SUNY Buffalo Department of Computer Science *Technical Report 87–10.*

Almeida, M. J. and S. C. Shapiro. 1983. Reasoning about the Temporal Structure of Narrative Texts. *Proceedings of the 5th Annual Conference of the Cognitive Science Society, University of Rochester.* Hillsdale, NJ: Lawrence Erlbaum.

Anderson, J. R. 1977. Memory for Information about Individuals. *Memory and Cognition* 5:430–422.

Anderson, J. R. 1978. The Processing of Referring Expressions within a Semantic Network. *Theoretical Issues in Natural Language Processing (TINLAP–2)* New York: Association for Computing Machinery.

Asher, N. 1986. Belief in Discourse Representation Theory. *Journal of Philosophical Logic* 15:127–189.

Asher, N. 1987. A Typology for Attitude Verbs and Their Anaphoric Properties. *Linguistics and Philosophy* 10:125–197.

Barr, A., and J. Davidson, eds. 1981. Representation of Knowledge. In A. Barr and E. Feigenbaum, eds. *Handbook of Artificial Intelligence,* 141–222. Los Altos, CA: Walter Kaufmann.

Barnden, J. A. 1986a. A Viewpoint Distinction in the Representation of Propositional Attitudes. *Proceedings of the 5th National Conference on Artificial Intelligence (AAAI–86; Philadelphia),* Vol. 1, 411–415. Los Altos, CA: Morgan Kaufmann.

Barnden, J. A. 1986b. Imputations and Explications: Representational Problems in Treatments of Propositional Attitudes. *Cognitive Science* 10:319–364.

Barnden, J. A. 1989. Towards a Paradigm Shift in Belief Representation Methodology. *Journal of Experimental and Theoretical Artificial Intelligence* 2:133–161.

Brachman, R. J., R. E. Fikes, and H. J. Levesque. 1983. Krypton: A Functional Approach to Knowledge Representation. *Computer* 16:67–73; also in Brachman and Levesque 1985:411–429.

Brachman, R. J., and H. J. Levesque, eds. 1985. *Readings in Knowledge Representation.* Los Altos, CA: Morgan Kaufmann.

Brachman, R. J., and J. G. Schmolze. 1985. An Overview of the KL-ONE Knowledge Representation System. *Cognitive Science* 9:171–216.

Brachman, R. J., and B. C. Smith. 1980. Special Issue on Knowledge Representation. *SIGART Newsletter,* No. 70.

Castañeda, H.-N. 1966. 'He': A Study in the Logic of Self-Consciousness. *Ratio* 8:130–157.

Castañeda, H.-N. 1972. Thinking and the Structure of the World. *Philosophia* 4:3–40; reprinted in 1975 in *Critica* 6 (1972) 43–86.

Castañeda, H.-N. 1975a. Identity and Sameness. *Philosophia* 5:121–150.

Castañeda, H.-N. 1975b. *Thinking and Doing: The Philosophical Foundations of Institutions.* Dordrecht: D. Reidel.

Castañeda, H.-N. 1977. Perception, Belief, and the Structure of Physical Objects and Consciousness. *Synthèse* 35:285–351.

Castañeda, H.-N. 1984. Philosophical Refutation. In J. H. Fetzer, ed., *Principles of Philosophical Reasoning,* 227–258. Totawa, NJ: Rowman & Allanheld.

Castañeda, H.-N. 1989. Philosophy as a Science and as a Worldview. In A. Cohen and M. Dascal, eds. *The Institution of Philosophy*. Peru, IL: Open Court.

Cercone, N. and G. McCalla, eds. 1987. *The Knowledge Frontier: Essays in the Representation of Knowledge*. New York: Springer-Verlag.

Dennett, D. C. 1978. Intentional Systems. In D. C. Dennett, *Brainstorms*, 3–22. Montgomery, VT: Bradford Books.

Dennett, D. C. 1982. Beyond Belief. In A. Woodfield, ed., *Thought and Object*, xvi–95. Oxford: Clarendon Press.

Fodor, J. A. 1975. *The Language of Thought*. New York: Thomas Y. Crowell Co.

Frege, G. 1892 [1970]. On Sense and Reference. Trans. M. Black. In P. Geach and M. Black, eds., *Translations from the Philosophical Writings of Gottlob Frege*, 56–78. Oxford: Basil Blackwell.

Hardt, S. L. 1987. Conceptual Dependency. In Shapiro 1987:194–199.

Haugeland, J. 1985. *Artificial Intelligence: The Very Idea*. Cambridge, MA: MIT Press.

Hobbs, J. R. 1985. Ontological Promiscuity. *Proceedings of the 23rd Annual Meeting of the Association for Computational Linguistics (University of Chicago)*, 61–69. Morristown, NJ: Association for Computational Linguistics.

Kamp, H. 1984. A Theory of Truth and Semantic Representation. In J. Groenendijk, T. M. V. Janssen, and M. Stokhof, eds., *Truth, Interpretation and Information*, 1–41. Dordrecht: Foris.

Kamp, H. (forthcoming), *Situations in Discourse* (Austin, TX: University of Texas Center for Cognitive Science).

King, M., and M. Rosner, eds. 1986. Special Issue on Knowledge Representation. *Proceedings of the IEEE* 74:1299–1454.

Kramer, B. M., and J. Mylopoulos. 1987. Representation, Knowledge. In Shapiro 1987:882–890.

Kumar, D. 1990. An Integrated Model of Acting and Inference. In D. Kumar, ed., *Current Trends in SNePS: Lecture Notes in Artificial Intelligence, No. 437*, 55–65. Berlin: Springer-Verlag.

Kumar, D., S. Ali, and S. C. Shapiro 1988. Discussing, Using and Recognizing Plans in SNePS, Preliminary Report—SNACTor: An Acting System. In P. V. S. Rao and P. Sadanandan, eds., *Modern Trends in Information Technology: Proceedings of the Seventh Biennial Convention of South East Asia Regional Computer Confederation*, 177–182. New Delhi: Tata McGraw-Hill.

Landman, F. 1986. Pegs and Alecs. In J. Y. Halpern, ed., *Theoretical Aspects of Reasoning about Knowledge*, 45–61. Los Altos, CA: Morgan Kaufmann.

Levesque, H. J. 1986. Knowledge Representation and Reasoning. In J. F. Traub, ed., *Annual Review of Computer Science*, Vol. 1:255–287. Palo Alto: Annual Reviews.

MacGregor, R. and R. Bates. 1987. The Loom Knowledge Representation Language. *Proceedings of the Knowledge-Based Systems Workshop (St. Louis, MO)*; also, *Technical Report ISI/RS-87-188*. Marina del Rey, CA: USC/Information Sciences Institute.

Maida, A. S., and S. C. Shapiro. 1982. Intensional Concepts in Propositional Semantic Networks. *Cognitive Science* 6:291–330. Reprinted in Brachman and Levesque 1985:170–189.

Martins, J. P., and S. C. Shapiro. 1983. Reasoning in Multiple Belief Spaces. *Proceedings of the 8th International Joint Conference on Artificial Intelligence (IJCAI-83; Karlsruhe, W. Germany)*, Vol. 1, 370–373. Los Altos, CA: Morgan Kaufmann.

Martins, J., and S. C. Shapiro. 1988. A Model for Belief Revision. *Artificial Intelligence* 35:25–79.

McKay, D. P., and S. C. Shapiro. 1981. Using Active Connection Graphs for Reasoning with Recursive Rules. *Proceedings of the 7th International Joint Conference on Artificial Intelligence (IJCAI–81; Vancouver )*:368–374.

Meinong, A. 1904. Über Gegenstandstheorie. In R. Haller, ed., *Alexius Meinong Gesamtausgabe*, Vol. II: 481–535. Graz, Austria: Akademische Druck- u. Verlagsanstalt, 1971. English translation ("The Theory of Objects") by I. Levi et al., in R. M. Chisholm (ed.), *Realism and the Background of Phenomenology* (New York: Free Press, 1960): 76–117.

Moser, M. G. 1983. An Overview of NIKL, The New Implementation of KL-ONE. In C. Sidner, et al., eds., Research in Knowledge Representation for Natural Language Understanding, Annual Report. *BBN Report No. 5421*. Cambridge, MA: Bolt Beranek and Newman.

Mylopoulos, J., and H. J. Levesque. 1984. An Overview of Knowledge Representation. In M. L. Brodie, J. Mylopoulos, and J. W. Schmidt, eds., *On Conceptual Modeling* 3–18. New York: Springer-Verlag.

Pollock, J. 1988. My Brother, The Machine. *Noûs* 22:173–212.

Rapaport, W. J. 1978. Meinongian Theories and a Russellian Paradox. *Noûs* 12:153–180; errata, *Noûs* 13 (1979):125.

Rapaport, W. J. 1981. How to Make the World Fit Our Language: An Essay in Meinongian Semantics. *Grazer Philosophische Studien* 14:1–21.

Rapaport, W. J. 1985. Meinongian Semantics for Propositional Semantic Networks. *Proceedings of the 23rd Annual Meeting of the Association for Computational Linguistics ( University of Chicago )*, 43–48. Morristown, NJ: Association for Computational Linguistics.

Rapaport, W. J. 1985/1986. Non-Existent Objects and Epistemological Ontology. *Grazer Philosophische Studien* 25/26:61–95.

Rapaport, W. J. 1986a. Logical Foundations for Belief Representation. *Cognitive Science* 10:371–422.

Rapaport, W. J. 1986b. Searle's Experiments with Thought. *Philosophy of Science* 53:271–279.

Rapaport, W. J. 1987. Logic, Predicate. In Shapiro 1987:538–544.

Rapaport, W. J. 1988a. Syntactic Semantics: Foundations of Computational Natural-Language Understanding. In J. Fetzer, ed., *Aspects of Artificial Intelligence*, 81–131. Dordrecht, Holland: Kluwer Academic Publishers.

Rapaport, W. J. 1988b. To Think or Not to Think. *Noûs* 22:585–609.

Rapaport, W. J., E. M. Segal, S. C. Shapiro, D. A. Zubin, G. A. Bruder, J. F. Duchan, and D. M. Mark. 1989. Cognitive and Computer Systems for Understanding Narrative Text. *Technical Report 89–07* SUNY Buffalo Dept. of Computer Science.

Rapaport, W. J., and S. C. Shapiro. 1984. Quasi-Indexical Reference in Propositional Semantic Networks. *Proceedings of the 10th International Conference on Computational Linguistics ( COLING–84; Stanford University )*, 65–70. Morristown, NJ: Association for Computational Linguistics.

Rapaport, W. J., S. C. Shapiro, and J. M. Wiebe. 1986. Quasi-Indicators, Knowledge Reports, and Discourse. SUNY Buffalo Department of Computer Science *Technical Report 86–15*.

Russell, B. 1905. On Denoting. Reprinted in R. C. Marsh, ed., *Logic and Knowledge* 39–56. New York: Capricorn, 1956.

Schank, R. C. 1975. *Conceptual Information Processing*. New York: Elsevier.

Schank, R. C., and C. J. Rieger. 1974. Inference and the Computer Understanding of Natural Language. *Artificial Intelligence* 5:373–412. Reprinted in Brachman and Levesque 1985:120–139.

Schank, R. C., and C. K. Riesbeck, eds. 1981. *Inside Computer Understanding: Five Programs Plus Miniatures.* Hillsdale, NJ: Lawrence Erlbaum.

Searle, J. R. 1980. Minds, Brains, and Programs. *Behavioral and Brain Sciences* 3:417–457.

Sells, P. 1987. Aspects of Logophoricity. *Linguistic Inquiry* 18:445–479.

Shapiro, S. C. 1978. Path-Based and Node-Based Inference in Semantic Networks. In D. Waltz, ed., *Theoretical Issues in Natural Language Processing (TINLAP–2)*, 219–225. New York: Association for Computing Machinery.

Shapiro, S. C. 1979. The SNePS Semantic Network Processing System. In N. V. Findler, ed., *Associative Networks: The Representation and Use of Knowledge by Computers*, 179–203. New York: Academic Press.

Shapiro, S. C. 1982. Generalized Augmented Transition Network Grammars for Generation from Semantic Networks. *American Journal of Computational Linguistics* 8:12–25.

Shapiro, S. C., ed. 1987. *Encyclopedia of Artificial Intelligence.* New York: John Wiley & Sons.

Shapiro S. C. 1989. The CASSIE Projects: An Approach to Natural Language Competence. In J. P. Martins and E. M. Morgado, eds. *EPIA 89: 4th Portugese Conference on Artificial Intelligence Proceedings: Lecture Notes in Artificial Intelligence, No. 390.* 362–380. Berlin: Springer-Verlag.

Shapiro, S. C., J. P. Martins, and D. P. McKay. 1982. Bi-Directional Inference. *Proceedings of the 4th Annual Conference of the Cognitive Science Society*, 90–93. Hillsdale, NJ: Lawrence Erlbaum.

Shapiro, S. C., and D. P. McKay. 1980, Inference with Recursive Rules. *Proceedings of the 1st National Conference on Artificial Intelligence (AAAI–80; Stanford University)*, Vol. 1:151–153. Los Altos, CA: Morgan Kaufmann.

Shapiro, S. C., and W. J. Rapaport. 1987a. SNePS Considered as a Fully Intensional Propositional Semantic Network. In Cercone & McCalla 1987:262–315.

Shapiro, S. C., and W. J. Rapaport. 1987b. Knowledge Representation for Natural Language Processing. *Presentations from the 1987 Natural Language Planning Workshop, Northeast Artificial Intelligence Consortium Technical Report WR–8703*, 57–77. Griffis Air Force Base, NY: Rome Air Development Center.

Shapiro, S. C., and W. J. Rapaport. 1988. Models and Minds: A Reply to Barnden. *Northeast Artificial Intelligence Consortium Technical Report TR–8737*. Syracuse University, March 1988. Reprinted 1988–89, as Models and Minds. *Computer Science Research Review*, 24–30. SUNY Buffalo Dept. of Computer Science.

Smith, B. C. 1982. Prologue to "Reflection and Semantics in a Procedural Language". In Brachman and Levesque 1985:32–39.

Stich, S. 1983. *From Folk Psychology to Cognitive Science: The Case Against Belief.* Cambridge, MA: MIT Press.

Vere, S. A. 1987. Planning. In Shapiro 1987:748–758.

Vilain, M. 1985. The Restricted Language Architecture of a Hybrid Representation System. *Proceedings of the 9th International Joint Conference on Artificial Intelligence (IJCAI–85)*, 547–551. Los Altos, CA: Morgan Kaufmann.

Weischedel, R. M. 1986. Knowledge Representation and Natural Language Processing. *Proceedings of the IEEE* 74:905–920.

Wiebe, J. M., and W. J. Rapaport. 1986. Representing *De Re* and *De Dicto* Belief Reports in Discourse and Narrative. *Proceedings of the IEEE* 74:1405–1413.

Wilks, Y. 1986. Relevance and Beliefs. In T. Myers, K. Brown, and B. McGonigle, eds., *Reasoning and Discourse Processes*, 266–289. London: Academic Press.

Winograd, T. 1975. Frame Representations and the Declarative/Procedural Controversy. In D. G. Bobrow and A. M. Collins, eds., *Representation and Understanding: Studies in Cognitive Science*, 185–210. New York: Academic Press. Reprinted in Brachman and Levesque 1985:358–370.

Wyatt, R. W. 1990. Kinds of Opacity and Their Representations. In D. Kumar, ed., *Current Trends in SNePS: Lecture Notes in Artificial Intelligence, No. 437*, 123–144. Berlin: Springer-Verlag.

# 11 Implementing the Intentional Stance

Yoav Shoham

## 11.1 Agent-Oriented Programming

The interaction between AI and philosophy is as old as AI itself (which, admittedly, is not saying a whole lot). Presumably that interaction has been mutually beneficial, or else it would not have lasted. I will leave it to others to say whether and where philosophy has benefited from AI. Instead I will take this opportunity to acknowledge the influence of philosophy on my research in general, and in particular on my current work on what I have termed *agent-oriented programming* (AOP).

This article has two essential components. The first is a general, non-technical description of the AOP concept. The second is an abbreviated discussion of some technical details involved in implementing the concept.

The term "agents" is used a lot these days. This is true in AI, but also outside it, for example in connection with databases and manufacturing automation. Although increasingly popular, the term has been used in such diverse ways that it has become meaningless without reference to a particular notion of agenthood. Some notions are primarily intuitive, others quite formal. Some are very austere, defining an agent as a finite automaton or a Boolean circuit, and others ascribe to agents sensory-motor, epistemic, and even natural-language capabilities.

I propose viewing "artificial agents" as formal versions of human agents, possessing formal versions of knowledge and belief, abilities and choices, and possibly a few other mentalistic-sounding qualities. The result is a computational framework I will call *agent-oriented programming* (AOP).

The name is not accidental, as AOP can be viewed as an extension of the *object-oriented programming* (OOP) paradigm. I mean the latter in the spirit of Hewitt's original Actors formalism (1977), rather than in the more specific sense in which it used today. Intuitively, whereas OOP proposes viewing a computational system as made up of modules that are able to communicate with one another and that have individual ways of handling incoming messages, AOP specializes the framework by allowing the modules, now called agents, to possess knowledge and beliefs about themselves and about one another, to have certain capabilities and make choices, and possibly other similar notions. A computation consists of these agents informing, requesting, offering, accepting, rejecting, competing with, and assisting one another. The table below summarizes the relation between AOP and OOP.

| Basic unit | Obect | Agent |
|---|---|---|
| Parameters defining state of basis unit | unconstrained | knowledge, beliefs, commitments, capabilities, choices, ... |
| Process of computation | message passing and response methods | message passing and response methods |
| Types of message | unconstrained | inform, request, offer, promise, decline, ... |
| Constraints on methods | none | honesty, consistency, ... |

This is the programming-paradigm perspective on AOP. An alternative view of AOP is as an applied formal language. From this perspective it may be viewed as a generalization of epistemic logics, which have been used extensively in AI and distributed computation in recent years. These logics, which were imported directly from analytic philosophy, describe the behavior of machines in terms of notions such as knowledge and belief. In computer science these mentalistic-sounding notions are actually given precise computational meanings, and are used not only to prove properties of distributed systems, but to program them as well. A typical rule in such 'knowledge-based' systems is "if processor A does not KNOW that processor B has received its message, then processor A will not send the next message." AOP augments these logics with formal notions of choices, abilities, commitments, and possibly others. A typical rule in the resulting systems will be "if agent A BELIEVES that agent B has CHOSEN to do something harmful to agent A, then A will REQUEST that B change its intention." In addition, temporal information is included to anchor belief, choices, and so on in particular points in time.

Here again we benefit from some ideas in philosophy. As in the case of knowledge, there exists work in exact philosophy on logics for choice and ability. More centrally, however, we borrow ideas from the *speech-act* literature in philosophy and linguistics (Austin 1965, Searle 1969, Grice 1989). Speech-act theory categorizes speech, distinguishing between informing, requesting, offering, and so on; each such type of communicative act involves different presuppositions and has different effects. Speech acts have been applied in AI, in natural-language research as well as in plan recognition. In a sense, AOP too can be viewed as a rigorous implementation of a fragment of direct-speech-act theory.

Intentional terms such as "knowledge" and "belief" are used in a curious sense in the formal AI community. On the one hand, the definitions come nowhere close to capturing the full linguistic meanings. On the other hand, the intuitions about these formal notions do indeed derive from the everyday, commonsense meaning of the words. What is curious is that, despite the disparity, the everyday intuition has proven a good guide to employing the formal notion in some circumscribed applications. AOP aims to strike a similar balance between computational utility and common sense.

It should be understood that this document describes a concept rather than a finished product. I believe that the concept is sound and that it can form a basis for future computer environments. I am also aware that some of the issues involved in implementing it are nontrivial and must be settled before a practical system is built. I will describe work we are carrying out that addresses these issues. The description here will be brief; a fuller description may be found in Shoham 1990 and related publications.

The rest of the document is organized as follows. I first provide further motivation for the AOP paradigm by looking at two intended applications. I then outline the research program, including a sketch of the progress we have made to date. I conclude with a brief comparison with related work.

## 11.2   Two Scenarios

Below are two semi-futuristic scenarios. Although they are couched in different settings, the two illustrate similar points. They each involve communicative acts such as informing, requesting, committing, permitting, and commanding, and require agents to reason about the mental state of other agents.

### 11.2.1   Manufacturing Automation

Alfred and Brenda work at a car manufacturing plant. Alfred handles regular-order cars, and Brenda handles special-order ones. The plant has a welding robot, Calvin. The overly busy plant foreman has written a coordinating program, Dashiel. The following scenario develops.

8:00   Alfred requests that Calvin promise to weld ten bodies for him that day; Calvin agrees to do so.

8:30 Alfred requests that Calvin accept the first body, Calvin agrees, and the first body arrives. Calvin starts welding it and promises Alfred to notify him when it is ready for the next body.

8:45 Brenda requests that Calvin work on a special-order car which is needed urgently. Calvin reponds that it cannot right then, but that it will when it finishes the current job, at approximately 9:00.

9:05 Calvin completes welding the Alfred's first car, ships it out, and offers to weld Brenda's car. Brenda ships it the car, and Calvin starts welding.

9:15 Alfred enquires why Calvin is not yet ready for his (Alfred's) next car. Calvin explains why, and also that it (Calvin) expects to be ready by about 10:00.

9:55 Calvin completes welding Brenda's car, and ships it out. Brenda requests that it reaccept it and do some painting, but Calvin refuses, explaining that it does not know how to paint. Calvin then offers to weld another car for Alfred, and proceeds to weld Alfred's cars for a while.

12:15 Brenda requests that Calvin commit to welding four more special-order cars that day. Calvin replies that it cannot, since that conflicts with its commitment to Alfred, who still has six unwelded cars. Brenda requests Alfred to release Calvin from its commitment to Alfred. Alfred refuses. Brenda requests that Dashiel (remember Dashiel?) order Calvin to accept her important request and revoke its commitment to Alfred. Dashiel orders Calvin to weld two of Brenda's cars, and then as many of Alfred's as time allows.

Important features: Requesting, offering, committing, maintaining consistency of commitments, commanding.

### 11.2.2 Airline Reservation

This example is a minor modification of one due to John McCarthy (1990), who uses it to illustrate his Elephant2000 programming language. The example involves three agents: a passenger P, an airline clerk C, and C's supervisor S. P and S are human, and C is a program. Or is it the other way around? Or perhaps all three are programs.

*March*

P to C: Please inform me what flights you have from San Francisco to New York on April 18.

C to P: Flight #354 departs at 08:30, flight #293 departs at 10:00, flight #441 departs at noon....

P to C: Please book me on #354.

C to P: That is sold out.

P to C:   Please book me on #293.

C to P:   That is confirmed; your reservation number is 112358.

P to C:   Please book me also on #441.

C to P:   That conflicts with #293; I am not allowed to double book a passanger.

P to C:   Please get permission to do so.

C to S:   I request permission for the following double booking....

S to C:   Permission denied.

C to P:   Sorry, I cannot get approval.

          *April 18, at the airport*

P to C:   Please issue me a boarding pass for flight #293.

C to P:   Here you are.

Important features: Capabilities, questions, answers, requests, making a commitment (confirming the reservation), the persistence of the commitment, honoring the commitment.

## 11.3   Overview of the Research Program

The preceding scenarios made reference to mentalistic notions such as beliefs and commitments. As AI researchers our goal is to make engineering sense out of these abstract concepts. The result will be the agent-oriented programming paradigm. The AOP framework will include three primary components:

• A restricted formal language with clear syntax and semantics to describe mental state. The mental state will be defined uniquely by several modalities, such as B (belief) and CMT (commitment).

• An interpreted programming language in which to program agents, with primitive commands such as REQUEST and INFORM. The semantics of the programming language will rely in part on the semantics of mental state. Specifically, both the preconditions and postconditions of each communicative act will be defined in terms of the mental states of the agents concerned.

• A compiler from the agent-level language to an abstract model of processes, or an "agentifier."

In the remainder of this essay I concentrate on the first two components.

## 11.4  Mental State

The first step in the enterprise is to define agents, that is, to define the various components of mental state. There is not a unique "correct" definition of mental state, and different applications can be expected to call for specific mental properties. Here we discuss what could be viewed as a bare-bones theory of mental state, a kernel that will in the future be modified and augmented. The discussion here will summarize work carried out jointly with Becky Thomas and Anton Schwartz, and described more fully in Shoham et al., 1991.

In related past research by others three modalities were emphasized: belief, desire, and intention (giving rise to the pun on BDI agent architectures). Although we started out by exploring similar notions, with time we lowered our sights. In this document I will concentrate on two primitive modalities—belief and commitment—and two derived ones—choice and capability—which we have found more basic (strictly speaking, capability is a relation between the mental state and the environment; more on that later).

By restricting the components of mental state to these modalities I have in some informal sense excluded representation of motivation. Indeed, I will not assume that agents are "rational" beyond assuming that their beliefs, commitments, and choices are internally and mutually consistent. This stands in contrast to other work on agents' mental state, which makes further assumptions about agents acting in their own best interests, and so on. Such stronger notions of rationality are obviously important, and in the future we may wish to add them. However, neither the concept of agenthood nor the utility of agent-oriented programming depend on them.

Although I discuss formal definitions, I leave out many details. In particular, I have omitted almost all discussion of formal semantics (I have left in only terse outlines, for the benefit of the readers who particularly care about such matters; others may skip those few and short segments).

### 11.4.1  Time

The basis for our language is a simple temporal language. The particular temporal logic we adopt here is an explicit-time point-based logic; the construction would be similar for other choices. We take time to be a linear order. In fact, here we will assume the integers as a model for time; this too is a convenience one might decide to do without later. A "time line" associates with each time point a set of propositions, those that are true at that time.

**Syntax**   Assume a set $TC$ of time point constants, a set $P$ of predicate symbols (each with a fixed arity $\geq 0$), a set $F$ of function symbols (each with a fixed arity $\geq 0$), and set $V$ of variables. The set of terms is defined as follows: a variable is a term, and if $f$ is an $n$-ary function symbol and $\text{trm}_1$, ..., $\text{trm}_n$ are terms, then $f(\text{trm}_1, \ldots, \text{trm}_n)$ is also a term. The set of well-formed formulas is then defined as follows. If $t_1, t_2 \in TC$ then $t_1 < t_2$ is a wff. If t is a time point symbol, $r$ is an $n$-ary predicate symbol, and $\text{trm}_1$, ..., $\text{trm}_n$ are terms, then $f(\text{trm}_1, \ldots, \text{trm}_n)^t$ is a wff. If $\varphi$ and $\psi$ are wffs and $v$ is a variable, then $\varphi \wedge \psi$, $\neg \varphi$ and $\forall v \varphi$ are all wffs. We will use the standard abbreviations $\vee$ and $\supset$. (In this simple construction we do not even allow quantification over time points.)

**Semantics** (outline)   The models for sentences are conventional: time point constants are interpreted as integers[1], variables and 0-ary function symbols as objects, other function symbols as functions from time and objects to objects, and predicate symbols as functions from to time to tuples of objects. If $M$ is such an interpretation, then $P(\text{trm}_1 \ldots \text{trm}_n)^t$ is true in it iff $(M(\text{t}, \text{trm}_1), \ldots, M(\text{t}, \text{trm}_n)) \in M(\text{t}, \text{P})$.

### 11.4.2   Belief

We now augment the language with a modal operator B, denoting belief. The standard logic of belief (Halpern and Moses 1985) simply adds to the language the sentence $B\varphi$, for any sentence $\varphi$ in the language. The most common logic of belief is the KD45 system (Chellas 1980), which in addition to the axioms of propositional calculus and two inference rules satisfies the following axioms:

$B\varphi_1 \wedge B(\varphi_1 \supset \varphi_2) \supset B\varphi_2$

$B\varphi \equiv BB\varphi$

$\neg B\varphi \equiv B \neg B\varphi$

$\neg B(\varphi \wedge \neg\varphi)$

---

[1] In this document we assume the integers as the temporal structure, but one could assume otherwise.

We will complicate the logic in only a minor way by adding to the operator two more arguments: the agent who is doing the believing, and the time of belief. Furthermore, possible worlds will also have a temporal dimension, and will in fact each be a time line.

**Syntax**  Given a temporal logic as before, we assume another set of constants AG, the agent constants. We now add one wff-formation rule: if t is a time-point constant, a is an agent constant, and $\varphi$ is a sentence in the language, then $B^t(a, \varphi)$ is also a sentence in the language. For example, $B^3(a, B^{10}(b, \text{like}(a, b)^7))$ will mean that at time 3 agent a believes that at time 10 agent b will believe that at time 7 a liked b.

We assume B to be an KD45 operator; among other properties this includes:

$$B^t(a, \varphi_1) \wedge B^t(a, \varphi_1 \supset \varphi_2) \supset B^t(a, \varphi_2)$$

$$B^t(a, \varphi) \supset B^t(a, B^t(a, \varphi))$$

$$\neg B^t(a, \varphi) \supset B^t(a, \neg B^t(a, \varphi))$$

$$\neg B^t(a, \varphi \wedge \neg \varphi)$$

**Semantics** (outline)  A B-structure is a tuple $(L, m)$ where $L$ is a set of time lines, and $m$ is a function that specifies for every time point and agent an accessibility relation $R_{B_{t,a}}$ on L. Each such accessibility relation is transitive and Euclidean, and B is defined to be the necessity operator for this modality.

### 11.4.3  Belief versus Knowledge

In this document we will not assume that agents possess knowledge that is distinct from their beliefs. The distinction usually made between the two is that while known facts must in fact be true, believed facts need not be. It is possible to add another modality K to represent knowledge, with the extra property $K^t(a, \varphi) \supset \varphi$. In fact, we have made a proposal to view belief as a defeasible form of knowledge, and actually defined the B operator in terms of K; see details in Shoham and Moses 1989. However, since on the one hand the proposal is sufficiently novel to attract controversy, and on the other hand one can define a coherent and useful notion of mental state without distinguishing between knowledge and belief, we will not pursue this issue here.

### 11.4.4   Commitment

So far we have used largely well-known constructions: the temporal logic is standard, the logic of belief is standard, and their combination, although somewhat novel, is nonetheless straightforward. We now depart more radically from past constructions and introduce new modal operator, CMT.

Unlike B, CMT is a ternary operator: $\mathrm{CMT}(a, b, \varphi)$ will mean that agent a is committed to agent b about $\varphi$ (of course, we will add a temporal component to represent the time of commitment). This interagent flavor of commitment contrasts with past accounts of the same concept, which viewed it as an intra-agent phenomenon. Notice that the agent is committed about the truth of a sentence, not about his taking action. In fact, we will not introduce in the logic a separate category of entities called "action." For example, strictly speaking, rather than say that the robot is committed to taking the action "raise arm" at time t, we will say that the robot is committed to the proposition "the robot raises its arm at time t." However, since actions are such a natural concept and in fact are dealt with in a special way, in the actual programming language we will introduce them as syntactic sugar. Both in the logical treatment here and in the programming language later, since actions are facts, they are also instantaneous (we have adopted for now a point-based logic). In order to represent durational actions, we must currently break them into consecutive, instantaneous ones; it will be important, and not too hard, to avoid this in future extensions.

**Syntax**   We augment the syntax of the language as follows: If a and b are agent terms, t is a temporal term and $\varphi$ is a sentence, then $\mathrm{CMT}^t(a, b, \varphi)$ is also a sentence.

We take CMT to be a KD4-operator (Chellas 1980); among other properties, this gives us the following:

$$\mathrm{CMT}^t(a, b, \varphi_1) \wedge \mathrm{CMT}^t(a, b, \varphi_1 \supset \varphi_2) \supset \mathrm{CMT}^t(a, b, \varphi_2)$$

$$\mathrm{CMT}^t(a, b, \varphi) \supset \mathrm{CMT}^t(a, b, \mathrm{CMT}^t(a, b, \varphi))$$

$$\neg \mathrm{CMT}^t(a, b, \varphi \wedge \neg \varphi)$$

**Semantics** (outline)   A B-CMT-structure is the result of adding to a B-structure a second function, which specifies for each time point $t$ and each ordered pair of agents $a, b$ a second accessibility relation on time lines,

$R_{CMT_{t,a,b}}$. Each such accessibility relation is transitive and serial, and CMT is defined to be the necessity operator of this modality.

### 11.4.5 Belief and Commitment

Beliefs and commitments must not only be internally consistent, they must also be mutually consistent. First, we assume that an agent is completely aware of his commitments:

$$CMT^t(a, b, \varphi) \equiv B^t(a, CMT^t(a, b, \varphi))$$

$$\neg CMT^t(a, b, \varphi) \equiv B^t(a, \neg CMT^t(a, b, \varphi))$$

Note that an agent is not necessarily aware of which commitment are made to him, only of commitment he has toward others. Second, we assume that agents only commit in good faith:

$$CMT^t(a, b, \varphi) \supset B^t(a, \varphi)$$

Note that as a corollary we have that commitments must be consistent:

Fact: $CMT^t(a, b, \varphi) \supset \neg CMT^t(a, c, \neg \varphi)$

### 11.4.6 Choice

The freedom to choose among several possible actions is central to the notion of agenthood, and earlier on in the research we indeed took choice to be a primitive notion. The current definition of commitment provides an alternative, however: choice is defined to be simply commitment to oneself:

$$CH^t(a, \varphi) =_{def} CMT^t(a, a, \varphi)$$

It should be added that, as is the case in general in language, the word "choice" is multifaceted, and it is not our aim to capture all senses of the word. The sense of choice here is akin to that of "decision"; an agent has chosen something if he has decided that that something be true. In particular, no connection is assumed here to any notion of motivation, such as desire or intention.

### 11.4.7 Capability

Also intimately bound to the notion of agenthood is that of capability. I may choose to move my arm, but if I am not capable of it then it will not move. I will not ask a two-year-old, nor a mobile robot, to climb a ladder, since I do not believe they are capable of it.

Unlike the notions discussed so far, capability is not a purely internal property of the agent. In fact, there are philosophical views which completely dissociate capability from mental state. We, however, choose to view the notion as a certain relation between the agent's mental state and the world. One could introduce an independent operator to denote capability, but we have decided to define it away. The intuition behind the following definition is that "to be able to X" means to have the power to make X true by merely choosing that it be so:

$$CAN^t(a, \varphi) =_{def} CH^t(a, \varphi) \supset \varphi$$

To be sure, this definition departs from common sense quite sharply on certain points, but so far we have not found ourselves hurt by this gap. For example, although we get that $\neg CH^t(a, \varphi) \supset CAN^t(a, \varphi)$, (i.e., one is capable of anything by merely not choosing it), that turns out to be quite innocuous; what counts are the choices that are *not* ruled out. And while $\varphi \supset CAN^t(a, \varphi)$ (i.e., one is capable of anything that happens to be true), the typical statements refer to beliefs about capabilities, such as $B^t(a, CAN^{t'}(b, \varphi))$, which is not entailed by $\varphi$. Of course, we do get $B^t(b, \varphi) \supset B^t(b, CAN^t(a, \varphi))$, but we see no harm in assuming that anyone can bring about something that we believe will happen anyway.[2]

The definition does have some very intuitive properties, such as the following

Fact: $CMT^t(a, b, \varphi) \supset B^t(a, CAN^t(a, \varphi))$

As with the previous notions we are open to other definitions, but until we encounter difficulties we intend to adopt the simplest systems. Again, the game we are playing is not to determine whether a particular definition can be shown to contradict common sense or linguistic convention, but whether restricted definitions will support significant applications.

---

[2] It is possible to add a necessity operator in the definition, as in $CAN^t(a, \varphi) =_{def} \Box(CH^t(a, \varphi) \supset \varphi)$, where $\Box$ is interpreted as truth in all worlds. However, while there is a better match with intuition under this definition, we have so far found no other advantage to it, and so for now we have decided against this more complex definition.

### 11.4.8  The Persistence of Mental States

So far all the restrictions on mental attitudes referred to attitudes at a single instant of time. We conclude the discussion of mental state by discussing restrictions on how mental states change or persist over time.

Consider, for example, belief. Our axioms so far allow models in which at one time an agent believes no propositional sentences but tautologies, at the next time he has a belief about *every* sentence, and at the time following that he is again very agnostic. We have the intuition that beliefs tend to be more stable than that. We will now place a strong condition on belief; we will assume that agents have perfect memory of and faith in their beliefs, and only let go of a belief if they learn a contradictory fact. Beliefs therefore persist *by default*. Furthermore, we will assume that the *absence* of belief also persists by default, although in a slightly different sense: if an agent does not believe a fact at a certain time (as opposed to believing the negation of the fact), then the only reason he will come to believe it is if he learns it. In a forthcoming publication with Fangzhen, where we consider also the persistence of knowledge and ignorance, we assume that the persistence of knowledge is absolute: what you know now you always will. The persistence of ignorance is, again, only by default.

How to capture formally these two kinds of default persistence is another story, and touches on issues that are painfully familiar to researchers in nonmonotonic temporal reasoning and belief revision. In fact, a close look at the logical details of belief (or knowledge) persistence reveals several very subtle phenomena, which have so far not been addressed in the literature. We will use the following seemingly formal sentences:

$$B^t(a, \varphi) \wedge \neg LEARN^t(a, \neg\varphi) \supset B^{t+1}(a, \varphi)$$

$$\neg B^t(a, \varphi) \wedge \neg LEARN^t(a, \varphi) \supset \neg B^{t+1}(a, \varphi)$$

However, much more needs to be added in order for the right persistence to take place; a more detailed treatment will appear elsewhere.

Commitments, too, should persist; they wouldn't be commitments otherwise. As in the case of belief, however, the persistence is not absolute. Although by default commitments persist, there are conditions under which commitments are revoked. These conditions presumably include explicit release of the committer by the committee, or alternatively a realization on the part of the committer of the impossibility of the commitment. Cohen and Levesque (1990) actually propose a more elaborate second condition, one that requires common belief by the committer and committee of the impossibility; however, further discussion of their position and arguments against it would be too long a detour.

We will use the sentence

$$CMT^t(a, b, \varphi) \land \neg REVOKE^t(a, b, \varphi) \supset CMT^{t+1}(a, b, \varphi)$$

but again we caution that more needs to be done in order to preclude unwarranted revoking of a commitment.

Since choice is defined in terms of commitment, it inherits the default persistence. Notice, however, an interesting point about the persistence of choice: while an agent cannot revoke commitments he made to others, he can cancel commitments that were made to him—including commitments he made to himself, namely choices. An agent can therefore freely modify his choices.

Finally, capabilities, too, tend to not fluctuate wildly. In fact, in our work so far we have assumed that capabilities are fixed: what an agent can do at one time it can do at any other time. However, we have allowed to condition a capability of an action on certain conditions that hold at the time of action.

## 11.5   Agent Programs and Their Interpretation

The behavior of agents is governed by programs; each agent is controlled by his own, private program. Agent programs are in many respects similar to standard programs, containing primitive operations, control structures, and input-output instructions. What makes them unique is that the control structures refer to the mental-state constructs defined previously, and that the IO commands include methods for communicating with other agents.

In Shoham 1990 I define a precise basic language for programming agents, called AGENT0; here I only outline the features of a generic agent language.

**Programs**   An agent program consists of two parts, *initialization* and *commitment rules*. The initialization defines the capabilities of the agent, its initial beliefs (that is, beliefs at the particular initial time point, but *about* any time) and initial commitments. In other words, this part initializes the

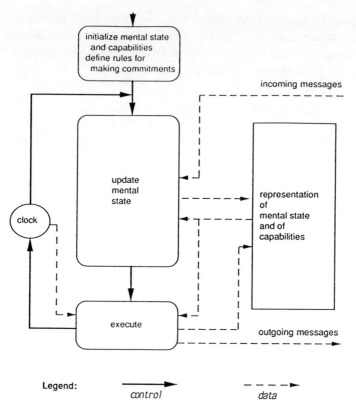

**Figure 11.1**
Flowchart of a generic agent interpreter

mental state (strictly speaking, capability is a relation between mental state and the world, but we ignore this detail in this essay).

Commitment rules determine how commitments are added over time. Conditions for making a commitment always refer to the "current" mental state and the "current" incoming messages. Actions to which an agent is committed always refer to a particular future point in time. The order between the commitment rules is completely unimportant and has nothing to do with the times of action specified in the various rules.

**Interpreter**   Figure 11.1 presents a flowchart of the generic agent interpreter. In many respects agent programs are similar to conventional ones.

In a conventional programming language the syntax defines the legal operations, and the program specifies which of those are to be carried out and in which order. To this end the programmer is provided with data and control structures. This much is true of agent programs as well. In regular languages, however, there is a simple mapping between the structure of the program and the order of execution; typically, a linear sequence of commands translates to the same execution order. In contrast, in agent programs there is complete decoupling between the order among different commitment rules and the time of execution; each commitment rule can refer to an action at any future time. In fact, somewhat paradoxically, agent programs never contain direct instructions to execute an action. Rather, agents are continually engaged in two types of activity: making commitments about the future, and honoring previous commitments whose execution time has come (and which have not been revoked in the meanwhile).

In order to implement this process we will make assumptions of two kinds:

1. We assume that the platform is capable of passing message to other machines addressable by name. The program itself will define the form and timing of these messages.

2. Central to the operation of the interpreter is the existence of a clock. The main role of the clock is to initiate iterations of the two-step loop at regular intervals (every 10 milliseconds, every hour, etc.); the length of these intervals, called the "time grain," is determined by the programmer. The other role of the clock is to determine which commitments refer to the current time, and must therefore be executed.

We are currently making the very strong assumption that a single iteration through the loop lasts less than the time grain; in the future we will relax this assumption, and correspondingly will complicate the details of the loop itself.

I will not describe the process of updating the mental state; I only comment that this process is governed in part by the constraints on belief and commitment discussed earlier (What does an agent do when informed of a fact that contradicts its current beliefs? When requested to commit to an action which is incompatible with a current commitment? When informed that it no longer has a certain capability?) and in part by the commitment rules.

## 11.6  Concluding Remarks

I have described the general concept of Agent-Oriented Programming, and explored some of the details involved in defining the mental state of computational constructs and programming them. The influence of philosophy on this framework is apparent. Whether or not this turns out to be a case of AI benefiting from philosophy will depend, of course, on the success of the project. Recent developments—including the implementation of a prototype interpreter (Torrance and Viola 1991) and initial application programs—make me feel optimistic.

## Acknowledgments

AOP was inspired by much previous work, and has been continuously influenced by other ongoing work. Thanks to all members of the Nobotics group at Stanford. Becky Thomas and Anton Schwartz have collaborated on the definition of mental state, Fangzhen Lin on the logic of persistence, Jun-ichi Akahani on the development of an interpreter, and Jean-Francois Lavignon on the definition of the target language for the compiler. Special thanks to John McCarthy for enlightening conversations. I am indebted also to Michael Bratman, Phil Cohen, Mike Genesereth, Pat Hayes, David Israel, Kurt Konolige, Hector Levesque, Nils Nilsson, Martha Pollack, Stan Rosenschein, Rich Thomason, and undoubtedly many more people whom I have at the moment forgotten and from whose work and comments I have benefited.

## References

J. L. Austin. 1955 (1975). *How to Do Things with Words.* Harvard University Press.

B. F. Chellas. 1980. *Modal Logic: An Introduction.*

P. R. Cohen and H. Levesque. 1990. Intention is choice with commitment. *Artificial Intelligence,* 42(3).

P. Grice. 1989. *Studies in the Ways of Words.* Harvard University Press.

J. Y. Halpern. 1987. Using reasoning about knowledge to analyze distributed systems. In J. F. Traub, editor, *Annual Review of Computer Science, Volume 2.* Annual Reviews Inc.

C. Hewitt. 1977. Viewing control structures as patterns of passing messages. *Artificial Intelligence,* 8:323–364.

J. R. Searle. 1969. *Speech Acts: An Essay in the Philosophy of Language.* Cambridge University Press, Cambridge.

Y. Shoham. 1990. Agent oriented programming. Technical Report STAN–CS–90–1335, Computer Science Department, Stanford University.

Y. Shoham and Y. Moses. 1989. Belief as defeasible knowledge. In *Proceedings 11th IJCAI*, 1168–1172.

Y. Shoham, S. R. Thomas, and A. Schwartz. n.d. The mental state of a basic agent. n.p.

M. Torrance and P. Viola. n.d. The agent0 programming manual, 1991. Stanford technical report.

# 12 The Dinosaur Debate: Explanatory Coherence and the Problem of Competing Hypotheses

Paul Thagard

## 12.1 Introduction

In recent years, few scientific issues have been more intensely debated than why the dinosaurs became extinct. Alvarez et al. (1980) proposed that the collision of a massive meteorite with the earth at the end of the Cretaceous era could explain recently discovered deposits of iridium as well as the extinction of the dinosaurs. Subsequent investigations turned up other evidence supporting the collision hypothesis. Other researchers, however, have been unconvinced by the Alvarez arguments, preferring to explain dinosaur extinction by more gradual processes such as sea-level changes and preferring to explain the iridium deposits by volcanic action (Hallam 1987).

The aim of this paper[1] is not to help settle the question of why dinosaurs became extinct, but rather to contribute to an understanding of its logic. The philosophy of science ought to help illuminate a controversy that has generated so much research and argumentation, but I shall argue that available accounts of scientific methodology are largely irrelevant. In contrast, I shall describe a new theory of explanatory coherence that fits well with the kinds of arguments made both for and against the collision hypothesis. The theory has been implemented in a connectionist computer program called ECHO that evaluates sets of hypotheses in parallel, preferring those that are most coherent with the evidence and with each other. ECHO has been used in detailed analyses of the arguments of two proponents of the collision hypothesis (David Raup and Luis Alvarez) and two of its opponents (Anthony Hallam and Robert Bakker). Application of ECHO to the dinosaur debate is much improved by the development of a new principle of explanatory coherence that is offered in response to recent worries of Gilbert Harman (1989) concerning when hypotheses constitute competing alternatives. ECHO.2 is the extension of ECHO that implements the new principle of explanatory coherence concerned with competition.

[1] This research was supported by a grant from the McDonnell Foundation to Princeton University. LISP and C versions of ECHO are available from the author. I am grateful to Gil Harman for helpful conversations.

## 12.2   A Theory of Explanatory Coherence

Arguments concerning why the dinosaur became extinct involve four major strategies. By far the most common is for writers to point to evidence explained by the hypotheses they favor. For example, the collision hypothesis is supported by the finding of iridium deposits laid down around the time that the dinosaurs became extinct, while the sea-level hypothesis is supported by evidence that end-Cretaceous extinctions were gradual rather than cataclysmic. Another positive strategy is to offer an explanation of why the favored hypothesis might be true. For example, Raup's Nemesis hypothesis would explain why the collision occurred. On the negative side, a common strategy is to point to evidence that runs contrary to the opposing hypotheses, for example saying that the collision hypothesis implies the existence of a huge crater that has not been found. Finally, one can attack the explanatory claims of alternative hypotheses by denying the validity of the evidence adduced in their support.

These four strategies can be understood in terms of a theory of explanatory coherence discussed at much greater length elsewhere (Thagard 1989). The initial statement of the theory used the following seven principles of explanatory coherence. S is a system of propositions P, Q, and $P_1 \ldots P_n$. Local coherence is a relation between two propositions. I coin the term "incohere" to mean that two propositions are incoherent, which is stronger than saying that they do not cohere.

*Principle 1. Symmetry.*
   (a)  If P and Q cohere, then Q and P cohere.
   (b)  If P and Q incohere, then Q and P incohere.

*Principle 2. Explanation.*
   If $P_1 \ldots P_m$ explain Q, then:
      (a)  For each $P_i$ in $P_1 \ldots P_m$, $P_i$ and Q cohere.
      (b)  For each $P_i$ and $P_j$ in $P_1 \ldots P_m$, $P_i$ and $P_j$ cohere.
      (c)  In (a) and (b) the degree of coherence is inversely proportional to the number of propositions $P_1 \ldots P_m$.

*Principle 3. Analogy.*
   (a)  If $P_1$ explains $Q_1$, $P_2$ explains $Q_2$, $P_1$ is analogous to $P_2$, and $Q_1$ is analogous to $Q_2$, then $P_1$ and $P_2$ cohere, and $Q_1$ and $Q_2$ cohere.
   (b)  If $P_1$ explains $Q_1$, $P_2$ explains $Q_2$, $Q_1$ is analogous to $Q_2$, but $P_1$ is disanalogous to $P_2$, then $P_1$ and $P_2$ incohere.

*Principle 4. Data priority.*
Propositions that describe the results of observation have a degree of acceptability on their own.

*Principle 5. Contradiction.*
If P contradicts Q, then P and Q incohere.

*Principle 6. Acceptability.*
(a) The acceptability of a proposition P in a system S depends on its coherence with the propositions in S.
(b) If many results of relevant experimental observations are unexplained, then the acceptability of a proposition P that explains only a few of them is reduced.

*Principle 7. System coherence.*
The global explanatory coherence of a system S of propositions is a function of the pairwise local coherence of those propositions.

Principle 2, Explanation, is the one most relevant to the dinosaur debate, since it covers cases where hypotheses explain evidence or are themselves explained by higher level hypotheses. Clauses 2(a) and 2(b) state that hypotheses that explain a proposition cohere with that proposition and with each other. Clause 2(c) is a simplicity principle, suggesting that the greater the number of hypotheses needed to explain a proposition, the less they cohere with it and with one another. Principle 3, Analogy, does not appear to me to be relevant to the dinosaur debate, since the participants make little use of analogical explanations. In contrast, the fourth principle, Evidence, is important, since there is much contention concerning whether what is explained by particular hypotheses should in fact be treated as evidence. The best example in the dinosaur debate concerns how long it took the dinosaurs to become extinct. The collision hypothesis explains a sudden extinction, while the sea-level hypothesis explains a more gradual extinction.

Principle 5, Contradiction, marks competing hypotheses as incoherent with each other if they are contradictory given background assumptions. The collision hypothesis and the sea-level hypothesis are not logically contradictory, since it is possible that both a massive collision and sea-level dropping contributed to dinosaur decline. But scientists lend to assume that only one of these will win out as the correct explanation of why dinosaurs became extinct. Section 12.4 will propose a principle of competition that justifies treating the collision and sea-level hypotheses as incoherent even though they are not contradictory.

The last two principles state that the previous five principles establishing local relations of explanatory coherence are all that is needed to determine the overall coherence of a set of propositions and the acceptability of particular propositions. These contentions have been put to the test by development of a computer program that allows simulation of judgments of explanatory coherence.

## 12.3  ECHO

Connectionist networks consist of units, roughly analogous to neurons, that are connected by excitatory and inhibitory links (Rumelhart and McClelland 1986). ECHO is a Common LISP program that constructs networks for evaluating the explanatory coherence of sets of propositions. Propositions that cohere are represented by units connected by excitatory links, while ones that incohere have units connected by inhibitory links. For input, ECHO is given formulas describing the explanatory relations of propositions. If two hypotheses H1 and H2 together explain a piece of evidence E1, ECHO is given the LISP input:

(EXPLAIN '(H1 H2) E1).

In accord with the second principle of explanatory coherence, ECHO then sets up symmetric excitatory links between units representing H1 and E1, H2 and E1, and H1 and H2. If H1 and H3 are contradictory, ECHO gets the input:

(CONTRADICT 'H1 'H3).

This sets up a symmetric inhibitory link between H1 and H3. That E1 and E2 are to be treated as pieces of evidence is represented by the input:

(DATA '(E1 E2))

In accord with principle 4, Evidence, links are then set up from a special evidence unit to E1 and E2.

Connectionist networks make decisions by repeatedly updating the activation of units in parallel until the whole network settles into a stable state in which the activation of each unit has reached asymptote. ECHO adjusts the activation of a unit $u_j$ by considering all the units to which it is linked.

An excitatory link with an active unit will increase the activation of $u_j$, while an inhibitory link with a unit with positive activation will decrease it. Activation of units starts at 0 and is allowed to range between 1 and $-1$. The equation used to update activation is:

$$a_j(t + 1) = a_j(t)(1 - \theta) + \begin{cases} net_j(max - a_j(t)) & \text{if } net_j > 0 \\ net_j(a_j(t) - min) & otherwise \end{cases} \qquad (1)$$

Here $\theta$ is a decay parameter that decrements each unit at every cycle, min is minimum activation $(-1)$, max is maximum activation $(1)$, and $net_j$ is the net input to a unit. This is defined by:

$$net_j = \sum_i w_{ij} a_i(t) \qquad (2)$$

Repeated adjustments of activations results in a stable state where some units end up with high activation and others with activation below 0.

## 12.4   The Problem of Competing Hypotheses

Proponents of the collision hypothesis for dinosaur extinction do not just consider it to be somewhat better than alternative hypotheses; they actually *reject* the alternatives. Rejection in ECHO is modeled by units representing rejected hypotheses being reduced to activations less than 0, which requires these units to have inhibitory links with accepted units. In the dinosaur case, the unit that represents the collision hypothesis should inhibit units representing volcano and sea-level hypotheses. But principle 5, Contradiction, does not suffice to establish incoherencies in this case, since the hypotheses do not strictly speaking contradict each other. Thagard (1989) recommended a liberal interpretation of that principle that justified treating propositions as contradictory if people treated them as incompatible, but Harman (1989) convincingly argues that the problem of competing hypotheses is more serious than I realized.

Harman presents a detective case in which there are four hypotheses:

(1) Albert died because he was strangled.

(2) Albert died because he was poisoned.

(3) Albert died because his heart stopped beating.

(4) Albert died because of lack of oxygen going to his brain.

Normally, the strangling hypothesis will compete with the poisoning hypothesis, but not with the heart stopping or lack of oxygen hypotheses. Yet there are no logical contradictions here, since Albert might have been both poisoned and strangled. Harman rightly challenges my remark that scientists treat the collision and sea-level dropping hypotheses as contradictory because the co-occurrence of asteroid collision and sea-level dropping is unlikely: introduction of probabilistic matters is inconsistent with the spirit of explanatory coherence theory, which is intended to apply to cases where probabilistic information is unavailable.

The solution to the problem presented by Harman is to treat principle 5 more strictly and abandon the attempt to interpret "contradiction" loosely enough to cover competing hypotheses such as the strangling and poisoning ones in the Albert case. Instead, we should assume that *hypotheses that explain the same evidence compete with one another unless there is reason to believe otherwise.*[2] Hence there need be no special relation between two hypotheses for them to be incoherent, since hypotheses that both explain a piece of evidence are judged to incohere unless there are reasons to think that they cohere. Such reasons, of course, should be in accord with other principles of explanatory coherence stated above. We can now state the following principle intended to supplement the seven principles of explanatory coherence stated above:

*Principle C. Competition.*
   If P and Q both explain proposition R, and if P and Q are not explanatorily connected, then P and Q incohere. Here P and Q are explanatorily connected if any of the following conditions holds:
   (a)  P is part of the explanation of Q,
   (b)  Q is part of the explanation of P,
   (c)  P and Q are together part of the explanation of some proposition T.

Clauses (a) and (b), stating that hypotheses do not compete if one explains the other, provide the basis for our intuition that Albert's being poisoned does not compete with the heart-stopping and no-oxygen hypotheses. We all know enough about human physiology to be able to say that poisoning can cause hearts to stop which can cause the cessation of oxygen flow to the brain. Our background knowledge does not suggest any similar explanatory relation between strangling and poisoning. In a very unusual case, however, there might be some piece of evidence whose explanation required

---

[2] This principle was inspired by a remark of Keith Holyoak to Greg Nelson that people probably take hypotheses to be competing unless they have reason to believe otherwise.

**Table 12.1**
Algorithm for implementing Principle C

---

1. Compile a list of pairs of potentially competing hypotheses:
   (a)  For each proposition R, compile a list of all the hypotheses that explain R.
        Create a list of pairs of the explainers of R.
   (b)  Return a list L of pairs of potentially competing hypotheses.
2. Prune the list L by eliminating any pair (P   Q) such that any of the following conditions holds:
   (a)  P is in the list of explainers of Q,
   (b)  Q is in the list of explainers of P,
   (c)  P and Q are cohypotheses,
3. For each pair (P   Q) in the pruned list L, create an inhibitory
   link between P and Q with a weight equal to:

$$\frac{inhib * (\textit{number of propositions explained by both P and Q})}{(\textit{number of cohypotheses of P and Q in the explanations of propositions that they both explain})/2}$$

Notes:
(i) inhib is a constant representing the default inhibition.
(ii) A unit U in ECHO is represented by a LISP atom with a property list that includes entries for units representing propositions that (1) explain, (2) are explained by, and (3) are cohypotheses of the proposition represented by U.
(iii) H1 and H2 are *cohypotheses* if H1 and H2 are together part of the explanation of some other proposition.

---

both poisoning and strangling, in which case clause (c) would apply and eliminate competition between poisoning and strangling. Note that in (c) the proposition R might be the proposition R: if P and Q together explain R, then they do not compete to explain R.

ECHO.2 implements this principle by finding for each proposition R pairs of hypotheses P and Q that explain R but are not explanatorily related to each other. Then an inhibitory link between P and Q is constructed. Table 12.1 gives the algorithm; the other algorithms used by ECHO are stated elsewhere (Thagard 1989, Thagard and Nowak 1990). The equation in part 3 of table 12.1 ensures that in the limiting case where P and Q each explain R without any help, and R is the only proposition that they both explain, then the inhibition is the same as that between units representing contradictory hypotheses. The equation captures the following intuitions: the more propositions that P and Q both explain, the more they compete, but the greater the number of the additional assumptions used in these explanations, the less they compete. If P and Q each independently explains E only with the assistance of numerous other hypotheses, then they incohere to a lesser extent; compare principle 2 (c), according to which the degree of *coherence* is lessened by the number of hypotheses that *together* explain a proposition. By virtue of the algorithm in table 12.1, ECHO.2

tends to create more inhibitory links than did ECHO.1, the old version, which created them only when told that two propositions are contradictory.

## 12.5   Application to the Dinosaur Debate: Raup

ECHO has now been applied to numerous cases of scientific and legal reasoning, including Lavoisier's argument for his oxygen theory against the phlogiston theory, Darwin's argument for evolution by natural selection, Wegener's argument for continental drift, Copernicus's argument versus Ptolemy, and Newton's argument against Descartes (Thagard 1989, in press; Thagard and Nowak 1988, 1990; Nowak and Thagard in press). In order to show its applicability to the dinosaur debate, I have analyzed the basic structure of the arguments of four participants. Two analyses, of the arguments by Raup and Hallam, will be described here. My analyses are not exhaustive, and do not capture the authors' arguments in full detail, but I have tried to represent the basic structure of their arguments for and against the collision hypothesis. No attempt will be made to use ECHO to adjudicate the debate, although I hope the analysis offered will help to highlight the key points of contention. We will see that ECHO.2 reaches appropriate conclusions about what hypotheses are competitive.

Raup (1986) uses the collision hypothesis to explain dinosaur extinction and mineral deposits, and he uses the Nemesis hypothesis of the sun's having a twin star to explain periodic extinctions. He also considers alternative hypotheses for both end-Cretaceous extinctions and periodic extinctions. Volcanic action is the primary source he considers for the minerals at the Cretaceous boundary, while the possible existence of a tenth planet is an alternative to Nemesis. (He only briefly mentions the sea-level decline hypothesis that is important to Hallam's case below.) Table 12.2 presents the propositions derived from the analysis of Raup that seem to me to be central to his case. Propositions starting "GE" are pieces of negative evidence that contradict observed evidence. Note that ECHO.2 uses only the propositions names; the content is provided for information only.

ECHO.2 creates a unit representing each of these hypotheses and constructs a network by linking the units using the inputs shown in table 12.3, which omits LISP quote symbols for legibility. These produce the network displayed in figure 12.1, in which excitatory links are shown by solid lines and inhibitory links are shown by dotted lines. ECHO.2 produces inhibitory links between CH1 and VH1 and between NH1 and PH1 in accord

**Table 12.2**
Propositions used for simulation of Raup

| | |
|---|---|
| Evidence relevant to collision and the periodic extinctions: | |
| E1 | Extinctions occur in cyclic patterns, peaking at 26 million-year intervals. |
| E2 | Cratering increases periodically, about every 28 million years. |
| GE3 | Astronomers have observed Nemesis. |
| E3 | Nemesis has not been found. |
| GE4 | Astronomers have observed Planet X. |
| E4 | Planet X has not been found. |
| E5 | Dinosaurs became extinct around 65 million years ago. |
| E6 | Irdium deposits were laid down around 65 million years ago. |
| E7 | Shocked quartz deposits were laid down about 65 million years ago. |
| E8 | Osmium deposits were laid down about 65 million years ago. |
| E9 | No huge crater has been found. |
| GE9 | There is a huge crater on the earth's surface. |
| Collision hypotheses: | |
| CH1 | A comet collided with the earth around 26 million years ago. |
| CH2 | The crater from the collision is hidden by water or lava flows. |
| Nemesis hypotheses: | |
| NH1 | Our sun has a companion star, Nemesis, that passes close to the sun every 26 million years and deflects comets toward the earth. |
| NH2 | Astronomers have not looked thoroughly enough for Nemesis. |
| Alternative to Nemesis: the tenth planet: | |
| PH1 | A tenth planet causes periodic comet showers. |
| PH2 | Astronomers have not looked thoroughly enough for the tenth planet. |
| Hypothesis opposed to collision: | |
| VH1 | Volcanic eruptions led to dinosaur extinction. |

with the competition principle C; no explicit contradiction input for these propositions is given. Figure 12.2 shows the connectivity of CH1, the main collision hypothesis. The weights on the excitatory links (thick lines) vary based on the number of hypotheses used in the particular explanations, in accord with Principle 2(c); the default is .04. In accord with the equation in table 12.1, the weight on the inhibitory link (thin line) between CH1 and VH1 is 3 times the default inhibitory weight of $-.06$ because the two propositions compete in the explanation of three propositions: E5, E6, and E7.[3]

---

[3] There is nothing special about the values of .04 for excitation, $-.06$ for inhibition, and .05 for decay which are standardly used in ECHO.2, both in the dinosaur simulations and in the much larger ones of Copernicus and Newton reported elsewhere (Nowak and Thagard, in press). Automated sensitivity analyses that tried 1000 different combinations of values for the three key parameters, each varied between .01 and .1, determined that Raup's conclusion of accepting the collision hypothesis and rejecting the volcanic hypothesis is generally modeled correctly so long as the absolute value of inhibition is greater than the value of excitation. Each simulation, including network creation and settling, takes about 7 seconds on a Sun 4 workstation. Similar results were obtained by 1000 runs of the Hallam simulation described later.

**Table 12.3**
Input for Raup simulation

---

Note: LISP quotes are omitted.

Explanations by collision:
  (EXPLAIN (CH1) E5)
  (EXPLAIN (CH1) E6)
  (EXPLAIN (CH1) E7)
  (EXPLAIN (CH1) E8)
  (EXPLAIN (CH1) GE9)
  (EXPLAIN (CH1 CH2) E9)

Explanations by volcanoes:
  (EXPLAIN (VH1) E5)
  (EXPLAIN (VH1) E6)
  (EXPLAIN (VH1) E7)

Explanations by Nemesis:
  (EXPLAIN (NH1) E1)
  (EXPLAIN (NH1) E2)
  (EXPLAIN (NH1) GE3)
  (EXPLAIN (NH1 NH2) E3)
  (EXPLAIN (NH1) CH1)

Explanations by tenth planet:
  (EXPLAIN (PH1) E1)
  (EXPLAIN (PH1) E2)
  (EXPLAIN (PH1) GE4)
  (EXPLAIN (PH1 PH2) E4)
  (EXPLAIN (PH1) CH1)

Contradictions:
  (CONTRADICT E3 GE3)
  (CONTRADICT E4 GE4)
  (CONTRADICT E9 GE9)

The evidence:
  (DATA (E1 E2 E3 E4 E5 E6 E7 E8 E9))

---

The network thus constructed contains nineteen units and thirty-nine symmetrical links. It settles into a stable state in sixty-two cycles of activation updating. Since this network models Raup's pro-collision views, we would expect the main collision hypothesis CH1 to win out over its principle rival, the volcano hypothesis VH1, and it does. Figure 12.3 presents graphs of the activations of the units over the sixty-two cycles before all the units have reached asymptote. Notice that VH1 gets some initial activation, but is suppressed by the superior CH1. The asymptotic activation values are shown in figure 12.2. Evidence units starting with "E" rise steadily because of links to the special evidence unit which always has activation 1. GE propositions are driven down by the E propositions they contradict. The Nemesis and tenth planet hypotheses receive equal

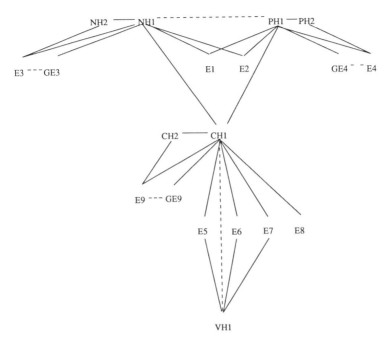

**Figure 12.1**
Network representing Raup's argument. E1–E8 are evidence units. CH1 is a unit
representing the collision hypothesis, while VH1 represents the volcano hypothesis. Solid
lines are excitatory links while dotted lines are inhibitory.

activation, .33. The final state of the network, with these hypotheses tied
and collision winning out over volcanism, well represents Raup's overall
conclusion (Raup 1986: 93, 145).

## 12.6   Application to the Dinosaur Debate: Hallam

But what of the active opposition to the collision hypothesis? ECHO.2 has
been used to model two of its most vociferous critics, Robert T. Bakker
(1986) and Anthony Hallam (1987). Both contend that dinosaur extinction
can be better explained by the less catastrophic hypothesis of a decline in
sea level. They explain the geological phenomena of mineral deposits at the
K/T (Cretaceous/Tertiary) boundary as arising from heavy volcanic activity. Hallam's account is particularly comprehensive, so I shall present
ECHO's simulation of his argument.

290 Paul Thagard

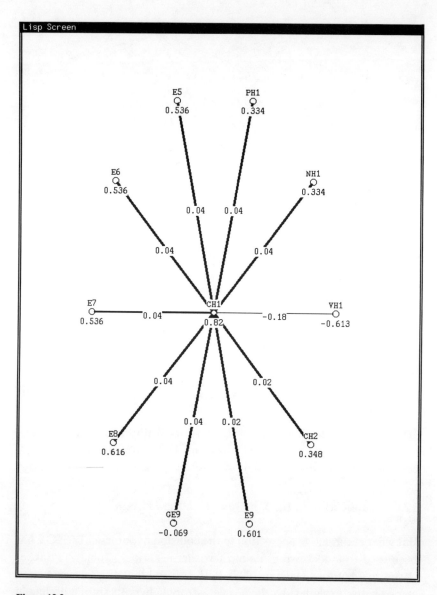

**Figure 12.2**
Connectivity of collision hypothesis unit CH1. The numbers under the units are their
activation values after the unit has settled. Thick lines indicate excitatory links, while thin
lines indicate inhibitory links. Numbers on the lines indicate the weights on the links.

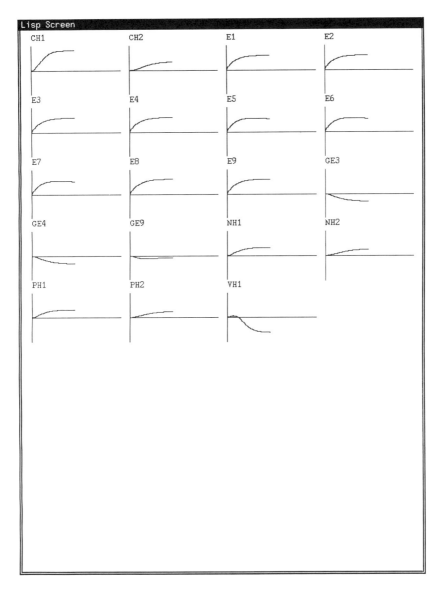

**Figure 12.3**
Activation history of Raup network. Each graph shows the activation of a unit over 62 cycles of updating, on a scale of −1 to 1, with the horizontal line indicating the initial activation of 0.

**Table 12.4**
Propositions used in simulation of Hallam

Evidence:
| | |
|---|---|
| E0 | Dinosaurs became extinct at the end of the Cretaceous. |
| E1 | There is iridium enrichment exactly at the Cretaceous/tertiary boundary. |
| E2 | Boundary clay contains tektite-like microspherules. |
| E3 | Boundary clay contains smectite. |
| E4 | Boundary clay contains soot. |
| E5 | Boundary clay contains shocked quartz. |
| E6 | End-Cretaceous extinctions were selective. |
| E7 | Planktonic forams and coccolithophorids became extinct at the K/T boundary. |
| E8 | Microspherules are not unique to the K/T boundary. |
| E9 | No impact crater has been found. |
| GE9 | Impact produced a large crater. |
| E10 | Strontium isotope ratio changed at the K/T boundary. |
| E11 | There was an influx of turbidities into the deep sea at the K/T boundary. |
| E12 | Kaolinite is found at the K/T boundary. |
| E13 | There is evidence of extensive volcanicity at the K/T boundary. |
| E14 | End-cretaceous extinctions were gradual. |
| GE14 | End-cretaceous extinctions were sudden. |
| E15 | Multiple impacts produced multiple craters. |
| GE15 | No multiple craters have been found. |

Collision hypotheses:
| | |
|---|---|
| CH1 | At the time of the K/T boundary, there was a massive asteroid impact that threw up a huge dust cloud. |
| CH2 | There were a succession of impacts. |

Terrestrial hypotheses:
| | |
|---|---|
| TH1 | Massive volcanic eruptions produced layers at the K/TH boundary. |
| TH2 | K/T microspherules have a variety of origins. |
| TH3 | Forest fires occur persistently. |
| TH4 | Sea level falling at the end of the Cretaceous caused dinosaur extinction. |
| TH5 | The geomagnetic field changed at the end of the Cretaceous. |

Table 12.4 lists the propositions derived from an analysis of Hallam (1987), and table 12.5 presents the CONTRADICT and EXPLAIN input to ECHO.2 that establishes excitatory and inhibitory links. Figure 12.4 portrays the resulting network. ECHO.2 sets up inhibitory links based on the following competitions that it detects:

CH1 competes with TH3 because of E4.

CH1 competes with TH2 because of E2.

CH1 competes with TH4 because of E0.

CH1 competes with TH1 because of E0, E1, and E5.

CH2 competes with TH1 because of E14.

CH2 competes with TH4 because of E14.

**Table 12.5**
Input for Hallam simulation

Note: LISP quotes are omitted.

Collision explanations:
(EXPLAIN (CH1) E0)
(EXPLAIN (CH1) E1)
(EXPLAIN (CH1) E2)
(EXPLAIN (CH1) E3)
(EXPLAIN (CH1) E4)
(EXPLAIN (CH1) E5)
(EXPLAIN (CH1) GE9)
(EXPLAIN (CH1) GE14)
(EXPLAIN (CH2) E14)
(EXPLAIN (CH2) GE15)

Contradiction:
(CONTRADICT E9 GE9)
(CONTRADICT E14 GE14)
(CONTRADICT E15 GE15)

Terrestrial explanations:
(EXPLAIN (TH1 TH4) E0)
(EXPLAIN (TH1) E1)
(EXPLAIN (TH2) E2)
(EXPLAIN (TH3) E4)
(EXPLAIN (TH1) E5)
(EXPLAIN (TH1 TH4) E6)
(EXPLAIN (TH4) E7)
(EXPLAIN (TH1) E8)
(EXPLAIN (TH4) E10)
(EXPLAIN (TH4) E11)
(EXPLAIN (TH4) E12)
(EXPLAIN (TH1) E13)
(EXPLAIN (TH1 TH4) E14)
(EXPLAIN (TH5) TH1)

The evidence:
(DATA (E0 E1 E2 E3 E4 E5 E6 E7 E8 E9 E10 E11 E12 E13 E14 E15))

Volcanic activity, TH1, and sea-level dropping, TH4, do not compete with each other because Hallam uses them *together* to explain the gradualness and selectivity of extinctions. Hence ECHO.2 recognizes them as co-hypotheses rather than as competitors. Notice that, just as Raup explains the collision hypothesis by Nemesis, Hallam conjectures that the increased volcanic activity might have come about because of a change in the geo-magnetic field. Figure 12.5, shows the connectivity of unit CH1, which, in contrast to figure 12.2, has negative activation at the end of the run. The reader can verify that the inhibitory links from CH1 to its competitors, TH1 and TH2, have weights in accord with the equation in the algorithm given in table 12.1.

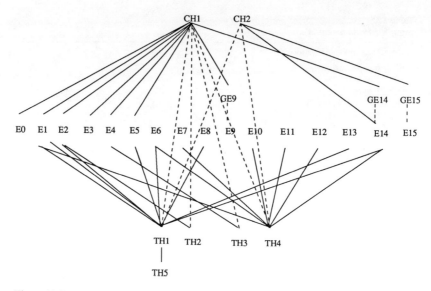

**Figure 12.4**
Network representing Hallam's argument. E0–E15 are evidence units. CH1 and CH2 are collision hypotheses, while TH1–TH5 are terrestrial hypotheses. Solid lines are excitatory links, while dotted lines are inhibitory.

Figure 12.6 displays the activation histories of the twenty-six units (with fifty-three links) over the ninety-five cycles of updating that the network requires to settle. Just as Hallam concludes, the terrestrial hypotheses TH1–TH5 displayed at the bottom dominate the collision hypotheses CH1–2 displayed in the top left corner. The main terrestrial hypotheses TH1 and TH4 both end up with activations greater than .8, while CH1 asymptotes below −.7. CH1 starts out with positive activation from the evidence it explains, but soon is forced down by the negative evidence and competing hypotheses. Figure 12.6 displays the links to CH1, whose activation is brought down both by the inhibitory links with TH1 and TH4 and by the excitatory links with the negative evidence units whose activations are negative. The simulation of Bakker gives similar results, except that his discussion is less comprehensive and emphasizes the question of rate of extinction.

Despite its comprehensiveness, it would be rash to expect Hallam's survey to settle the issue of why dinosaurs became extinct. Since his paper appeared, there has been much empirical and theoretical discussion of the

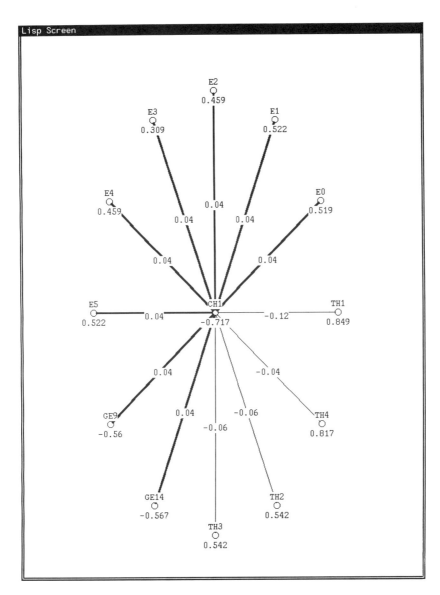

**Figure 12.5**
Connectivity of unit CH1 in the Hallam network. The numbers under the units are their activation values after the unit has settled. Thick lines indicate excitatory links, while thin lines indicate inhibitory links. Numbers on the lines indicate the weights on the links.

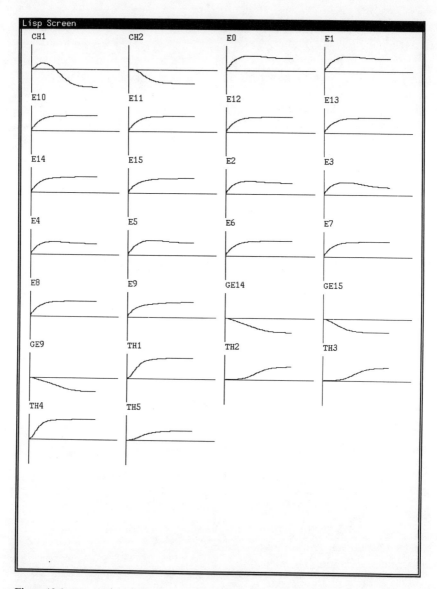

**Figure 12.6**
Activation history of the Hallam network. Each graph shows the activation of a unit over
95 cycles of updating, on a scale of −1 to 1, with the horizontal line indicating the initial
activation of 0.

topic. Luis Alvarez's (1987) survey of the field concluded that the evidence overwhelmingly favors the collision hypothesis. ECHO's simulation of his case results in high activation for the collision hypothesis and rejection of the sea-level and volcano explanations. Alvarez rejects the evidence that extinctions were gradual and argues that volcanoes could not have produced the iridium layer. It would be interesting to use ECHO.2 to model an objective observer taking in all the evidence and explanations advocated by both sides, but for now I am content to have modeled some of the leading disputants in the debate about dinosaur extinction.

## 12.7    Other Approaches in the Philosophy of Science

How might the dinosaur debate be viewed from other perspectives in the philosophy of science? In current philosophical and popular discussions of scientific method, five views are most frequently mentioned. These are the confirmation theory of philosophers such as Hempel (1965), the falsificationist account of Popper (1959), the theory of scientific revolutions of Kuhn (1970), the complex methodological account of Lakatos (1970), and Bayesian models based on probabilities (Salmon 1966). I shall briefly describe how each of these theories of scientific method misses crucial elements of the dinosaur debate.

According to confirmation theory, hypotheses are evaluated by deducing from them their observational consequences. A hypothesis is *confirmed* if the predictions derived from it are true, and a sufficiently confirmed hypothesis can be accepted. The dinosaur debate (and, I would argue, other scientific debates) does not fit this picture in several key respects. First, particular observations are not used to evaluate hypotheses such as that a meteorite collided with the earth. Rather, a hypothesis is evaluated using generalizations based on multiple observations. The typical unit of evidence is a generalization from many observations, for example that there is an unusually large amount of iridium in clay at the Cretaceous boundary. Second, the relation between a hypothesis and the evidence for it is looser than deduction. Rarely, and certainly not in the dinosaur debate, can scientists state their views in sufficient detail to enable a strict deduction of evidence from hypotheses. Rather, they speak more loosely of the hypothesis being used to "explain" or "give an account of" the evidence. Third, it is not enough to pay attention to what a hypothesis explains; scientists often also seek an explanation of the hypothesis itself. For example, Raup attempts to explain *why* there was a collision of a meteorite at the end of the Cretaceous by supposing that our sun has a twin star, Nemesis, that periodically causes asteroids to be directed toward the earth. Fourth, confirmation theory neglects the essentially *comparative* nature of theory evaluation. The collision hypothesis is usually assessed with respect to alternative explanations for dinosaur extinction such as sea-level changes and volcanic activity.

As an account of the dinosaur debate, Popper's falsificationism suffers all of these flaws and more. According to Popper, good scientists should not try to confirm their hypotheses, but should instead design rigorous tests and attempt to falsify them. In contrast, the participants in the dinosaur debate appear much more concerned with defending their own views by accumulating more evidence in their favor rather than with attempting to falsify them. Popper would see this as a sign of irrationality, but it is an inevitable consequence of the need to explore hypotheses thoroughly before considering their abandonment. Strict falsification never occurs in science, since one can always hold onto a hypothesis in the face of negative evidence by challenging assumptions about the validity of the evidence or about its relation to the hypothesis. As Lakatos (1970) argues, rejection of a theory typically occurs only when another theory comes along.

Lakatos's account maintains that the unit of evaluation is a whole research program, not a particular hypothesis. A progressive research program is one that exceeds its competitors in the prediction of novel facts. Although Lakatos's model is superior to both confirmation and falsification accounts in making theory evaluation comparative and dynamic, it misses the importance of having explanations *of* hypotheses as well as of generalizations, and its emphasis on novel facts provides no help in analyzing the ongoing dinosaur debate where new findings both for and against the collision hypothesis turn up almost weekly. Kuhn's very influential discussion of scientific revolutions also seems inapplicable, since proponents and opponents of the collision hypothesis are not enmeshed in different paradigms and are capable of extended, if occasionally acrimonious, argument.

Finally, I see no hope of analyzing the dinosaur debate in terms of subjective probabilities. To use Bayes's theorem to judge the probability of the collision hypothesis given the evidence for and against it, we would need to make judgments concerning, for example, the probability of the collision hypothesis prior to any evidence, the probability of the iridium deposits given the collision hypothesis, and the probability of the iridium deposits. Since these probabilities are indeterminate and do not play a role in any of the arguments put forward by participants in the dinosaur debate, a different sort of analysis is needed. The theory of explanatory coherence and the program ECHO.2 provide such an analysis.

Other AI programs have been used to model scientific reasoning. Comparison with relevant computational models can be found in Thagard 1989.

## 12.8   Conclusion

I have not attempted the presumptuous experiment of combining the evidence and explanations of Raup, Bakker, Hallam, and Alvarez into a single simulation. My concern has been merely to model their individual positions and thereby to shed light on the nature of the dispute. All four scientists can naturally be understood as arguing concerning the explanatory coherence of the collision hypothesis with respect to the evidence and alternative hypotheses. The issue is extremely complex, with evidence and counterevidence flowing in from several scientific disciplines. It is not surprising that different researchers have tended to focus on different subsets of the available evidence. I look forward to further attempts to synthesize the evidence and evaluate the explanatory power of the competing hypotheses.

### References

Alvarez, L. 1987. Mass extinctions caused by large bolide impacts. *Physics Today*, 40(7): 24–33.

Alvarez, W., F. Asaro, and H. Michel. 1980. Extraterrestrial cause for the Cretaceous-Tertiary extinction. *Science* 208: 1095–1108.

Bakker, R. 1986. *The dinosaur heresies*. New York: Morrow.

Hallam, A. 1987. End-Cretaceous mass extinction event: Argument for terrestrial causation. *Science*, 208: 1237–1242.

Harman, G. 1989. Competition for evidential support. *Proceedings of the Eleventh Annual Conference of the Cognitive Science Society*, 220–225. Hillsdale, NJ: Erlbaum.

Hempel, C. 1965. *Aspects of scientific explanation*. New York: The Free Press.

Kuhn, T. 1970. *The structure of scientific revolutions*. Second edition. Chicago: University of Chicago Press.

Lakatos, I. 1970. Falsification and the methodology of scientific research programs. In I. Lakatos and A. Musgrave, eds., *Criticism and the growth of knowledge*, 91–195. Cambridge: Cambridge University Press.

Nowak, G., and Thagard, P. (in press). Copernicus, Ptolemy, and explanatory coherence. In R. Giere (ed.), *Cognitive Models of Science, Minnesota Studies in the Philosophy of Science*, vol. 15. Minneapolis: University of Minnesota Press.

Popper, K. 1959. *The logic of scientific discovery*. London: Hutchinson.

Raup, D. 1986. *The Nemesis affair: A story of the death of the dinosaurs and the ways of science*. New York: Norton.

Rumelhart, D. E., J. R. McClelland, and the PDP Research Group. 1986. *Parallel distributed processing: Explorations in the microstructure of cognition*. 2 volumes. Cambridge, Mass.: MIT Press.

Salmon, W. 1966. *The foundations of scientific inference*. Pittsburgh: University of Pittsburgh Press.

Thagard, P. 1989. Explanatory coherence. *Behavioral and Brain Sciences*. 12:435–467.

Thagard, P. (in press). *Conceptual revolutions*. Princeton University Press.

Thagard, P., and G. Nowak, 1988. The explanatory coherence of continental drift. In A. Fine and J. Leplin, Eds., *PSA 1988*, vol. 1, 118–126. East Lansing, Mich.: Philosophy of Science Association.

Thagard, P., and Nowak, G. 1990. The conceptual structure of the geological revolution. In J. Shrager and P. Langley (eds.), *Computational models of discovery and theory formation*. San Mateo, CA: Morgan Kaufman, 27–72.

# Index